The Complete Idiot's Command Reference

Cool Desktop Keyboard Shortcuts for Files, Folders, and Windows

Function Name	Key Combination	What It Does
Select All	⌘+A	Selects ...
Duplicate	⌘+D	Creates ...
Move to Trash	⌘+Delete	Moves selected item to the Trash
Get Info	⌘+I	Opens the Get Info dialog box for the selected item
Make Alias	⌘+M	Creates an alias of the selected item
New	⌘+N	Creates a new folder
Open	⌘+O	Opens selected item
Show Original	⌘+R	Locates the original item for the selected alias
Close Window	⌘+W	Closes a window
Select a file	Arrow keys	Selects the icon appropriate for the key
Edit filename	Return	Highlights a file, folder, or disk name and enables you to edit it
Expand folder	⌘+right arrow	Expands the contents of a folder in List view
Collapse folder	⌘+left arrow	Collapses the contents of a folder in List view
Select name	Letter keys	In lists, selects the item that begins with the typed letter

Application Keyboard Shortcuts

Function Name	Key Combination	What It Does
Copy	⌘+C	Copies the selected data and places it on the Clipboard
New	⌘+N	Creates a new document
Open	⌘+O	Brings up the Open dialog box from which you can open a document
Save	⌘+S	Saves current version of saved documents, opens Save As dialog for new documents
Paste	⌘+V	Places data from the Clipboard into a document at the current location
Cut	⌘+X	Removes the selected data and places it on the clipboard
Undo	⌘+Z	Undoes the last action

Cool Desktop Keyboard Shortcuts for Disks and File Servers

Function Name	Key Combination	What It Does
Eject	⌘+E	Ejects any selected removable media
Put Away	⌘+Y	Ejects a selected disk and moves selected servers into the Trash to remove them from the desktop

cut here

Cool Desktop Keyboard Shortcuts for Tasks

Function Name	Key Combination	What It Does
Stop process	⌘+.	Causes some processes to be interrupted
Mac Help	⌘+?	Opens the Mac Help Center
Find	⌘+F	Opens Sherlock to search your local drives
Search the Internet	⌘+H	Opens Sherlock to search the Internet
Turn on iMac	Power Key (iMac off)	Starts up the iMac if it is off
Shut down, sleep, and restart	Power Key (iMac on)	Brings up dialog box to shut down, sleep, or restart
Sleep	⌘+Option+Power Key	Causes the iMac to go into sleep mode
Wake up	Any key or Mouse button	Causes the iMac to wake up from sleep
Desktop screenshot	⌘+Shift+3	Captures a screenshot of the entire desktop
Window screenshot	⌘+Shift+4+ Caps Lock	Captures a screenshot of a window

Emergency Keyboard Shortcuts

Use These Only If You Have To!

Function	Key Combination	What It Does	When You Should Use It
Force quit	⌘+Option+Esc	Forces the active application to quit	Use this when an application hangs.
Warm restart	⌘+Control+Power	Restarts your iMac	Use this when your iMac is locked up and you can't do anything else.
Hard reset	DV iMacs; press Reset button (small button marked with black rectangle located near FireWire port) Non-DV iMacs; use Reset paperclip to press button (in small hole marked with black triangle located near Ethernet port)	Causes your iMac to be reset	Use this when nothing else works

Cool Startup Keyboard Shortcuts

Function Name	Key Combination	What It Does
Start up from DVD or CD drive	C	Hold C down while the iMac starts to start up from the disc in the DVD or CD-ROM drive
Start up without extensions or control panels	Shift	Hold the Shift key down while the iMac is starting up to start up without loading extensions or control panels.
Rebuild desktop	⌘+Option	Hold keys down during startup to rebuild desktop files.
Zap PRAM	⌘+Option+P+R	Erases contents of parameter RAM.

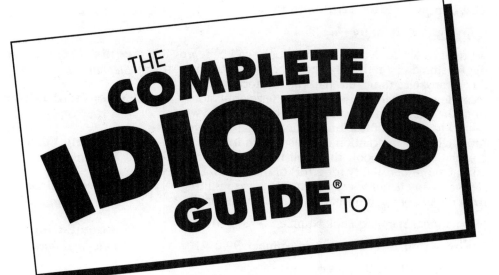

iMac

WITHDRAWN

by Brad Miser

que®

A Division of Macmillan USA
201 W. 103rd Street, Indianapolis, IN 46290

The Complete Idiot's Guide to iMac

Copyright © 2000 by Que

International Standard Book Number: 0-7897-2195-3

Library of Congress Catalog Card Number: 99-067107

Printed in the United States of America

First Printing: February 2000

02   01   00   4   3   2   1

Trademarks

Warning and Disclaimer

Associate Publisher
Greg Wiegand

Acquisitions Editor
Stephanie McComb

Development Editor
Nick Goetz

Managing Editor
Thomas Hayes

Project Editor
Leah Kirkpatrick

Copy Editor
Julie McNamee

Indexer
Aamir Burki

Proofreader
Harvey Stanbrough

Technical Editor
Terry Rawlings

Team Coordinator
Sharry Gregory

Interior Designer
Nathan Clement

Cover Designer
Michael Freeland

Illustrator
Judd Winick

Copy Writer
Eric Borgert

Production
Steve Geiselman

Contents at a Glance

Contents

4 Folders Aren't Manila Anymore   41

5 Ordering from the Menus   55

About the Author

Brad Miser is a Mac fanatic. From his first Macintosh, which was his beloved Mac SE, to the latest and greatest Mac, the DV iMac, Brad loves his Macs. He will talk Mac with anyone who will listen (and even some who won't) and has directly helped dozens of people better use their Macs. He hopes he has helped many more through his books. One of his life goals is to see how many Macs he can have at one time (currently 5 and counting) before his office collapses from the weight of the hardware.

Brad is an engineer (who likes to write—you must be kidding) who develops technical proposals for a major aircraft engine manufacturer (tea, anyone?). He has also been a development editor for Macmillan Computer publishing. He has written several books including *The Complete Idiot's Guide to iBook*, *The Complete Idiot's Guide to iMac*, *Guide to Mac OS 9*, and *Using Mac OS 8.5*.

Brad would love to hear from you about your experience with this book (the good, the bad, and the ugly). You can write to him at bradm@iquest.net.

Dedication

To the men and women who have given the last full measure of devotion so the rest of us can be free.

Acknowledgments

Although only one person's name appears on the cover of this book, developing a book is never a one-person job. It takes a team of people working together to take a book from its initial conception until it ends up in your hands. While it can't adequately compensate these people for their support on this project, it's time for some thank-yous to the following people:

Amy, Jill, Emily, and Grace Miser, for supporting me while I spent time and energy on this book, much of which would have gone to them otherwise.

Marta Justak, for putting the deal together and for providing invaluable advice, support, and encouragement every step of the way.

Stephanie McComb for giving me a chance to write this book and for working with me on it.

Nick Goetz for providing valuable feedback and managing the development process.

Terry Rawlings for catching my technical goofs and adding value to this book.

Macmillan's production team for putting the book together and making it "real."

Apple's iMac Development Team for creating another insanely great product that was a joy to write about.

Tell Us What You Think!

As the reader of this book, *you* are our most important critic and commentator. We value your opinion and want to know what we're doing right, what we could do better, what areas you'd like to see us publish in, and any other words of wisdom you're willing to pass our way.

As an Associate Publisher for Que, I welcome your comments. You can fax, email, or write me directly to let me know what you did or didn't like about this book—as well as what we can do to make our books stronger.

Please note that I cannot help you with technical problems related to the topic of this book, and that due to the high volume of mail I receive, I might not be able to reply to every message.

When you write, please be sure to include this book's title and author as well as your name and phone or fax number. I will carefully review your comments and share them with the author and editors who worked on the book.

Fax: 317.581.4666

E-mail: `office_que@mcp.com`

Mail: Greg Wiegand
          Que
          201 West 103rd Street
          Indianapolis, IN 46290 USA

Complete Idiot's Guide to the iMac

Introduction

It's hip, it's cool, it's now, it's happening. It's the iMac. In addition to its stylish, leading-edge design, the iMac is a powerful and fully functional computer. Even better, with Digital Video (DV) iMacs, you can watch DVD movies and even create and edit your own digital cinema masterpieces. And using the AirPort wireless networking capability, you can even connect to the Internet and to other computers with no cables to tie you down. Computers just don't get any better than this.

The iMac runs the best operating system, the Macintosh Operating System (better known as the Mac OS). In fact, the iMac is a Macintosh. This means that in addition to being powerful and having a ton of features, the iMac is easy to use (well, easy as far as computers go anyway). Even so, I am betting you have things you would rather do than trying to figure out how things work on your own, which leads me to the next section....

Why You'll Be Glad You Have This Book

This book is all about helping you make the most of the iMac in a fast, easy, and fun way. Rather than having to take the time and effort to learn all about your great computer on your own, you can use this book to speed you up the iMac learning curve. And it is better to learn faster and more easily, right? Having some fun along the way is just icing on the icake. (Sorry about that, but I just had to do it.)

The individual chapters of this book are designed to give you a good understanding of the topics, but the main point is to teach you how to *do* things as quickly and as easily as possible. You will find lots of steps to guide you through tasks; you will get a lot more from this book if you follow these steps as you read. This book is about learning by doing. You'll be glad you have this book because you will be able to *do* faster and more easily than you would have otherwise.

How Does This Book Work?

This book works however you want it to work. Each chapter is dedicated to particular aspects of the iMac. The first part covers the essentials of using the iMac; you should read through all of these chapters and practice the tasks you find there. The second part of the book is devoted to the Internet; you'll learn how to connect to the Net and how to use email and the Web. The third part covers fun activities, such as using desktop photos and creating your own alert sounds. The fourth part provides information that enables you to take your iMac to the next level. (I never have understood what that phrase means, but it sure sounds good.) Lastly, the appendix will be useful for those few times when your iMac will not behave itself.

As you read through the book, you will notice certain words are in bold. The bold indicates you are supposed to do something, such as click, select, or press. You don't have to worry about any funky conventions, such as special bold, italicized, or capitalized words in specific situations. The only things that might not be obvious to you are the keyboard combinations I mention throughout the book. When you see something like ⌘+Option+K, it means hold the ⌘ and Option keys down while you type the K key.

You will see some special sidebar elements throughout the book. The information in these sidebars is always related to the text in which they appear. There are three types of sidebars (each has its own icon), and the following sidebars explain what they are (using sidebars to explain sidebars—clever, huh?).

Take an iLook

These sidebars provide additional explanation, background, or different ways of doing things. You should take time to read these sidebars.

Be an iMac Wizard

These sidebars provide advanced information you don't necessarily have to read. Of course, I think reading them is worth your time, but it really is up to you to decide. In these sidebars, you will find additional nice-to-know information as well as lots of tips to help you work faster and smarter.

iWarning You

These sidebars contain warnings and cautions about things that can cause you grief. Since you are using an iMac, there aren't many of these sidebars, but you should pay attention to the few you will encounter.

Also, these sidebars tell you about a few features version 9 of the Mac OS has that version 8.6 does not. If you are using Mac OS 8.6, these sidebars will tell you what is different about 8.6 as compared to Mac OS 9. Using this information, you can account for differences between the book and what you see on your iMac.

Finally, the chapters begin and end with special summary sections that tell you what is coming and remind you what you read about.

That's about it. I hope you enjoy this book and learn a lot about your iMac. And if you have a good time along the way, so much the better....

Part 1

Start Using Your iMac Now!

You've got your hands on one of the coolest pieces of technology ever made. The Apple iMac looks great—it is stylish enough to make the biggest fashion snob look twice. However, unlike the latest Armani suit or Gucci handbag, the iMac can do lots more than simply look good. Also unlike a suit or handbag, you may need a little bit of help getting started with your iMac.

That is where this part of the book comes in. As you read through these first seven chapters of the book, you will learn a lot about how to use your iMac. You'll learn everything from how to start and stop the machine to how to create and print a document. You might think of this part as the iMac basics, but with computers, nothing is ever really basic. So, get going. Your iMac is waiting for you....

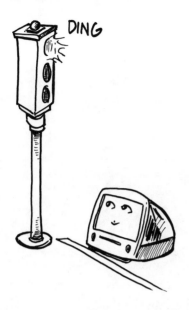
DING

Chapter 1

On Starting, Stopping, and Things In-Between

In This Chapter

➤ Understand why the iMac is such an excellent computer

➤ Learn how to point and click your way to iMac Nirvana

➤ Use the Mac OS Setup Assistant to configure your iMac

➤ Turn your iMac off

Congratulations! You are using one of the most amazing pieces of technology ever created. Apple's iMac has a dual personality—and both of them are good! The iMac is a powerful computer, and it is easy to use. It is eminently practical, and at the same time, very stylish. It is a compact package, and yet it contains everything you need to create, explore, and even play. The iMac has it all, and since you have an iMac, so do you!

Living in the Fast Lane with the iMac

Before you jump in and start iMacing it, take a few moments and learn your way around. Your iMac is a sophisticated computer, and it has been extremely well designed. It has the features you need to make the most of what you do, including running applications, playing games, and surfing the Internet. In both the way it works and the way it looks, the iMac makes a statement.

Kick the Chips

The iMac is a compact, stylish machine you will be proud to have in your home, office, or classroom (see Figure 1.1).

Figure 1.1

The iMac works as good as it looks.

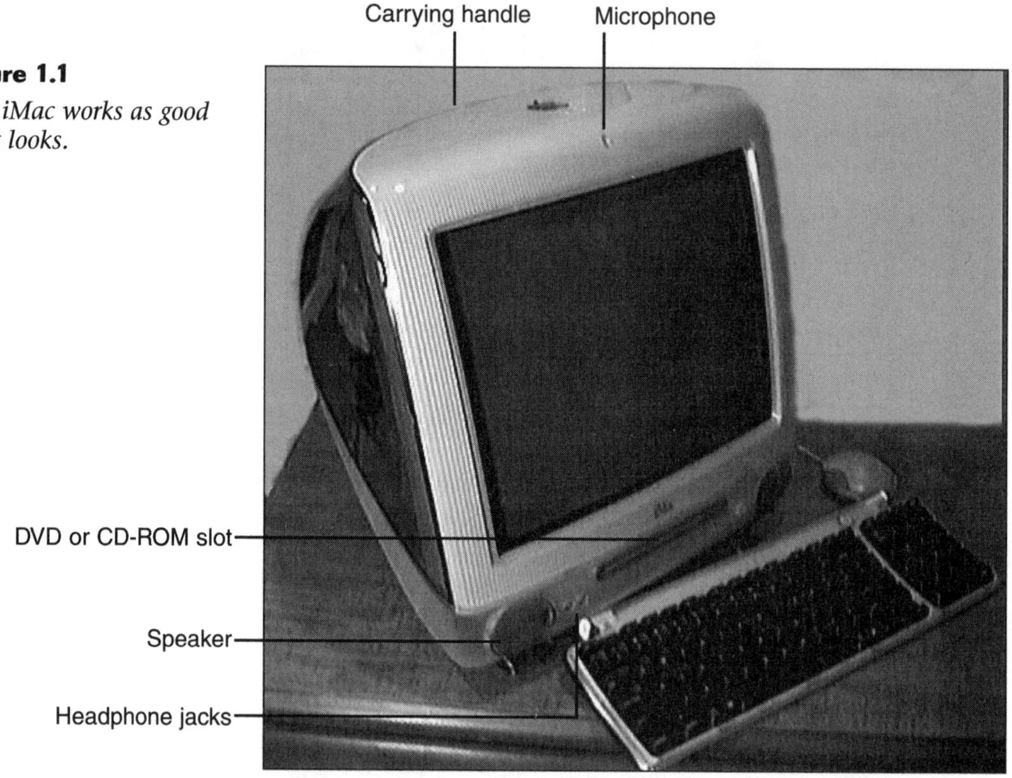

Carrying handle   Microphone

DVD or CD-ROM slot

Speaker

Headphone jacks

Two major versions of the iMac have been released. The iMac you see in Figure 1.1 is one of the Digital Video (DV) iMacs Apple released in the fall of 1999. The major improvements of these versions of the iMac as compared to earlier versions are a DVD drive (that enables you to view DVD movies as well as use DVD-ROM discs), larger hard drives, faster processors, an AirPort card slot (for wireless networking), and FireWire ports (which are high-speed ports that are primarily intended for digital video applications). There are also cosmetic differences; for example, DV iMacs have translucent cases.

On the right side of the iMac, you will find ports you need to connect your iMac to networks, the Internet, and peripheral devices (see Figure 1.2). Another difference between DV iMacs and non-DV iMacs is that DV iMacs do not have a cover over their ports.

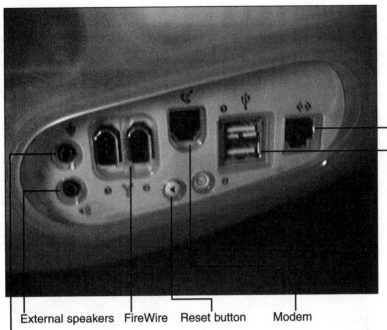

Figure 1.2

Along the right side of the iMac, you will find ports that enable you to connect your computer to other computers and peripheral devices.

Ethernet

USB

External speakers   FireWire   Reset button   Modem

External mic

Take an iLook

What's a Version?

Although I say there have been two versions of the iMac, understand that there have been several iterations of the non-DV iMacs. Each iteration featured minor improvements, such as a faster processor. Technically speaking, there have been more than two versions of the iMac, but all the iterations of the non-DV type share the same features. The DV iMacs were the first ones to which significant features were added.

There is also a USB port on each side of the keyboard (see Figure 1.3). Finally, at the back of the case, a removable cover conceals the AirPort slot (to which you can add an AirPort card) and a slot for additional memory.

Figure 1.3

You can also attach USB devices to the ports at each end of the keyboard.

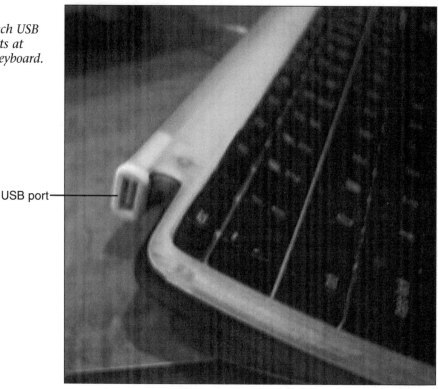

USB port

Previous versions of the iMac, which I call non-DV iMacs, share many of the same features as their more modern cousins. In fact, it can be hard to tell the two versions apart. They look quite similar (see Figure 1.4). The easiest way to tell if you have a non-DV iMac is to look on the right side of the machine. If you see a hinged cover over the ports, you are looking at a non-DV iMac. Non-DV iMacs also have a CD-ROM tray instead of an open DVD or CD-ROM slot.

Functionally, the two versions are very similar. DV iMacs can do a few more things primarily because of the DVD drive, FireWire ports, and AirPort card slot. Other than these things, the versions work quite similarly. This book is based on a DV iMac, but I will use the iWarning You sidebars to let you know when you are reading about a feature that non-DV iMacs can't do (there aren't a whole lot of them).

Finally, at the least expensive end of the current iMac lineup are machines that are between non-DV iMacs and DV iMacs. These machines share some of the features of DV iMacs, such as an open slot rather than a tray, but not all of them—mainly a CD-ROM drive instead of a DVD drive and no FireWire ports. If you have one of these machines, much of the DV-specific information in this book won't apply to you (again, don't worry because you can do most of what DV iMacs can do). You will be able to take advantage of some of the new iMac features, such as AirPort.

Figure 1.4

This is a non-DV iMac; hard to tell the difference, isn't it!

Drop Your Anchor at These Ports

You use the modem port to attach a phone line to the iMac's built-in modem. Use the Ethernet port to attach your iMac to high-speed networks. You use the USB ports to attach many different kinds of peripheral devices to your iMac (such as your mouse, the keyboard, printers, or Zip drives); you can also attach a USB hub to the ports to allow you to connect more than four USB devices at the same time. You can attach external speakers or headphones to the external speaker and headphone jacks. DV iMacs can attach digital video and other FireWire devices to the FireWire ports; you can also install and use an Air Port card for wireless networking. You will learn about all these ports in this book.

Talk the Talk

As great as your iMac's hardware is, its only purpose is to support its software. Before you jump into things, it's a good idea to take a tour of what you will see when you start up your iMac so you know what to expect. It will also help you with the rest of the book if you get a good grip on the lingo now.

When you first start your iMac, you will see the desktop. The desktop is the main area from which you will manipulate folders and files, launch applications, use disks, open files, and so on (see Figure 1.5).

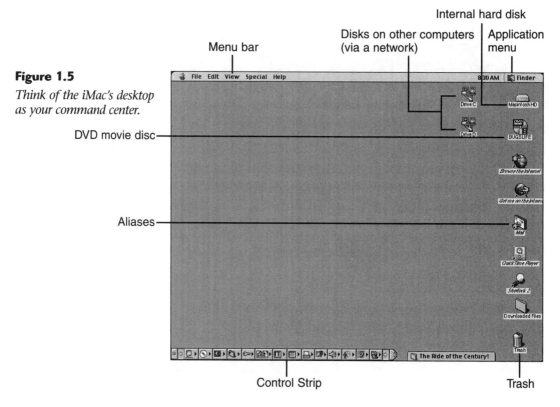

Figure 1.5

Think of the iMac's desktop as your command center.

Internal hard disk

Disks on other computers (via a network)

Application menu

Menu bar

DVD movie disc

Aliases

Control Strip

Trash

The desktop has the following features and functions:

Mounted

When you load a CD or DVD in your iMac and it appears on the desktop, it's said to be *mounted*. In fact, when any drive or other computer appears on your desktop and you can access them, they are mounted on your iMac.

➤ **Hard disk**—All the folders and files on your iMac are stored on its internal hard drive.

➤ **Disks on other computers**—You can use a network to share disks on other computers.

➤ **DVD or CD disc**—DVD discs enable you to watch movies on your iMac; you can also access programs and other files that are stored on DVD-ROM discs. You can use CD-ROM and CD audio discs in your DVD drive as well. Non-DV iMacs can't use DVD discs, but they have a CD-ROM drive in which you can use CD-ROM and CD audio discs.

➤ **Icons**—All files and folders on your iMac are represented by icons. Icons are small pictures that represent the files or folder they reference. To do something with a file or folder, you use its icon.

➤ **Trash**—You use the Trash to delete files and folders from your iMac.

➤ **Control Strip**—The Control Strip provides easy access to some of your iMac's controls.

➤ **Menu bar**—Many commands you will use are listed in menus. Many of the menu bars on the desktop and in programs you will see contain menus that have the same commands.

As much as I hate to lay some terminology on you this early in the book, I'm afraid I have to. The following are some terms you need to understand as you move ahead:

➤ **Mac OS**—Your iMac is a member of the Macintosh family of computers; these computers all run the Macintosh Operating System (Mac OS). An operating system is the set of software that provides the system-level functions of a computer. The Mac OS is one of the best operating systems because it is so easy to use. There have been many versions of the Mac OS, the latest of which is Mac OS version 9.

➤ **Applications**—Applications, also known as programs, are the software you will use to do work, access the Internet, play games, and so on. Your iMac comes with a number of applications you will learn to use as you read through this book.

➤ **File**—A file is an individual item on your computer. Files can be documents, applications, and other software.

➤ **Folder**—A folder is a container in which you can store files and other folders.

Walk the Walk

Now that you know your way around, go ahead and fire up your iMac. After you have your keyboard and mouse connected and the iMac plugged in to an electrical outlet (see in installation card that came with your iMac if you need help with this), press the **Power** key (this is the round button located in the upper-right corner of the keyboard). You hear the Mac startup sound, and your iMac begins to start up. You see a series of icons marching across the bottom of the screen. After a few moments, your desktop appears (it may look a bit different from the one shown previously in Figure 1.5, and that is perfectly fine). This means your iMac is ready to do your bidding.

Version Control

Earlier iMacs shipped with Mac OS 8.5 or 8.6. This book is based on Mac OS 9. I use these caution sidebars to explain OS 9 features you won't see if you are using version 8.5 or 8.6.

Applications and Documents

Applications are programs you use to create, open, and modify documents. Documents can contain text, graphics, photos, sound, and even video.

Doing Things the iMac Way

Now that your iMac is up and running, you can quickly learn the basics of how it works. One of the reasons the Mac OS is so easy to use is that everything is represented graphically—you don't have to worry about typing long series of text commands.

On the iMac, It Is Polite to Point

To use something, you point to it with the arrow (called the pointer) using the mouse. If you have never used one, a mouse can take a bit of getting used to. Moving the mouse moves the pointer. If you move the mouse away from you, the pointer moves up; pull it toward you and the pointer moves down the screen. Move the mouse left and the pointer moves left (I bet you can figure out how to move the pointer to the right.) If you need to move the pointer farther, but you have run out of desk room or arm length, pick up the mouse and move it back toward you. The arrow won't move because the mouse is not rolling along your desktop. When you set the mouse down, the arrow will be in the same place it was when you picked the mouse up. You will need to do this occasionally. Go ahead and move the pointer around the screen until you get comfortable with the mouse.

Round Mouse

The round mouse was introduced with the original iMac. Although this mouse looks cool, it can be hard to use because there is little tactile feedback about how the mouse is oriented. You may find yourself moving it in one direction while the pointer moves in another because the mouse is rotated in your hand. If this continues to trouble you, you can buy a shaped cover to go over the mouse or your can replace the mouse with a different kind. You can also replace it with a different device entirely, such as a trackball.

Point, Click, Do, Two, Three

You use the button at the "back" of the mouse to tell the iMac when you have found what you want to work with. (In Mac lingo, pressing the mouse button is known as clicking.) Almost everything you do on the iMac requires the following three steps:

1. Use the mouse to point to the item with which you want to work.
2. Click the mouse button to select the item.
3. Do what you want to do with that item.

Choosing Commands from Menus

As you work with your iMac, you will constantly be choosing commands from menu bars like the one you see at the top of your desktop. A command you will frequently use is the Open command, which amazingly enough opens the item you have selected. Use the **Open** command on your hard disk to see what it contains.

Point to the hard drive icon and click to select it (it will become highlighted). Now point to the **File** menu and click the mouse button. The menu opens. Now point to **Open** so it is highlighted and click the mouse button. Your hard disk opens showing that it contains several folders.

You Highlight My Life

Whatever you select on the iMac, whether it be a folder, file, or even text in a document, becomes highlighted with a color (you will learn how to set the highlight color later in the book). This makes it easy to see what will be affected by the next action you take.

More Lingo

When you read that you need to click something, that is shorthand for pointing to the item and then clicking the mouse button to select it. When you need to open a menu and choose a command, you need to do steps similar to those you did to open your hard disk: point to the menu, click to open the menu, and then choose the command by pointing to it and clicking.

Now choose a folder and open it the same way (remember to select it, then point to the **File** menu, click, and then click the **Open** command). Close the folder by opening the **File** menu again; this time, choose **Close**. Then choose **Close** again to close the hard drive's window.

Set Up Your iMac with the Mac OS Setup Assistant

The Mac OS tries to be as helpful as possible. For example, there are two Assistant programs that help you set various settings on your iMac. One of these, the Mac OS Setup Assistant, helps you with some basic settings, such as the time and date.

15

The More Things Change...

While I was writing this book, Apple was beginning to ship yet a third setup utility to help you. This one is called *Setup Assistant* and combines some, but not all, of the functions of the other two assistants plus adds an online registration option. This setup program has a nice multimedia introduction and then moves you into the various screens in which you can enter information; it may have started the first time you turned on your iMac. The screens you see in that application are slightly different than those you see in this book. However, the information is similar and it works just like the Mac OS Setup Assistant. If you find yourself in the Setup Assistant, quit it by pressing ⌘+Q. Then follow the steps in this chapter to run the MacOS Setup Assistant.

The first time you start your iMac, you are taken into the Mac OS Setup Assistant. If you are not in the Assistant, open it now. Open the hard drive, and then open the **Assistants** folder. Now open the **Mac OS Setup Assistant** and you will see the Mac OS Setup Assistant window.

Read the text in the window. When you are ready to move to the next screen, point to the right triangle located in the lower-right corner of the window and click it. In the next screen, read the text, point to the region for which you want the basic settings of your iMac to be compatible, and click the mouse button. When the region is selected, it is highlighted with a color. When you have selected the correct region, click the right-facing triangle to move to the next screen.

Continue moving through the screens and adding the information you are asked for. When you are prompted to enter text, use the keyboard to type it in. To move into a text box, point in it and click the mouse button. You will see a flashing vertical line; this means you can begin to type.

The following are items that may not be completely obvious to you (you won't see a bullet for each screen because many of them are pretty obvious):

➤ **Time and Date**—Your iMac uses the time and date to keep track of many things. In the Time and Date screen, you set the time and date it will use. If you are on daylight savings time, click the round button next to Yes (this kind of button is called a radio button). Click on the first digit in the time next to the **What time is it?** question. Click on the up and down arrows to set the hour. Then click on the minutes and set them in the same way. Continue by setting the seconds. Then set the date. When you are done, click the right-facing arrow.

➤ **Geographic Location**—When you are setting your geographic location, don't worry if you can't find your city in the list. Choose the city that is in your time zone and is as close as possible to your location.

➤ **Finder Preferences**—In this screen, make sure the **No** radio button is selected.

➤ **Shared Folder**—You can easily share the folders and files on your iMac with other computers by connecting your iMac to a network. If you are going to connect to a network, click the **Yes** radio button and give your shared folder a name.

➤ **Printer Connection**—Just click through the Printer Connection screens. You will learn how to set up a printer in Chapter 7, "The Paperless World—Bah!"

After you have answered all the assistant's questions, you will see the Conclusion screen. Click the **Go Ahead** button to set up your iMac.When you see the screen telling you Assistant is complete, click the **Quit** button. You will return to the desktop.

With the help of the trusty Mac OS Setup Assistant, your iMac now has the basic configuration settings it needs. Go ahead and practice some of the skills you have learned so far; point to folders and files and then click the mouse button to select them. Open folders and close them. Get used to moving the pointer around.

Take an iLook

Continue?

At the end of the set-up process, you will see a Continue button. If you click that one, you will move into the Internet Setup Assistant. If you can't wait to get on the Internet, jump to Chapter 8, "So Why Is There an "i" in iMac?" You will be much better off if you read through the chapters of the book between here and there first, however.

Shutting It Down

When you are done fooling around, point to the **Special** command on the menu bar and click the mouse button. The menu opens and the list of available commands appears. Point to the **Shut Down** command to highlight it. Click the mouse button. Your iMac turns itself off.

Always turn your iMac off in this way because when you do so, your iMac performs certain stopping tasks to protect its components as well as your data.

The Least You Need to Know

➤ With its powerful processor and excellent features, your iMac enables you to work, play, and explore the world.

➤ Working with something on the iMac is a matter of point (using the mouse), click (press the mouse button), and do.

➤ The Mac OS Setup Assistant can help you configure the basic settings your iMac needs to do its work.

➤ Use the **Shut Down** command on the **Special** menu to turn your iMac off.

Chapter 2

You Never Need to Dust This Desktop

In This Chapter

➤ Point, click, double-click, and drag your way to iMac happiness

➤ Use the Mac help system

➤ Make the mouse work the way you want it to

➤ Use the Energy Saver control panel to be environmentally correct

As you learned in Chapter 1, "On Starting, Stopping, and Things In-Between," the iMac's desktop is where much of the action happens. From the desktop, you open folders and files, change settings, and even get rid of undesirable elements (using the Trash). In this chapter, you will build on your already considerable iMac skills.

Working Your Desktop

You remember the three basic steps when working with the folders and files on your iMac, right? Come now, you must remember. Okay, say it with me: *point, click, do, two, three*.... There, I knew you would remember. Take some time to practice these skills by working through the next few sections.

Open and Close a Folder

In the previous chapter, you opened your hard disk's icon to see what it contained. For practice, open the Applications folder on your hard disk; this is the folder where, you guessed it, applications that come with the iMac are stored. Using the point, click, and do steps, open this folder.

Choosing a Command

I'm lazy and like to type as few characters as possible. From now on, when I tell you to choose a command, know that what I mean is for you to open the appropriate menu, point to the command to highlight it, and then click the mouse button to execute the command.

Point to the hard drive icon, click it, open the **File** menu, and choose the **Open** command (by highlighting it on the menu and clicking the mouse button). Your hard disk opens and you can see its contents.

Now follow similar steps to open the Applications folder. Point to that folder, click to select it, and from the **File** menu, choose **Open**. Nothing to it, is there?

To close the folder, open the **File** menu and choose **Close**.

Open and Close a Document

When you work with many applications, such as a word processor or spreadsheet, you create a document. One the iMac, a document is stored in a file (one file equals one document). Opening a document is similar to opening your hard disk and folders. The difference is that when you open a file, the application that created that file opens and you can work with the document.

Not All Files Are Created Documents

Although all documents are files, not all files are documents. Applications are files as are the various items that make up the OS, such as control panels, extensions, and such (you will learn about these later). Basically, everything on your iMac is stored in a file.

To see how documents work, open the Applications folder again. Open the AppleWorks folder. Now open the "Read Me" AppleWorks 5 document. (Notice that a document's icon looks different than a folder's icon.) When you open the document, you will see that an application opened; in this case the application is SimpleText (which is a basic word processor). Notice that the menu bar has changed—it is now the menu bar containing the commands available in SimpleText.

When you open a document on the iMac, it automatically knows which application it should open so you can work with that document. When you open the document, your iMac opens the appropriate application and places you in your document so you can get to work immediately.Read the ReadMe file, and then quit SimpleText by opening the **File** menu and choosing **Quit**. The document closes, the application quits, and you end up back at the desktop.

Double-Click Your Way Around

Although it's easy to use the Open command to open folders and files, there is a much better and faster way—the double-click. When you double-click something, it is the same as choosing the **Open** command from the **File** menu. Point to a folder—it doesn't matter which one you use because you are just practicing. This time, instead of clicking once, click twice. The folder opens. Now double-click a document to open it. The double-click is a useful trick, and in time, it will become natural to you.

Some people have a hard time getting the double-click down at first. They sometimes wait too long between clicks or they double-click too fast. If you are having a difficult time making the double-click work for you, don't worry. You can change the timing of the double-click to suit your finger speed (you'll learn how in a few pages).

Take an iLook

The Common Menus

All applications (as well as the desktop) are supposed to have a File menu and an Edit menu. File menus contain commands for working with files (such as Open, Close, Save, and so on) as well as quitting the application. Edit menus contain commands for editing the contents of something.

Create a Document

Creating your own documents is not much harder than opening someone else's. Use SimpleText to create a note to your self explaining how much you love your iMac. Open the Applications folder and open the SimpleText application (take this opportunity to practice your double-click). You will see a new, empty document with a flashing cursor; this indicates where you are in the document. Type something you want to say. Perhaps you can describe how cool your iMac is. Or maybe you can write a letter to your friends to explain why they should rush out and get their own copy of this book. For now, just put some text in your new document.

Whenever you create or change a document, you need to save it (the first time you save it, a file is created). Open the **File** menu and choose **Save As**. The Save dialog box appears; as you work with documents, you will see the Save dialog box a lot. It enables you to name your file and tell the iMac where you want the file saved. Type a name for your new document. (You can call it whatever you like as long as the name is 31 characters or fewer.) Click the **Desktop** button—this tells the iMac to save the file on your desktop (see Figure 2.1). Click **Save** to save your document.

Figure 2.1

Get used to seeing Save dialog boxes; there are a lot of them in your future.

——Clicking **Desktop** moves you there.

——Click **Save** to save your file.

Where you tell your iMac to save a file in the Save dialog can be a little confusing at first. The large pane in the dialog shows your current location. You can change locations by opening the folders you see in this pane. To open a folder, double-click it in the pane and you will see its contents. Keep opening folders until you get to the location at which you want to save your file. If you get too deep, you can always click the **Desktop** button to move to your desktop again.

Copy and Paste—To Use It Is to Love it

The iMac is all about doing things as easily as possible. For example, you should never have to retype something or recreate a graphic that is used in any document stored on your iMac. You can easily move text or graphics around in a document or from one document to another using the Copy and Paste commands. Just for fun, paste some text from the document you just created into a new document...

Open the document you just created (if you haven't quit SimpleText, it is already open). Now place the pointer at the beginning of some text you want to use in another document. Press the mouse button down and move the mouse while you continue to hold down the button (this is called *dragging*). As you move your mouse, text is highlighted (which means it is selected, right?). When the text you want to reuse is highlighted, release the mouse button (see Figure 2.2). Open the **Edit** menu and choose **Copy**. The text is copied to the clipboard (no, you can't see this part).

The Mystical Clipboard

When you copy or cut text or a graphic, it is stored in the iMac's clipboard file. This is a file used for temporary storage, and it only stores the last item you cut or copied.

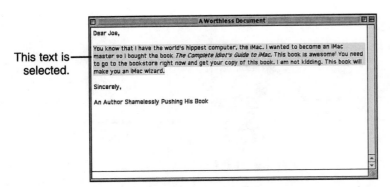

This text is selected.

Figure 2.2

You can select text and then copy and paste it into another document. (No retyping!)

Now create a new document by opening the **File** menu and choosing **New.** Open the **Edit** menu and choose **Paste**. Yahoo! The text from the other document is now in your new document. The copy (or cut) and paste technique works with text, graphics, and even sound and video! And you can use it to move items between documents as well as within the same document.

Drag Files and Folders All Over the Place

When you are working on the desktop, you will need to move files and folders around. You may want to reorganize things. Or you may want to store a set of documents in a particular folder. On the iMac, you move things by dragging them.

To drag something, point to it and press the mouse button, but don't release it. (You could call this a half-click, I suppose.) The item remains highlighted. Keeping the mouse button down, move the mouse—like magic, the item moves with the pointer. When you get to the new location for it, release the mouse button and the item is "dropped" in the new location. This works for files, folders, and anything else you see on the desktop.

Take an iLook

To Copy or Cut, That Is the Question

Notice that on the Edit menu, there is also a Cut command. The difference between Cut and Copy is that Copy leaves what you have selected in the document while Cut removes it from the document.

Be an iMac Wizard

Copy Instead of Move

If you want to copy something rather than move it, hold down the **Option** key while you drag it. A copy is made in the new location.

Use a DVD or CD

CD or DVD?

If you have a non-DV iMac, you have a CD-ROM drive instead of a DVD drive. This means you can't use any sort of DVD disc in the CD-ROM drive; you can only use CD-ROM discs and audio CDs in it. If you have an older non-DV iMac, then you have a CD tray that slides out of the iMac rather than an open slot. To insert a CD, push the button on the front of the CD tray. The tray pops out. Gently slide it all the way out. Place the CD, label side up, on the spindle (you may have to gently push it down over the spindle) and push the tray back into the drive. In a moment, the CD's icon appears on the desktop and you can use it.

If you have a DV iMac, your iMac has a DVD-ROM drive you can use to read movie DVDs, data DVD-ROMs (that contain applications, documents, photos, sounds, and so on), data CD-ROMs, and audio CDs.

Autoplay

The programs on some CDs and DVDs begin to run as soon as you insert the disc. If you insert a music CD, it begins to play automatically.

Insert a disc (try the *Bug's Life* DVD that came with your iMac) into the open DVD slot (label side up) and push it about a quarter of the way in. Your iMac grabs the disc and takes it all the way into the slot. In a moment, you will see the DVD's icon on your desktop. When you do, you can open the DVD to use its contents.

Trash It

The Trash can icon on the desktop has one basic purpose: to remove items from your iMac. If the item is a file or folder, you delete it by placing it in the Trash (and then emptying the Trash). If the item is a disk of some kind, you eject it by placing it in the Trash (no, this doesn't make sense and may be the most confusing single task you do on an iMac).

If you want to delete a file or folder from the iMac so it no longer consumes precious hard disk space, use the Trash. Deleting something is a two-step process. Place the item in the Trash and then empty the Trash.

To delete something, drag it onto the Trash—when it's in the right position, the Trash icon becomes highlighted. When that happens, release the mouse button and the item is placed in the Trash (the Trash icon changes to show you that something is inside it). At this point, your item is still stored on your iMac; you can open the Trash (it is actually a folder) and retrieve the item by dragging it out of the Trash. When you are ready to really be rid of it, open the **Special** menu and choose **Empty Trash**. You will see a warning that explains that you are about to delete something. Click **OK** and the item is deleted from the disk.

To remove a DVD or CD (or other removable disk, such as a Zip or floppy disk), drag its icon to the Trash until the Trash icon becomes highlighted. When you release the mouse button, the disc is ejected and you can remove it from the drive.

You may find it less confusing to select the disc you want to eject and then open the **Special** menu and choose **Eject**. This does the same thing as dragging it to the Trash, but it makes more sense.

Getting a Little Help from Your iFriend

The Mac OS has an excellent built-in help system that will, well, help you.

The Mac OS also includes a tutorial you can run that will help you practice your iMac skills. To run it, open the **Help** menu and choose **Tutorial**. Follow the onscreen instructions from there.

Help Yourself to Help

The Mac OS has an integrated help system you can use when you get stuck and can't figure out how to do something or when you just want to learn more about particular subjects. There are several ways to access this help.

From the **Help** menu, choose **Mac Help** to open the Mac Help window (see Figure 2.3). To get help in specific areas, click one of the links that appear in the left pane of the window. (Links appear in blue and are underlined—just click a link to move to that area.) To search for help with a specific topic, enter a text phrase in the search box and click **Search**.

Be an iMac Wizard

No Need to Close Help

You don't need to close help to go back to what you were doing. You can leave it open on the screen you are reading and switch back to the application or area in which you need help (choose it from the Application menu). That way you can follow any steps shown in the help window without having to remember what they are.

Figure 2.3

Everyone needs a little help now and then—and your iMac is there for you.

Enter text to search for here.

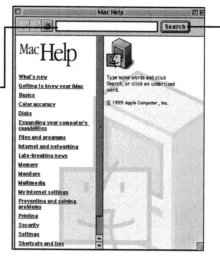

Click here to begin the search.

As an example, search for help on listening to music CDs. Type music CDs in the search box and click **Search**. After a few moments, the results of your search will appear (see Figure 2.4). Click the most promising link. You will move to another screen that contains information about your topic. You will also see links to Web sites and to other parts of the help system. You may also see links that say do something for me, such as, "Open AppleCD Audio Player for me." When you click these sort of links, the iMac does certain tasks for you.

Figure 2.4

Searching for music CDs *finds a lot of good information.*

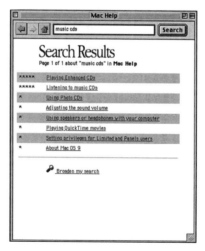

Tweak the Mouse

You may find that using the mouse seems to be more difficult than it needs to be, especially the speed at which you have to double-click. You can change the way the mouse works with the Mouse control panel. (Control panels are special parts of the system software that enable you to control how your iMac works.)

To change your mouse settings, open the **Apple** menu, choose **Control Panels**, and then choose **Mouse** from the menu. You will see the Mouse control panel (see Figure 2.5). There are two areas in which you can control how the mouse works.

Figure 2.5

You can set the mouse to suit your own hand comfort.

Use the **Mouse Tracking** slider to choose a tracking speed. The faster the tracking speed, the less you have to move your mouse to make the pointer move the same distance, but the more dexterity is required to control it accurately. The slower the setting, the easier it is to precisely position the pointer, but the longer it takes to move the pointer around the screen and the more you will have to reposition your mouse.

Set the double-click speed with the **Double-Click Speed** slider. When you change this setting, the "finger" in the window shows you how close together the clicks need to be to register as a double-click.

After you set the mouse options to suit your preferences, close the control panel by choosing **Quit** from the **File** menu. You can come back and make changes to the setting at any time, so don't be afraid to experiment.

Manage Your Power

I'm sure you want to be environmentally friendly, right? Your iMac can help. Rather than turn it off and on to save power (thus preserving the environment and saving your energy dollars), your iMac has power management tools you can use to minimize its power consumption.

Your iMac has a sleep mode in which it almost shuts down. The screen goes blank, the hard disk spins down, and so on. This mode uses almost no power, so you should put your iMac to sleep whenever you aren't going to use it for awhile. To put your iMac to sleep, you can choose **Sleep** from **the Special** menu, choose **Sleep Now** from the **Energy Control Strip** module, or press ⌘**+Option+Power** key. When

Non-DV iMacs

The pulsing sleep indicator was introduced on DV iMacs and the newest non-DV iMacs. If you have an older non-DV iMac, you will see a steady orange light rather than the cool pulsing light on the DV iMacs.

your iMac sleeps, the sleep indicator (which is also the Power key that is located just to the left of the right speaker) pulses with an orange light. To wake your iMac up, press a key, or click the mouse button..

Your iMac can also put itself to sleep after a specific period of inactivity so you don't have to remember to put it to sleep yourself. You can use the Energy Saver control panel to specify how long your iMac is idle before it goes to sleep as well as other energy saving settings. From the **Apple** menu, choose **Control Panels**, and then **Energy Saver**. Click **Show Details** to show all the sleep options you have (see Figure 2.6). Use the sliders to set the amount of idle time before your iMac implements its sleep functions. Use the top slider to set the idle time after which the system will go into sleep mode. If you want the screen to dim (also called display sleep) before the whole system sleeps, check the **Separate timing for display sleep** check box and set the slider. If you want the hard disk to spin down at a time other than when the rest of the system goes to sleep, check the **Separate timing for hard disk sleep** check box and use its slider to set the idle time.

Figure 2.6

Using the Details window of the Energy Saver control panel, you can set the amount of idle time that passes before the iMac sleeps.

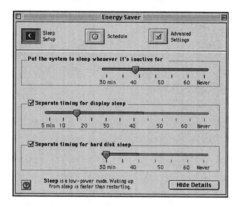

There are two other buttons on the Energy Saver control panel:

➤ **Schedule**—Click the **Schedule** button, and you make your iMac automatically start up and shut down at a specific time each day. You can also make it shut itself off instead of going to sleep.

➤ **Advanced Settings**—Clicking this button enables you to access various advanced power management settings. You aren't likely to need many of these options, but you should look at them to see whether they will be useful in your situation. One of the most useful is when you are connected to a network. If you want your iMac to automatically reconnect to these other computers, use the check boxes in the **Other Options** area.

When you are done changing the energy saving settings, close the control panel by opening the **File** menu and choosing **Quit.**

Take an iLook

Dim Screen

If your screen dims, rather than the iMac going to sleep, you won't see the sleep indicator. To bring your screen back to life, move the mouse.

The Least You Need to Know

➤ Working with files and folders on the desktop is a matter of point, click, and do or point and double-click.

➤ Learning to drag things around is also essential.

➤ The iMac provides a lot of built-in help—you will be ahead of the game if you use it.

➤ You can use the Mouse control panel to change the way your mouse works.

➤ Learn to use the power management features of the iMac to be a good citizen and to save yourself a few bucks on your electric bill.

Chapter 3

Looking at the iMac Through Gray-Colored Windows

In This Chapter

➤ Learn about window types

➤ Master document windows

➤ Learn about dialog boxes, alerts, and special windows

Windows, windows, everywhere.... When you work with your iMac, you'll constantly be using all sorts of windows. Windows are the, well, windows that you look through to see whatever you happen to be working with at the time, whether it is a document, folder, disk drive, control panel, or whatever. Understanding and using windows effectively will help you master the iMac.

What Kind of Windows Have i?

You will see many different types of windows as you work with your iMac. You don't need to worry about all the details of each type; you just need to learn to recognize the different windows and what they enable you to do.

Folder Windows

Folder windows are one of the most important types of windows you will see. Whenever you are working on the desktop, you're dealing with folder windows. This includes when you are opening a disk, when you're opening a regular folder, or when you're opening one of the special types of folders, such as the System Folder. You can see an example of a folder window in Figure 3.1. Folder windows are so important, I have dedicated the entire next chapter to them (see Chapter 4, "Folders Aren't Manila Anymore").

Figure 3.1

Folder windows contain many neat features you will learn to appreciate as you work with your iMac.

Document Windows

Whenever you open a document, you will see your data (text, graphic, movie, and so on) in a window. Document windows share many characteristics with the other kinds of windows you use. In addition, document windows usually have some special features that are unique to the applications that created them.

Dialog Boxes

Okay, you caught me trying to sneak something not called a window in here. Well, technically speaking, *dialog boxes* are windows. These special purpose windows are used all over the iMac. They can contain information, buttons, pop-up menus, check boxes, radio buttons, text entry areas, and so on. A dialog box (commonly referred to as a *dialog*) is used when you need to provide some input or settings for the application or control panel with which you are working. Dialog box windows usually have only a small subset of the features of document and folder windows.

Alert Windows

When your iMac wants to tell you something, such as when an error has occurred, it displays an alert window. Alert windows usually have an OK button that causes the dialog box to go away, although some have a Restart button, which you need to use to restart your iMac.

Special Windows

There are certain types of applications you don't use to create documents, but have windows associated with them; the Graphing Calculator is one example. The Chooser is another special window, as are all control panels. Mostly, these windows have similar features to folder windows and dialog boxes, but they have fewer of them.

My, My, How Good Your Documents Look Through These Windows!

Every time you open an existing document or create a new one, you see a document window that is created by the application you use to work with that document. Many document windows share common characteristics. For example, document windows created by AppleWorks (see Figure 3.2) and document windows created by Microsoft Word (see Figure 3.3) have many similar features even though the features of those applications are quite different. After you learn to use the features of one application's document windows, you pretty much know how to use the features of a document window in any application.

Floating Windows

Floating windows are always in the forefront of the screen no matter what you do. The Control Strip and Application menu are floating windows; when they are open, you can always get to them because they remain "on top" of all other windows.

Close box   Title bar   File name   Zoom box   Collapse box

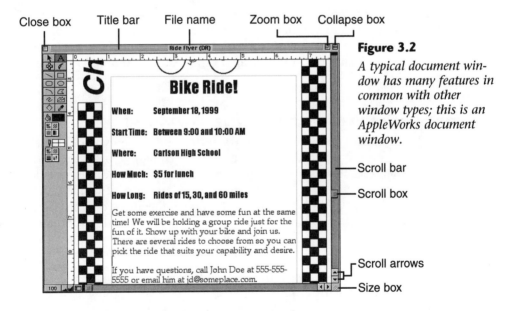

Figure 3.2

A typical document window has many features in common with other window types; this is an AppleWorks document window.

Scroll bar

Scroll box

Scroll arrows

Size box

Bike Ride!

When: September 18, 1999

Start Time: Between 9:00 and 10:00 AM

Where: Carlson High School

How Much: $5 for lunch

How Long: Rides of 15, 30, and 60 miles

Get some exercise and have some fun at the same time! We will be holding a group ride just for the fun of it. Show up with your bike and join us. There are several rides to choose from so you can pick the ride that suits your capability and desire.

If you have questions, call John Doe at 555-555-5555 or email him at jd@someplace.com.

33

Figure 3.3

Now check out this Microsoft Word document window—although Word is quite a bit different than AppleWorks, its document windows share many of the same features.

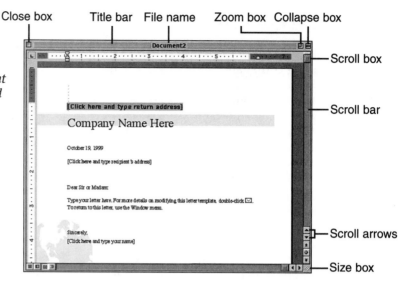

As you work with different applications, you will notice that not all document windows have the same features. That is because each application creates its own document windows. Applications that have more features and functions tend to have document windows that also have more features and functions. For example, Microsoft Word has a boatload of features, so its document windows also have a lot of features. On the other hand, a simple application such as SimpleText has a rather plain window.

Opening, Moving, and Closing Windows

Opening a document window is fairly straightforward. When you double-click a document to open it, its application opens and the document appears in a document window. When you create a new document from within application, the document

Another Way to Move

You can also move windows around by dragging them by any of their borders.

appears in a blank document window. To see how this works, find a document on your iMac and double-click it to open it. It doesn't matter which document you pick at this point. You'll see a document window. That is all there is to it.

In case the document isn't where you want it to be on your screen, it's easy to move it around. Simply click the document's title bar, hold the mouse button down, and drag the window where you want it. (If you don't remember where the title bar is, refer to Figure 3.3.)

Closing the document window won't provide much of a challenge for you either. All you have to do is click the **Close** box located in the upper-left corner and the document window disappears. (If you haven't saved the changes to a document, you'll see a dialog box prompting you to save those changes before the document window disappears.)

Resizing, Zooming, and Collapsing Windows

After you have a document window open, you can adjust its size—the size of a document window determines how much of the document you see. Click the Size box located in the lower-right corner of the window, hold the mouse button down, and drag the corner of the document window around until the window is the size you want it to be. Release the button and the window stays the size you made it.

Closing with Speed

If you want to close a window in the flash of an eye, press ⌘+**W**. This does the same thing as clicking the window's Close box. By the way, this works for all windows everywhere (on your iMac at least).

Now open a document window and make it really small. Then make it fill the screen. Now make it really small again. Play around as much as you like. (Unless you are desperate for something to do, I bet you won't do this very long.) When you are done playing, leave the window so small you can't see all the information in the document, just as I have done in Figure 3.4.

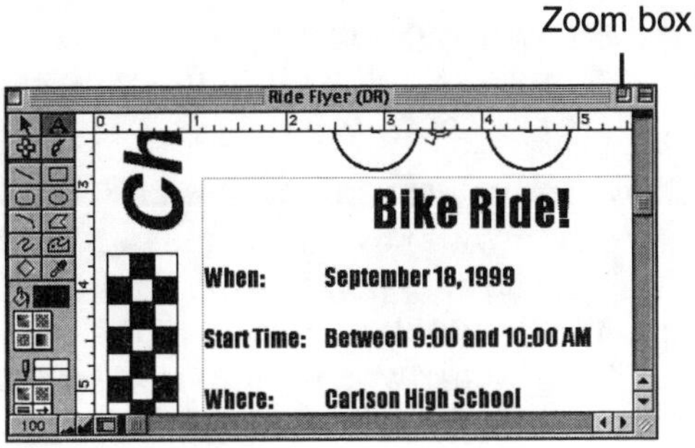

Zoom box

Figure 3.4

*This document window is so small not all the information in the document can be seen; a quick click of the **Zoom** box will fix that.*

Because your document contains such valuable information, you will probably want to see it all. You don't have to spend the time and effort to resize the window, however; you just click the **Zoom** box. The window jumps to a large enough size to display all the information it can, at least until the document window fills the screen. If you want to toggle back to the other size, click the **Zoom** box again, and the window returns to the size it was previously. The Zoom box always makes the document window toggle between "full size" (it fills up the screen) and the size it was before you clicked it.

What happens if you get sick of looking at a document? Is there some easy way to stop looking at it without actually closing it? Why, of course there is. (Would I have asked that question if there wasn't?) That's where the Collapse box comes in. To collapse a document window down to just its title bar, click the **Collapse** box (see Figure 3.5). This can be handy for getting windows out of the way so you can work on something else without closing the document. When you want to see the document again, click the **Collapse** box and the document springs back into being.

Figure 3.5

This document window has been collapsed down to its title bar using the Collapse box.

Ride Flyer (DR) ————Collapse box

If you don't want to have to find the Collapse box to collapse a window, you can make it so that double-clicking a window's title bar collapses it as well. Open the **Appearance** control panel, click the **Options** tab, and check the **Double-click title bar to collapse windows** check box. Now you can collapse an open window or display a collapsed one by double-clicking its title bar. (If you don't know how get to the Appearance control panel, just hang on because I'll show you how in a chapter or two.)

Moving Around Inside Windows

It is unlikely you will be able to see all of an open document at one time. Although the iMac screen is fairly large, your documents will usually be larger than one screen's worth. This is why all document and folder windows have scroll bars, scroll boxes, and scroll arrows. You can use the scroll tools to move up and down or left and right in the document to see all of its contents.

Which of the scroll tools you use depends on how far you want to move. If you want to move up or down (or left or right) by a small amount, such a few lines, use the scroll arrows. All you have to do is to point to the scroll arrow and click the mouse button. The document will scroll in the direction of the arrow line-by-line for as long as you hold the button down. When you want to stop scrolling, release the button and you'll be located in the new position in the document.

When you want to move in your document by a "screenful" at a time, click above or below (or to the right or to the left) of the scroll box. This makes the document scroll by a full screen in the direction in which you clicked.

Where Am I?

You can use the scroll box to tell approximately where you are in a document. If the scroll box is near the top of the scroll bar, you know you are looking at the top of the document. Similarly if the scroll box is at the bottom of the scroll bar, you know you are near the end of the document. In other words, the relative location of the scroll box in the scroll bar tells you your relative location in the document.

If you want to move to a particular point in a document, click the scroll box and drag it up and down or left and right until you see the portion of the document on which you want to work. Release the mouse button, and you'll see that part of the document.

Let's Dialog

Whenever your iMac needs some information from you, it displays a dialog box, commonly called a dialog. The purpose of a dialog box is to enable you to input information that your computer needs to do what you're asking it to do at that moment. For example, when you print, you'll see a Print dialog box. In this dialog box, you tell your computer how many pages to print, which pages of a document to print, and so on. When you open a file, you'll see an Open dialog box in which you tell the application which file to open.

As with document windows, dialog boxes share many of the same features, no matter what application you happen to be working in. For example, the Save As dialog box looks pretty much the same in any application you are using. As with document windows, each application may add its own features to dialog boxes, but after you get used to working with dialog boxes in one place, you can use them anywhere.

All dialog boxes share similar tools to enable you to input information. These include areas in which you type text, pop-up menus from which you make selections, radio buttons you click to select options, and buttons you click to either activate a command or move to another dialog box.

To see an example of one of the standard dialog boxes you will encounter, launch AppleWorks (open your hard drive icon, open the **Applications** folder, open the

AppleWorks folder, and then double-click the **AppleWorks** icon). From the **File** menu, choose **Save As**. In the resulting dialog box, you can name your file, tell AppleWorks where you want the file saved, and click the **Save** button to save the file (see Figure 3.6).

Moving with Speed

To quickly move up and down within your hard drive from within the Save As dialog box, click the pop-up menu at the top of the dialog box (marked with up- and down-facing triangles). You will see a pop-up list of all the folders from your current location up to your hard drive. To quickly move into one of those folders to save your document, select the folder from the pop-up menu. You move to that folder. Click **Save** and your document is saved into that folder.

Use this pop-up menu to quickly
move up through your disk.

Figure 3.6

This AppleWorks Save As dialog box shows many of the standard features you will see as you encounter dialog boxes in your favorite applications.

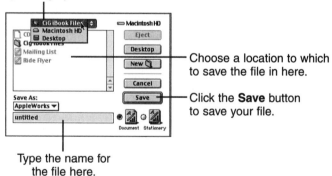

Choose a location to which
to save the file in here.

Click the **Save** button
to save your file.

Type the name for
the file here.

Consider This a Warning

As you use your iMac, things are bound to go wrong once in awhile. But don't worry, your iMac will take care of you. When something bad happens or if you try to do something you shouldn't do, your iMac often displays an alert window (sometimes called an alert box or just an alert). These windows don't have many features, usually just an OK button, a Restart button when your machine takes a nasty crash, or sometimes a Cancel button. When you see one of these dialog boxes, all you can do is either clear away the alert by clicking the **OK** or **Cancel** buttons, or if your machine has crashed, you'll have to restart it by clicking the **Restart** button).

Red Alert! Red Alert!

When there is a problem, don't expect your iMac to be quiet about it. When an alert window displays on your machine, your iMac also makes an alert sound. The sound it makes depends on the alert sound that is selected in the Sound control panel. You can choose from sounds that are installed automatically, and you can also add your own alert sounds. You'll learn how to do that later in this book.

The icons contained in warning dialog boxes change to reflect what is going on. If you run into a major problem, you might see the famous Macintosh bomb that indicates a serious problem has occurred on your machine. Your only choice in this one is to click the **Restart** button to restart your machine. If you try to do something that could be dangerous to something on your machine, you'll often see an exclamation point. This means you should be careful. If you try to do something you can't do, you'll see a stop sign. When you see this, back up and start over.

Closing Without a Close Box

Some windows (for example, alert windows) don't have a Close box. You close these windows with other things, such as an **OK** button. Sometimes you close a window with the **Quit** command (press ⌘+**Q**).

My, My, Aren't These Windows Special

Last, but certainly not least, are those windows I cleverly call the special windows. These windows don't really fit into the other categories you have learned about. The most important of these windows are control panels. Control panels are pieces of software that add additional capability to your iMac, and you use the control panel to determine how much of this capability is actually used in your machine. You will be using many different control panels as you use your iMac.

Control panel windows share a subset of the features that document windows have. Some control panels have a Close box, Zoom box, and Collapse box. Some control panels don't have the scroll tools because the material in the control panel fits in a single screen. Some control panels have different areas you can access by clicking a tab or choosing an icon from a window.

The Least You Need to Know

➤ Windows are the means through which you view everything on your iMac; this includes documents, files, and everything else.

➤ There are several major kinds of windows including folder windows, document windows, dialog boxes, alert windows, and special windows (such as control panels).

➤ Most windows contain similar features you will recognize as you move from window to window.

➤ To open a document window, just double-click a file or create a new document.

➤ To move a window, drag it by its title bar.

➤ Use the Size box, Zoom box, and Collapse box to make windows the size you want them to be.

➤ Use the scroll tools to move around inside windows.

THUNK

Chapter 4

Folders Aren't Manila Anymore

In This Chapter

➤ Learn folder basics

➤ Know the special features of folder windows

➤ View folders in more ways than you would ever want to

➤ Master setting views so your folders look right every time

➤ Use pop-up windows and spring-loaded folders because they are cool

---

There are literally thousands of different files on your iMac. Rather than piling them all over the place (like the dirty clothes in my room when I was kid), your iMac keeps all these files neatly organized in electronic folders. (You can store folders inside folders as well.) In fact, while you are working on the desktop, you will be using folder windows much of the time. Folder windows have unique capabilities when compared to other kinds of windows (such as the document windows you learned about in the last chapter).

The Desktop Is a Folder

Although it doesn't look much like other folders, your desktop is also a folder. When you store files on the desktop, you are actually storing them in a folder called Desktop. You will sometimes see this folder when you are in certain dialog boxes.

Folder Basics 101

Using an iMac means you will be working with folders—and lots of them. Learning to do the basics with folders will only take a few moments.

Making New Folders

As you create your own documents, you will want to create folders in which to store your masterpieces. You can create folders from anywhere on the desktop, such as on the desktop itself, in your hard disk folder, or from within any other folder. To create a new folder from anywhere in the finder, open the **File** menu and choose **New Folder**. You'll see a new, empty folder named, "untitled folder." This new folder works just like any other folder you see on the desktop. You can store documents in it, move it around, and so on.

Naming (and Renaming) Folders

I doubt you will want all the folders on your iMac to be named "untitled folder." Don't worry, you can name or rename a folder just about anything you want.

No Duplicate Names Please

You can't have two folders at the same level within the same folder or disk that have the same name. Your iMac is watching out for you and will not let you name a folder with a name that is already taken. If you try, you will see an alert window explaining this to you. And your iMac is no hypocrite either—it follows its own rules. If you create more than one new folder with the same name, the iMac adds a number to the end of the name (for example, "untitled folder 1") so none of the new folders has the same name.

To name a folder, point to its name and click. Wait a second or so, and the name becomes highlighted. (Note: If you haven't clicked anywhere else since you created the new folder, the name will already be highlighted so you can skip this part.) This tells you that you can edit the name to your heart's content; to delete the current name entirely, press **Delete**. Now type the name you want to use. When the name meets with your approval, press **Return**. The folder will now have the new name

The Need for Speed

To quickly create a new folder, hold down the ⌘ key and press **N**. This does exactly the same thing as choosing **New Folder** from the **File** menu.

I said you can name your folders *just about* anything you want to. There are a few special characters your iMac won't let you use, such as the colon (if you try it, the iMac will turn your colon into a hyphen). That is because your iMac uses the colon in the background to create pathnames, and it does not want you to confuse it by creating your own paths.

Also, you can only use folder names that are up to 31 characters long.

You can change the name of a folder in a similar way. Point to the folder's name and click. After the name becomes highlighted, click inside the name and you will see the "I-beam" symbol that tells you that you can edit the text. Click in the name and edit it, or use the arrow keys to move around and change the name. When you're done, press **Enter**.

Another Faster Way

If you click on a folder and press the **Enter** key, its name becomes highlighted immediately.

Moving Folders Around

You can move folders around. To do so, point to the folder, click and hold the mouse button down, and drag the folder to where you want it to be. When you are there, release the button and your folder is in its new home.

If you move a folder from one disk to another, the folder is copied instead of moved. When you copy a folder, the original copy remains in its current location and a copy is made in the new location.

If you want to move multiple folders at the same time, hold the **Shift** key down while you click each folder. They are all selected and you can move them as a group.

Putting Things in Folders

What good is an empty folder? The answer is not much. To place files within folders, click a file or folder so it is selected (it becomes highlighted) and drag it on top of the folder. When you are in the correct position, the folder becomes highlighted. Release the mouse button and the file or folder is placed inside the folder. (If you don't release the button right away, the folder may spring open—you'll learn more about this later in this chapter.)

Folder Windows Are Just Like Document Windows—Only More So

Although folder windows look similar to document windows, there are some significant differences between them. Folder windows offer many more tools than document windows do, and their tools are focused on working with files and folders rather than with data (see Figure 4.1).

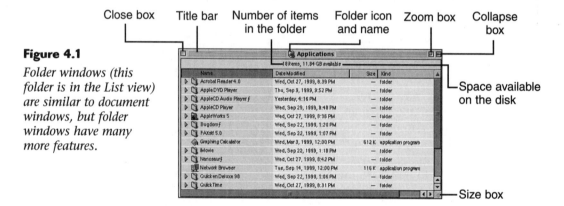

Figure 4.1

Folder windows (this folder is in the List view) are similar to document windows, but folder windows have many more features.

You learned about many of these window features in the previous chapter. The following are some that are unique to folder windows:

➤ **Folder icon**—In folder windows, the folder's icon appears in the Title bar, next to the window name. You can use this icon just as you can any other icon (by dragging it to another disk to copy the folder there, for example).

➤ **Disk information**—In At the top of each folder window, you will see the number of items contained in that folder and the amount of free space on the disk that contains that folder.

➤ **List information**—When you view a folder window in List view, you will see column heads and the sort order button at the top of the window, just under the disk information.

A Folder in Any Other View Looks Different

One of the most important differences between document windows and folder windows is that there are three types of views available in folder windows.

In the Icon view, folders and files are represented with icons (see Figure 4.2). You double-click an icon to open it.

Figure 4.2

Some icons are lovely to look at, but others are just plain boring.

Buttons are similar to icons except that to open an item, you single click its button rather than double-clicking its icon (see Figure 4.3) .

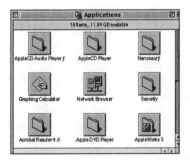

Figure 4.3

A folder in the Button view looks similar to one in the Icon view; the difference is one click versus two.

The List view presents the contents of an item in tabular format. This view provides the most information, but may not be quite as nice to look at as icons or buttons. However, in addition to providing the most information about your files, it is also the most efficient view. As you become a more experienced iMac user, you will probably work in the List view more than the others.

When you have a window open, you can switch among these view types for that window by choosing the view type from the Finder's **View** menu. For example, to see a folder in the Button view, open the **View** menu and then choose **As Buttons**.

45

Switching Views On-the-Fly

You can quickly change the view for a window by using a contextual menu. With the pointer inside a folder, hold down the **Control** key and click the mouse button. From the menu that pops up, choose **View** and then the kind of view you want from the submenu. (You will learn more about contextual menus in the next chapter.)

The Matrix

Your iMac uses an invisible grid on your desktop to locate the items on it. This grid is made up of invisible vertical and horizontal lines the iMac uses to keep everything lined up nice and neat.

The Icons Make the iMac

The Icon view is the simplest in many ways, in addition to being the best looking of the three view types. After all, who doesn't like to see all those pretty icons?

There isn't a whole lot you can do with Icon views; your two options are the following:

➤ **Icon Arrangement**—You can set the way your iMac aligns the icons in a window. **None** means that the Finder leaves the icons wherever you place them. **Always snap to grid** tells the Finder to line up icons according to the invisible grid on the desktop. **Keep arranged** tells the Finder to arrange icons by the parameter you select; you have a number of options from which to choose. (For example, if you choose **By Kind**, the Finder groups all applications together, all documents together, and so on.)

➤ **Icon size**—You can choose the size of the icons that are used in a window. Your choices are large or small.

You can choose among these options by using the View Options window. When you are in a folder in the Icon view, open the **View** menu and choose **View Options**. In the View Options window, choose the **Icon Arrangement** and **Icon Size** you want by clicking the radio buttons next to the options you choose (see Figure 4.4). (If you choose **Keep arranged**, you also need to choose an option from the pop-up menu.) Click **OK** and you see the results of your changes in the folder in which you were working.

Figure 4.4

The View Options window enables you to tell your iMac how to display icons.

Listing Files for All the World to See

The List view gives you the most information about a window's content, and it also has the most functionality of any of the views (see Figure 4.5). For example, you can choose which information is provided in the List view, and you can quickly see the contents of any folder.

Column headings Column width Sort order button

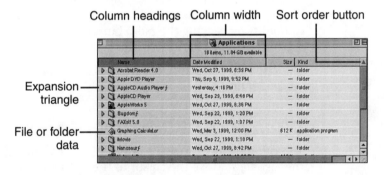

Expansion triangle

File or folder data

Figure 4.5

The List view provides the most powerful tools for managing your files, but it isn't much to look at!

In any List view, your iMac can display the following columns:

➤ File or folder name
➤ Date modified
➤ Date created
➤ Size
➤ Kind
➤ Label
➤ Comments
➤ Version

Make Your List

You probably don't want to see all the list data in every folder you open; only some of it will be useful to you. Fortunately, you can tell your iMac which information to display in the List view.

From within a folder in the List view, open the **View** menu and choose **View Options**. You will see a dialog box that is similar to the one you saw when you were working with the Icon view. To determine which columns you see in the List view, check the check box next to that column in the **Show Columns** area. For example, to show the **Size** column, check the check box next to that option. To hide a column, leave its check box unchecked.

While you have the View Options dialog box open, you can also do a couple more things. If you want relative dates to be used in the date columns (for example, Yesterday, 7:00 a.m. instead of Sun, Aug 22, 1999, 7:00 a.m.), choose the **Use relative date** check box. If you want folder sizes to be shown, check the **Calculate folder sizes** check box—I don't recommend this because it can really slow down your machine. Choose the icon size you want to be used in the list by clicking the radio button under the size you prefer. When you're done, click **OK**.

The List view for that folder is now customized to your own preferences. Neat, huh?

You Can Go Back Again

To resize the columns to their original width, open the **View** menu and choose **Reset Column Positions**. Click **OK** in the dialog box and the widths return to what they were before you monkeyed around with them.

Change the Width of a Column

You can quickly change the width of any column in the List view. Move the cursor to the right edge of the column name box for the column whose width you want to change. When the cursor changes from the arrow to the line with an arrow out of each side of it, click and drag the column to make it the width you want (see Figure 4.6). Release the button, and the column will have the new width.

Figure 4.6

It is easy to change the width of any column in the List view.

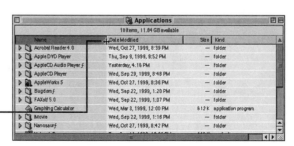

When you see this icon, drag to change the column width.

Expand a Folder

This List view enables you to view a folder's contents without actually opening it. Click the **Expansion triangle** (the right-facing triangle) next to the folder you want to expand. The contents of the folder are displayed and indented to the right for each level of folder (see Figure 4.7). The Expansion triangle is now pointing down to tell you that the contents of the folder have been expanded.

Expansion triangle

Name	Date Modified	Size	Kind
Acrobat Reader 4.0	Wed, Oct 27, 1999, 8:39 PM	—	folder
Apple DVD Player	Thu, Sep 9, 1999, 9:52 PM	—	folder
Apple DVD Player	Thu, Sep 9, 1999, 12:00 PM	378 K	application program
Apple DVD Player Guide	Mon, Feb 8, 1999, 12:00 PM	12 K	document
Apple DVD Player Read Me	Thu, Sep 9, 1999, 12:00 PM	12 K	SimpleText read-only do
AppleCD Audio Player f	Yesterday, 4:16 PM	—	folder
AppleCD Player	Wed, Sep 29, 1999, 8:48 PM	—	folder
AppleWorks 5	Wed, Oct 27, 1999, 8:36 PM	—	folder
About AppleWorks Help	Sat, Aug 29, 1998, 12:00 PM	252 K	document
AppleWorks	Wed, Aug 11, 1999, 12:00 PM	2.6MB	application program

Figure 4.7

Why bother to open a folder to see what is inside when you can simply expand it?

Click the **Expansion triangle** again to collapse a folder so you no longer see its contents.

Sort a List

You can change the order in which files and folders appear by sorting the folder. Click the column heading for the column by which you want to sort the list. The column heading is highlighted to show you this is the criteria used to sort the list, and the list will reorder itself based on the defined criteria for that parameter (for example, from most-recent to least-recent date modified, largest to smallest size, and so on). Click the **Sort order** button in the upper-right corner of the list area (above the scrollbar) to reverse the sort order (from ascending to descending or from descending to ascending).

Be an iMac Wizard

Expanding All Subfolders!

If you hold down the **Option** key while you click the Expansion triangle for a folder, all the folders within that folder are expanded or collapsed at the same time.

How Do You Want to View Your Folders Today?

There are two ways to set the views that will be used for your folder windows. You can set views preferences *globally* or *locally*. When you set views preferences globally, each time you open a window, it opens with the preferences you set. This means you don't have to change the view settings each time you open a window. When you don't want to use those global views preferences for a particular folder, you can set preferences locally for that folder.

This aspect of the iMac can be a bit confusing. To explain it another way, here is the general process you use to determine the views you use for your folders:

1. Set global views preferences for the Icon, Button, and List views. These preferences will be applied to every folder window you open.

2. For particular windows in which you don't want to use the global views preferences, you can override the global settings by setting the local preferences for the Icon, Button, or List views for that *particular* window.

Your iMac calls the global views preferences *Standard Views*. It calls local preferences *View Options*.

You should set the global preferences to your liking so folders, by default, appear with the settings you prefer. To do so, from the **Edit** menu, choose **Preferences**. You will see the Preferences window. Click the **Views** tab, and you will see the Views Preferences dialog box (see Figure 4.8).

Figure 4.8

With global views preferences, folders appear just the way you want them to—every time.

Re-Applying the Global View

If you decided you want to reapply the global view preferences to a folder you have customized, open the **View** menu and choose **View Options**. In the View Options window, click the **Set to Standard Views** button and your global preferences are reapplied to the folder with which you are working.

Choose the default settings for each view just like you did when you set them for a specific folder. For example, to set the global view for the List view, choose **List** from the **Standard View Options for** pop-up menu. Make the changes you want. Then move to the next view type. When you're done, close the window by clicking the **Close** box. Each time you open a folder, it will use the global preferences you just set—except when you override them.

You can override the global views settings for a particular folder by simply making the changes to that folder's view using the **View Options** command under the **View** menu. (You did this earlier in the chapter.)

Windows Are Popping Up All Over

Pop-up windows are a great way to keep files you frequently use easily accessible. Pop-up windows appear as tabs at the bottom of the desktop (see Figure 4.9). When you click a pop-up window's tab, the window pops open, and you can work within it. When you move out of the window, it pops back into a tab. You can quickly access files and folders in a pop-up window without using up a lot of screen space.

This pop-up window is open.   Size box

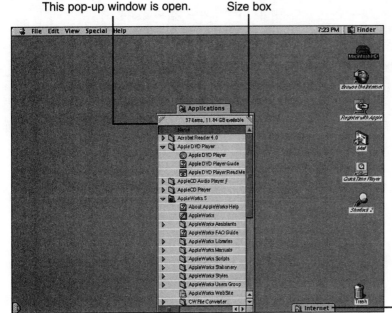

Figure 4.9

Pop-up windows appear as tabs across the bottom of your desktop; when you click a pop-up window, it pops open, and you can work within it.

This one is closed.

Creating a Pop-Up Window

To create a pop-up window, first open a folder. Open the **View** menu and choose **As Pop-up window**. The folder becomes an open pop-up window, located right next to the last pop-up window created or close to the left edge of the desktop if there are no other pop-up windows.

Another Way to Pop

You can also change a window into a pop-up window by dragging its title bar to the bottom of the desktop. When you get close to the bottom of the desktop, the folder is converted into a pop-up window. With this method, you can place the pop-up window anywhere along the bottom of the desktop.

You can set the width of the pop-up window by setting the width of the window you are changing into a pop-up window. The wider the window you are converting, the wider the pop-up window's tab will be.

Views Options in Pop-up Windows

All the views options you have for regular folder windows apply to pop-up windows also (for example, the Icon view).

Resize the pop-up window by dragging the Size box in the upper-left and upper-right corners of the window (look for the slanted hash marks). Dragging the sizing handles up or down determines how high the window pops up. Dragging them left or right determines how wide a pop-up window will be.

Click outside the folder to "pop" it closed.

To change a pop-up menu back into a "regular" folder window, drag the tab of the pop-up window up onto the desktop until you see an entire window. The window is now a "regular" window.

Using Pop-Up Windows

There is nothing to using pop-up windows, just try the following:

➤ To open a pop-up window, click its tab.

➤ To close a pop-window, click outside of it.

➤ To place a folder or file within a folder that uses a pop-up window, drag the file or folder into the pop-up window's tab, wait for the window to pop up, and then drag the file where you want it. Click outside the window and it pops back into a tab.

How Springy Are Your Folders?

When you drag a file or folder onto a spring-loaded folder, it springs open, and you can move the folder or file into the folder. This doesn't stop with the first spring-loaded folder you move into either. As you continue to drag items onto folders within a spring-loaded folder, those folders also spring open so you can quickly move a file or folder into any folder no matter how buried within other folders it is.

One of the good things about spring-loaded folders is that they snap closed after you move out of them, so you don't leave a trail of open folders behind you.

You can set the amount of time it takes for folders to spring open after you drag an item onto them. From the **Edit** menu, choose **Preferences**. Click the **General** tab, and you will see the General Preferences window. To turn spring-loaded folders on (it is on by default), check the **Spring-loaded folders** check box. Use the **Delay before opening** slider to adjust the amount of time you have to have for an item to be placed over a folder before it springs open.

The longer you set the time, the less springy the folder is and the longer you have to hold an item over a folder before it pops open. When you have it set, close the window. Experiment a bit to see what length of time is the most comfortable for you.

Using Folder Window Features

Folder windows have special navigation, window, and file management features you won't find with other windows. You can use these features in any of the views, and they work on any open folder window.

Moving Among Windows

To move up or down from the folder whose window is open, hold the ⌘ key down and click the window's title. A menu pops up that enables you to select any folder within your current folder or containing the current folder all the way up to the desktop.

Opening One Folder's Window While Closing the Current Window

Sometimes when you are opening folders looking for a particular file, you leave a trail of open windows that may not need to be open. To close the current window while you are opening the next folder, hold down the **Option** key while opening the folder. As the folder opens, the window you are currently in closes. This helps keep your desktop clean while you are burrowing down into folders.

Closing All Open Windows

You can close all the open windows on your desktop by holding down the **Option** key and clicking the **Close** box of one of the open folders.

The Least You Need to Know

➤ To create a folder, use the **New Folder** command on the File menu; to rename a folder, click its name, wait for the highlight to appear, and type a new name.

➤ Move a folder by dragging it by its title bar; to use a folder, just drop a file on it to place the file in it or double-click a folder to open it.

➤ There are three views for folders: Icon, Button, and List; the Icon view is the prettiest, but the List view is the most useful.

➤ You can choose a view for a folder from the **View** menu.

➤ In the List view, you can customize the information shown, sort the list, view folder contents without opening them, and so on.

➤ Use pop-up windows to access your favorite folders and files quickly.

➤ Use spring-loaded folders so you don't have to open a folder when you need to place something in it.

COULD I BRING THE PRINTER SETTINGS UP AND GET SOME WORD PROCESSING?

EXCELLENT, SIR.

Chapter 5

Ordering from the Menus

In This Chapter

➤ Understand what menus are and how to use them

➤ Learn about the special Finder menus

➤ Understand how to keep several applications open at the same time and how to switch from one to another

---

Menus are one of the major interface elements you will use while you work with your iMac. Why are they called menus? Because, just as with a restaurant menu, you choose things from lists that are presented to you. Rather than choosing blueberry pancakes or the five-eggs-and-four-pounds-of-meat special, with iMac menus, you choose various commands and options. If you have read through this book so far (and I know you have, right?), you have already seen and used a number of menus.

Know Thy Menus

As you use your iMac, you will use the following types of menus:

➤ **Pull-down menus**—Pull-down menus are the most common type of iMac menu, and they appear in all applications. In fact, there are standard pull-down menus that are supposed to be included in every application. These include the Apple, File, Edit, and Application menus. Pull-down menus get their name because you "pull them down" by clicking them. You can choose commands from the menus in their "pulled down" condition.

Missing Menus

Although all applications are supposed to have the standard menus, you won't always see them. Some applications, especially games, hide the menus while the application is running. You can usually make them appear by pressing the **spacebar** or the ⌘ key.

➤ **Pop-up menus**—Pop-up menus are used to provide you with a list of choices that "pop up" when you click the pop-up menu. From the pop-up menu, you can choose commands or options. Pop-up menus are most common within dialog boxes, but you see them other places as well.

➤ **Contextual menus**—Contextual menus are pop-up menus that change depending on the context in which they are activated. Contextual menus provide quick and easy access to the most likely commands you will use in certain situations. Plus, you can customize contextual menus so the commands you use most are just a click away.

➤ **Tear-off (floating) menus**—Some menus can be "torn off" the menu bar and become free-floating palettes from which you can choose commands or options.

➤ **Unique menus**—There are certain menus that are only available in specific areas. Your iMac uses several of these unique menus, including the Finder's View menu (which you used quite a lot in the previous chapter).

Contextual Menus and Applications: The Untold Story

CMs are also supported in many major applications, including Microsoft Office. To see if your favorite applications use CMs, just hold the **Control** key and click on something in that application. If CMs are supported, you will see one.

It's Easy to Order, So Order Now!

Using most iMac menus requires little explanation. To use pull-down menus, you simply click the menu to pull it down, highlight the command you want, and release the mouse button.

To use pop-up menus, you click the mouse button and highlight your choice from the menu that pops up. Release the button and the choice is made.

Putting Menus in Context

Contextual Menus (CMs) are one of the most powerful tools on the iMac. CMs provide a pop-up menu of commands that you can quickly access by clicking something while holding the Control key down. As their name implies, CMs change depending on the context in which you activate them. For example, when you activate a contextual menu in a window, you will see one set of commands. If you use a contextual menu on the desktop, you will see another set of choices.

CMs are also extensible, which means you can add items to CMs to fully customize them for the way you like to work. You can also add new functions to your iMac through CM files.

Using CMs is simple—just point to something, hold the **Control** key down, and click the mouse button. The CM pops up, and you can choose a command from it (see Figure 5.1).

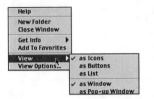

Figure 5.1

Contextual menus provide an easy and fast way to access context-specific commands.

If you have been following along at home, you have already seen some contextual menus (you used them to change the view for a folder). Try some more, just for the fun of it. Move the pointer over an empty space on the desktop. Hold the **Control** key down and click. You will see a variety of desktop commands, including Help, New Folder, View (with submenus), Clean Up, and so on. To activate a command, choose it from the menu.

Rolling Your Own Contextual Menus

Contextual menus are extensible; this means you can add new commands to existing contextual menus. You do this by placing contextual menu files in the Contextual Menu Items folder that is within the System Folder. (If you open this folder now, you will see several contextual menu files already in there.)

Take an iLook

Marking CMs

If you point to something, press the **Control** key, and see a small pop-up menu icon by the arrow, a contextual menu is available. If you don't see this, there is no CM available for whatever you are pointing to.

You can find additional contextual menu files on the Internet that add all sorts of commands to your contextual menus. Place these files in the Contextual Menu folder, restart your iMac, and the new commands will be available .

Adding the Ultimate Contextual Menu Tool: FinderPop

One of the most powerful additions you can make to your iMac is a utility called FinderPop. FinderPop makes the most out of contextual menus by adding many different commands to them and also by making it even easier for you to add your own commands. You can find FinderPop on the Internet, and even better, it is free! When you can access the Internet (you will get to that in the next part of the book), go to www.finderpop.com and download FinderPop. Install it and your contextual menus will never be the same.

The Special Menu Really Is Special

Unless you are brand new to the iMac, you have already used commands on the Special menu. The Special commands are fairly important, and most of them are pretty straightforward. The major commands on the Special menu that you need to know how to use are the following:

➤ **Empty Trash**—This command deletes the files that are stored in the Trash.

One nice-to-know feature of the Trash is that if you hold the **Option** key while you select **Empty Trash**, you will delete any locked items that are in the Trash. (Without using the Option key, you can't empty locked items from the Trash.) If you are having a hard time getting rid of a file in the Trash, try this.

➤ **Eject**—You can use the **Eject** command, or press ⌘+**E**, to eject any removable media that is mounted on the desktop and that is selected. This works with CD-ROMs, floppy disks, Zip disks, and other removable media.

You can also use the **Put Away** command on the **File** menu (⌘+**Y**) to eject a removable disk.

➤ **Erase Disk**—The Erase Disk command erases and formats hard, Zip, and floppy disks. When you choose the Erase Disk command, you have different options depending on the type of disk you are erasing (Zip, floppy, and so on).

➤ **Sleep**—The Sleep command puts your iMac to sleep. In Sleep mode, your iMac's hard drive stops spinning and the monitor powers down. In Sleep mode, your iMac uses much less power than it does in "awake" mode. And your iMac will be ready for you to use again much faster than if you have to start it up from the shut-down condition. All you have to do wake your iMac up is press a key. If you are going to be away from your iMac for a while, it is a good idea to put it to sleep. You can set your iMac to automatically go to sleep after a specific period of time. (You learned to do this in Chapter 2, "You Never Need to Dust This Desktop.")

Pressing ⌘+**Option+Power** key puts your iMac immediately into the sleep mode.

➤ **Restart**—The Restart command makes your iMac shut down all running processes and then restart all of its system software. Restarting is also called *warm starting* or *rebooting*. You will need to restart your iMac occasionally, such as when a program crashes or when you have made software changes (installing new software for example).

➤ **Shut Down**—You should always use the Shut Down command to turn you iMac off. This command ensures that all the processes running on your iMac are properly stopped and that the hard drive is ready to stop spinning (the drive heads are parked).

The Fast Way to Sleep, Quit, or Restart

If you press the **Power** key (the key in the upper-right corner of the keyboard—it has a partial circle with a line through it), you will see a dialog box that enables you to click **Restart**, **Sleep**, or **Shut Down** (the default). You can also cancel if you need to. A good way to shut down your iMac is to hit the **Power** key and then press **Return**.

The Application Menu—Confusing But Cool

Your iMac is able to *multi-task*. This means your iMac can do more than one thing at a time. For example, you can have several applications open simultaneously (see Figure 5.2). This prevents you from having to stop one application just because you want to work in another one for awhile. Plus, your iMac can do some tasks in the background while you are working within another application.

Application menu

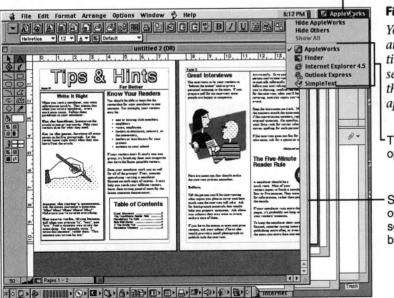

Figure 5.2

Your iMac can chew gum and walk at the same time—this desktop shows several open documents that are in different applications.

These applications are all open and running.

Some have documents open, which you can see in the background, but others don't.

59

Now for the confusing part. You can have open applications that do not have open documents. In this case, there are only two ways to tell that you are in that application. The first is to notice that the menu bar is for the application, not for the Finder (remember that the Finder's menu bar is the only one with the Special menu). The second way is to look at the **Application** menu (which I will show you in a moment).

If you try to click something on your desktop and nothing seems to happen, you were probably in an application with no documents open. I can't tell you how many people I have seen clicking madly on things and wondering why nothing was being selected. Usually, they were simply in an open application, but did not know it.

This concept is a bit tough to get used to, but with some practice and observation, you can "get it" and save yourself some frustration.

Using the Application Menu Like a Pro

You use the Application menu to manage all the open applications that are currently running on your iMac. The Application menu is always available to you; it is the last menu on the far right of the menu bar.

Click the **Application** menu. You will see a list of the applications currently running on your iMac; if the Finder is the only application running, that is all you will see listed. The application with the check mark next to it is the one that is currently "on top" or *active*, and its menu bar will be visible.

To bring a different application to the front, which you must do to work with it, simply choose it from the **Application** menu. The menu bar becomes the menu bar of the application that you selected, and the application's name and icon appear at the top of the **Application** menu (see Figure 5.3). Any open documents are also moved to the front so you can work in them.

Hide and Go Seek

If open windows of applications that are in the background distract you, choose **Hide Others** from the **Application** menu. The other applications are hidden from view (although they are still running).

If you want to move back to the application that was previously active, choose **Hide CurrentApplication** (where **CurrentApplication** is the name of the application that is active).

To see all the applications that are open, choose **Show All**.

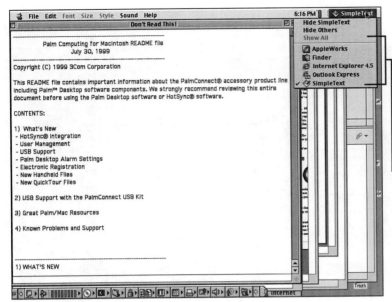

Figure 5.3

Now SimpleText is the active application—compare this figure to the previous one, in which SimpleText was in the background and AppleWorks was in the front.

Compare this Application menu to the one in the previous figure.

Make Your Own Application Menu

You can customize the Application menu. You can resize the menu to display as much or as little of the active application's name as you want. (If you make it small enough, you will see only its icon.) The most significant of these features is the ability to convert the Application menu into a floating menu or palette. In this mode, the Application menu is called the *Application Switcher*.

Resize the Application menu by dragging the left edge (the hash marks) to the right to make it smaller or to the left to make it bigger.

Drag down through the menu to tear it off the Finder's menu bar and make it into a floating window. The active application is highlighted (see Figure 5.4).

Even with the Application Switcher open, you can still use the Application menu in the same ways that you can when the Application Switcher is closed.

To switch to a different application, click its icon or name in the Application Switcher window.

Take an iLook

Is It Better to Click to Switch?

You can simply click in an open document to move into the application that was used to open it. You can also click the desktop to move back into the Finder. Whatever you click becomes the active application.

Figure 5.4

*When you "tear off" the **Application** menu, it becomes a floating window called the Application Switcher.*

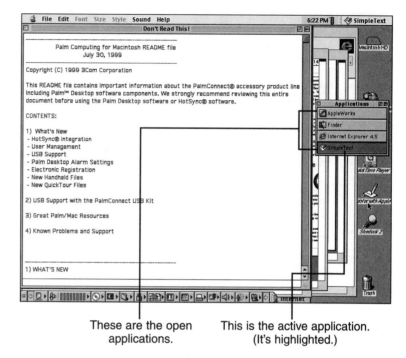

These are the open applications.

This is the active application. (It's highlighted.)

You can move the Application Switcher around, but it always floats on top of all other open windows. You can collapse it to its title bar by clicking its **Collapse** box.

Another way to switch between applications is to hold down the ⌘ key and press **Tab**. Keep pressing **Tab** (while holding down the ⌘ key) to move from one application to the next. When the application you want to switch to is highlighted, let the keys up and you will move into that application.

If you hold down the **Shift** key while you have the ⌘ key down and then press the **Tab** key, you move backward through the list of open applications. This comes in handy sometimes.

To view the Application Switcher in the Icon view, hold the ⌘ key down while you click the window's **Zoom** box.

To toggle the size of the icons, hold the **Option** key down while you click the **Zoom** box.

To change the orientation of the palette from vertical to horizontal, hold down the **Option** and **Shift** keys while you click the **Zoom** box.

To close the Application Switcher, click its **Close** box.

Take an iLook

The Floating Window Is Always with You

The floating Application Switcher remains where you last left it, even after you restart your iMac.

Learning to use the iMac's multitasking capability, the Application menu, and Application Switcher can save you the time you normally waste opening and closing applications. As long as your iMac has enough RAM to keep the applications you use open at all times, there is really no reason to quit an application. It is much better to use the **Application** menu and Application Switcher to quickly move into the application with which you want to work.

The Least You Need to Know

➤ There are several different types of menus, such as pull-down menus, pop-up menus, floating menus, and so on.

➤ All menus work similarly simply choose a command to activate it.

➤ There are several special Finder menus, including the Special and Application menus, that you need to know about to be iMac literate.

➤ Learning to use your iMac's multitasking capability can save you a lot of time that you would normally spend opening and closing applications; use the Application menu and Application Switcher to move among your open applications.

➤ If you find yourself clicking, but nothing seems to be happening, the most likely cause is that you are actually in an application. (Look at the Application menu and menu bar to see if this is the case.) The first click moves you back into the Finder, which seems to have done nothing if you aren't watching carefully.

Chapter 6

Stop All This Playing Around and Create Your First Document

In This Chapter

➤ Learn about AppleWorks and what it can do for you

➤ Use AppleWorks to create a flyer containing text and graphics

➤ Create a database to organize a mailing list

➤ Create mailing labels to send out the flyer

Now that you know your way around the iMac pretty well, I'll bet you are anxious to do something with it. After all, that is the point of having an iMac isn't it? You are going to use your iMac for all sorts of things, and one of the most common will be creating various types of documents. In this chapter, you'll learn how easy it is to create great documents with an iMac. If you follow along, you will create a set of documents using AppleWorks, which is a nice application that is included with your iMac.

Using AppleWorks—Not Exactly Like Using a Swiss Army Knife, But Pretty Close

AppleWorks is truly an all-in-one application. It enables you to do all of the following:

➤ Create documents with a word processing module

➤ Create and add graphics to your documents with the drawing and painting modules

➤ Calculate numbers with a spreadsheet module

➤ Store and manage information with the database module

➤ Communicate over the modem with a communications module

With AppleWorks, you can use these different modules in the same document. For example, you can use the database to store addresses that you can print on mailing labels you create in the word processing module.

Understand How AppleWorks Works

When you first open AppleWorks (which you will do in a few pages), you are prompted to create a new document. You see a list of document types you can create, including a word processing document, a drawing document, and so on. You select the document type from the list, and then choose to create a new document on your own or by using the AppleWorks Assistant.

A Program by Any Other Name

AppleWorks used to be called ClarisWorks because it was produced by Apple's software subsidiary Claris, which also produced other applications such as the FileMaker Pro database. A few years ago, Apple did away with Claris. (It became FileMaker, which is dedicated to the FileMaker Pro database.) Apple took ClarisWorks back and renamed it AppleWorks.

Don't worry about limiting yourself to one document type (such as a word processing document) because you can add any other type of element to that document. For example, if you choose a word processing document, you can easily add a drawing, a painting, or even a spreadsheet as a graphic on that document When you want to add another type of information, you can do it in one of two ways. You can either create a separate document and then import it into your document, or you can add a new element directly onto your base document. Don't worry; this amazing capability is harder to describe than it is to use.

Many of the AppleWorks commands are available through buttons on its toolbars as well as on its menus.

Learn Some Neat Features of AppleWorks

The following are some AppleWorks features you should learn to use:

➤ **AppleWorks Help**—Under the Help menu, you can get several different kinds of help. You can get Apple Balloon help, which presents pop-up balloons when you point to icons or commands. More useful is the AppleWorks Help Contents command, which brings up a hot-linked, fully searchable help system (just like the iMac's Help Center). On the Help menu you can also access Frequently Asked Questions (FAQs) and AppleWorks Assistants.

➤ **AppleWorks Assistants**—When you create a new document, you can choose to have an assistant walk you through creating the type of document you select. You can choose from different categories of documents, such as flyers or certificates, and then AppleWorks guides you as you create that document (see Figure 6.1).

Figure 6.1

AppleWorks Assistants can help you create many different kinds of documents; because there are so many, you will have a harder time choosing a document type than you will creating it!

➤ **Macros**—Macros are a series of steps you can record to perform certain tasks. Then you can play the steps back with a single click or selection from a menu. For example, perhaps there's a certain block of text you include in many of your documents. This can be your address, signature block, a standard contract clause, or anything else. Rather than having to retype this text in every document, you can have AppleWorks record the text in a macro. When you want to add this text to a document, you simply run the macro and the text is typed for you. You can get more sophisticated with macros also; basically, anything you can repeat can be done with a macro.

➤ **Toolbars**—AppleWorks uses a toolbar to enable you to quickly use certain commands. AppleWorks comes configured with a very nice toolbar that provides buttons for the most common tasks. The good news is that you can add your own buttons to the AppleWorks toolbar and you can create your own toolbars to completely customize AppleWorks to the way you work.

Use Your iMac to Host a Bike Ride

The best way to learn about AppleWorks is to use it to create your own documents. To get started, pretend you are coordinating a large bike ride for a bicycling group. To get riders to show up for the ride, you need to develop an informational flyer. Then you need to mail that flyer out to a lot of riders (the more the merrier).

Don't Like to Bike?

You may not care for my example, and if not, that is okay (although I can't imagine anyone not enjoying a good bike ride!). You can use the same process to plan and organize a party or other group event. Just plug your own information in as you follow along with the book.

Plan Your Project

I know you are so excited about AppleWorks that you want to rush in and get started. But you will be better off if you take a few moments and plan what you want to create. Planning helps you avoid wasting a lot of time because you aren't sure what you are going to do along the way.

In this example, you need to create the following documents:

➤ **Flyer**—The flyer describes the ride, provides the key details (date, time, and so on), and hopefully gets people excited about coming to the ride.

➤ **Contact database**—To keep things organized, you can create a database of all the people you want to invite to the ride. Because you will need some help supporting the ride, you also should get information for volunteers.

➤ **Mailing labels**—Your flyer is no good unless you get it to people; you can use your database to prepare mailing labels. (Who wants to hand-print envelopes?)

Be Speedy

The fastest way to create and name a folder is this: press ⌘+**N** to create the folder, and immediately type the new name. When you're done, press **Return** again to "set" the name.

Create a Folder to Keep Your Project Organized

Now it is time to put your iMac through its paces. Create a folder in which to keep all the ride-related documents so you don't have to search for them every time you need them. Open your hard drive, and from the **File** menu, choose **New Folder**. You will see a folder with the name highlighted. (Your iMac assumes you don't want to call your new folder, "untitled folder".) Rename it something like "The Ride of the Century!"

Because you will be accessing this folder often, convert it into a pop-up window so it's easy to get to. Open your folder and make it the size you think you'll need (drag the resize box). Now drag its title bar to the bottom edge of the desktop until the window becomes a tab (see Figure 6.2).

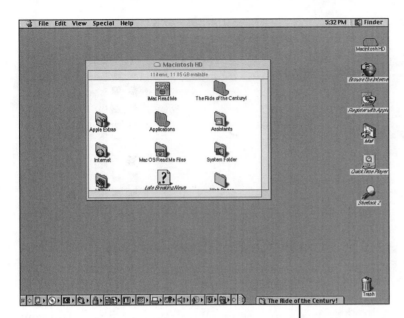

Figure 6.2
Use a pop-up window to make your folder easy to access.

Click the tab to make the window pop open.

Launch AppleWorks

Now that your organizational work is done, it's time to open AppleWorks and get to it. Open the Applications folder on your hard drive. Now open the AppleWorks folder and double-click the **AppleWorks** icon to open the application. You will see a splash screen that quickly disappears and leaves you in the New Document dialog box.

Creating a Flyer to Announce Your Ride

The first thing to create is a flyer that both encourages people to attend your ride and provides all the details they need to be able to do so.

Use the AppleWorks Assistant to create your flyer as fast and easy as possible. In the New Document dialog box, click the Use Assistant

Take an iLook

Register Early and Often

The first time you open AppleWorks, you are prompted to enter your name, company, and serial number. Fill in the first two, but don't worry about the serial number. You don't need it.

or Stationery radio button. (If you don't see this dialog box, open the **File** menu and choose **New**.) You see a list of Assistants in the left pane of the dialog box. Open the **Category** pop-up menu and choose **Flyers**. Now you will see a list of flyer templates on which you can base your own flyer. Click Flyer 5 and click **OK** to begin. You will see a nicely designed flyer that lacks only your custom information (see Figure 6.3).

69

Figure 6.3

The AppleWorks Assistant has done a lot of work for you; all you have to do is add the details!

Take an iLook

Document Type at a Glance

When AppleWorks creates a document, you can determine the type of document by the abbreviation in parentheses after the document name. DR stands for drawing, WP for word processing, and so on.

Save Once, Save Often

Start practicing good computing habits and save your document as soon as you create it. From the **File** menu, choose **Save As**. In the Save As dialog box, you need to tell your iMac what you want your document to be called and where you want to save it. Type a name for the document in the text box. (How about something imaginative like Ride Flyer?) Click the **Desktop** button. In the upper-left pane of the dialog box, double-click the **hard drive** icon. Scroll through the list of folders until you see the folder you created for your project. Double-click the folder to open it—when you click **Save**, your document is saved in this folder (see Figure 6.4).

Figure 6.4

The Save As dialog box appears the first time you save a document so get used to seeing it!

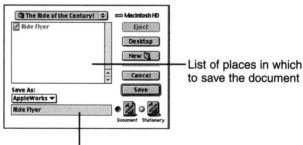

List of places in which to save the document

Type the document name here.

Add a Bike Graphic—This Flyer Is for a Bike Ride

Because this is a flyer announcing a bike ride, it is a good idea to add a graphic of a bike so people get the idea right away. You can import a picture of a bike, but AppleWorks provides some clip art you can quickly add to your projects as well.

Open the **File** menu, select **Library**, and choose **Transportation** from the hierarchical menu. The Transportation library window opens. Click **Bicycle** and you see a preview of the art in the upper part of the window. (It isn't much to look at, but what can you expect for something so easy?) Click the **Use** button, and the bike art appears in your flyer, albeit at a small size. Close the Transportation window (open the **File** menu and choose **Close**.)

Now make the bike graphic large so it really grabs people's attention. Click the bike, and selection handles (small, black boxes) appear on each corner. You can resize the graphic by dragging these handles, but there is a better way. With the graphic still selected (you should still see the selection handles), open the **Arrange** menu and choose **Scale By Percent**. In the Scale By Percent dialog box, enter the percent increase you want to use (use the same percentage in both directions). Type **300** in both text boxes and click **OK**. The bike graphic is now 300% larger than it was.

What Is the Add Button For?

You may have noticed the Add button in the Transportation window. You can create your own libraries and add your own creations to existing libraries. The Add button enables you to do either.

Selection Handles (AKA Grab Handles)

When you select an item, the black boxes at the corners enable to you "grab" a corner of the item so you can move that corner to resize the object. If you hold down the **Shift** key while you drag, the object is resized proportionally.

Now the bike is pretty large, but it is probably not in the best place. With the bike graphic selected, click inside the graphic and drag it to a new location on the flyer—try placing it in the center of the page at the top. When you do so, you may run into the default text the Assistant placed on the page (it begins with, "This attention-getting headline..."). Click that text to select it (look for the selection handles) and press **Delete**. Now you have plenty of room for the bike graphic (see Figure 6.5).

Figure 6.5

A nice bike graphic has been added to the flyer—using the AppleWorks library, this took only a few moments.

Where Are My Tools?

If you don't see the tools, open the **Window** menu and choose the **Show Tools** command.

Make Your Pitch

Now that you have a nice-looking flyer, it is time to add the meat to this skeleton. At the least, you should put all the details about the ride, such as the time and date, mileage to be ridden, where it starts, whether lunch is provided, any fees required, and so on.

You begin by inserting a text frame. Click the **Text** tool (the button with the capital "A" on the tool bar), move onto the document, and drag to create a text frame. Make it as large as you can, but stay inside the checkered border. (Remember that you can make the document window larger by using its **Size** box.)

I've Been Framed!

In AppleWorks lingo, a frame is a placeholder for another object. For example, if you place a graphic in a word processing document, you place it in a frame. In this case, you placed a text frame in a drawing document. Inside a frame, the tools appropriate for that frame are active—this is sort of like a document within a document.

Now type your text. Don't worry about formatting it as you type. It is better to put all the information in first and then make it look nice later (see Figure 6.6).

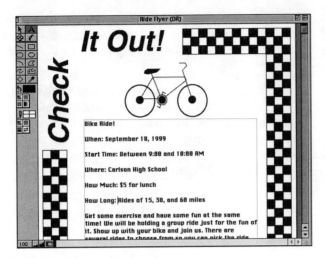

Figure 6.6

Now the flyer has all the pertinent information, but it doesn't look very nice—yet.

Now Make the Text Look Nice

AppleWorks provides many tools you can use to format text in all sorts of ways. You can change the fonts, add styles (such as bold or italics), make the text larger, and so on. Use the formatting options to make the text on your flyer look great.

To format text, first select it and then apply the formatting by choosing a command from a menu or by clicking a button. Select the flyer title by dragging through it so the text is highlighted. Choose a new font for it by opening the **Font** menu and choosing another font. Now open the **Size** menu and choose the size you want the text to be. To center the title text open the **Format** menu, choose **Paragraph**, choose **Center** from the **Alignment** pop-up menu, and click **OK**.

Take an iLook

Pop-Up Menus Work Too

You can also format the text by making choices from the text formatting pop-up menus just above the document's title bar.

Continue to format the text as you see fit. Generally, if you think it looks nice, others will too. However, go easy on it—if you use every font and style that is available to you, you are going way overboard and you will experience the kidnapper effect (where your document looks sort of like a kidnapper's ransom note).

Advanced Formatting

AppleWorks provides many advanced text formatting tools, such as tabs, text styles, and so on. Check out the AppleWorks help to explore how these work. They make formatting text much more efficient.

Edit Your Work—After All, No One Is Perfect

After your document has all the text it needs and is formatted the way you want it, it is time to do a final edit to make sure there are no mistakes.

Start by doing a spell check on your flyer. From the **Edit** menu, choose **Writing Tools,** and then **Check Document Spelling**. AppleWorks begins to check the spelling in your flyer. When it identifies a misspelled word (and unless you have better spelling skills than I do, it will!), you see the Spelling dialog box.

The suspect word is highlighted at the top of the dialog box. AppleWorks suggests possible spellings of that word in the pane just beneath the misspelled word. To replace the misspelled word with a correct one, press the ⌘ key and then the number of the correct word (or you can highlight the correct word and click **Replace**). If the word AppleWorks thinks is misspelled is okay, click the **Skip** button. If you want AppleWorks to remember the word so it doesn't flag it as an error in the future, click **Learn**. Finally, if you want to correct the word yourself, type the correct spelling in the **Word** text box and click **Replace**.

Save Me!

Get in the habit of saving your document frequently so you don't lose any work in the event something bad happens. Open the **File** menu and choose **Save** or press ⌘+**S**).

After you have acted on the misspelled word (replaced it, skipped it, and so on), AppleWorks moves to the next misspelling. When you have checked all the questionable words, the Replace button becomes a Done button. Click **Done** to end the spell check process.

Now read through your document to make sure the information is correct. Make any tweaks in the format or text, move the graphic around, and so on. When you are satisfied with it, save it one last time. You can also print it to do a final check. (You'll learn about printing in the next chapter.) Isn't it a beauty (see Figure 6.7)!

Zoom It!

If you want to see the full page, click the **Zoom** buttons in the lower left-hand corner of the AppleWorks window. These buttons look like little mountains. The smaller mountains (zoom out) make the document smaller and the larger mountains (zoom in) increase the document's size. Click the **Zoom Out** button until you can see the whole page. Zoom in on any elements at which you want to take a closer look.

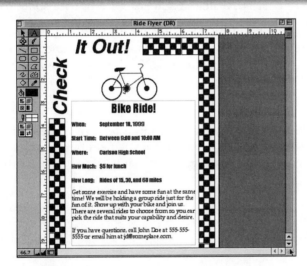

Figure 6.7

Here is the finished flyer—makes you want to jump on your bike, doesn't it!

Creating a Database for the Ride

After you have a flyer, you need to get it to people so they can put the ride on their calendars. A great way to do that is to create a database containing the names and addresses of the people you want to invite. Then you can print mailing envelopes so the flyer can be sent to all the people you are inviting.

As you might guess (because this is the AppleWorks chapter), AppleWorks enables you to do both of these tasks.

First, you need to create the database.

Decide what data you want to have in your database. Because you are going to use this information to create mailing labels, you need at least the names and addresses. You might also want to track who has volunteered to support the ride with you.

Create the Database

In AppleWorks, open the **File** menu and choose **New**. In the New Document dialog box, click **Database** and then click **OK**. The Define Database Fields dialog box appears. In this dialog box, you define the data fields you want in your database.

What's in a Name?

In database lingo, a field is a placeholder for data. Think of it as a box that holds data and you won't be far off. A field is a single piece of data about something.

A record is the set of all information that relates to one thing. For example, you might have a record for each person in your database. Each piece of information about that person (such as street address) is a field. A record usually has more than one field.

Create a first name field, by typing First Name in the **Field Name** box. Click the **Create** button to create the field. Create a last name field by typing Last Name in the **Field Name** box and then click **Create**. Do the same steps to add the following fields:

➤ Address
➤ City
➤ State
➤ Zip
➤ Volunteer

When you are done, you will see all the fields in your new database (see Figure 6.8). Click **Done** to close the dialog box.

From the **File** menu, choose **Save As**, enter a name for your database (try Mailing List), make sure you are in "The Ride of the Century!" folder, and click **Save**.

Add the Data

Now you have an empty Mailing List database, which is much like an address book that you haven't put any addresses in yet. You need to add information on the people you are going to invite.

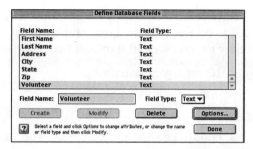

Figure 6.8

This database has all the information you need to send out your flyers.

Click in the **First Name** field and type a first name. Press **Tab**, which moves you to the next field, and type a last name. Press **Tab** and type the street address. Continue until you have filled in all the data for the first person.

From the **Edit** menu, choose **New Record**. You will see a second blank record. Fill in the data for the second person just like you did for the first one. Continue until all the people you want to invite are in your database. Don't worry if the data looks messy; you are just entering it for now. You will format it in the next section.

Creating Mailing Labels for the Flyers

Now that you have the database set up, all you have to do is create mailing labels.

With a database, you can view the records in different layouts (a layout is basically a window on your data). You can choose different layouts to view the same data. You can also create custom reports that contain all data or only part of it. For example, you can create online layouts for data entry or a list of names to print. For now, you should create mailing labels you can use to address the flyers.

Set Up the Labels

From the **Layout** menu, choose **New Layout**. In the New Layout dialog box, click the **Labels** radio button. From the **Labels** pop-up menu, choose the type of label you want to use. (AppleWorks comes with a lot of predefined label sizes; you can match the name on the pop-up label menu to the labels you will use.) In the **Name** text box, name the layout (try Mailing Labels). Click **OK**.

Next, you see the Set Field Order dialog box. This enables you to determine which fields appear on the labels and in what order they appear. Click **First Name** in the Field List

A Powerful Tool...

I have shown you only a small portion of the power of the AppleWorks database module. You can sort records, find specific records, make multiple layouts and reports, and so on. If you handle data, it is worth your while to learn some of these more advanced tools.

pane and then click the **Move** button to move it into the Field Order pane. Repeat this process for each field you want on the labels; include Last Name, Address, City, State, and Zip. When they are all listed in the Field Order pane, click **OK**.

You will see the fields in the order you specified.

Format the Labels

From the **Layout** menu, choose **Layout**. In this mode, you can design the layout you are working on. In this case, you need to reorganize the data so it looks like a mailing label. The dotted lines show you the limits of the mailing labels you set up. Keep all your data inside these lines so it all appears on the labels when you print them.

Click the **First Name** field and make it shorter by dragging the right-hand selection handles to the left. Make the Last Name field shorter and move it up so it is on the same line as the First Name. Move the Address field up so it is just below the name line. Now make the City, State, and Zip fields shorter also. Put these fields on the same line—you can add a comma between City and State fields if you want to. (Use the **Text** tool.)

You can print these labels on label stock and attach them to your flyers for easy mailing. Make sure you use the same label stock as you specified when you set up the label.

The Least You Need to Know

➤ AppleWorks is a powerful application that enables you to create documents by combining various elements, such as text, graphics, spreadsheets, and so on.

➤ To learn how to create AppleWorks documents, work through the sample documents in this chapter.

➤ Use the AppleWorks Help menu to get more information on AppleWorks; use the AppleWorks Help Contents to access a detailed help system in which you can search for the information you need.

Chapter 7

The Paperless World—Bah!

In This Chapter

➤ Learn about the various printer options for your iMac

➤ Understand what needs to be done to install a printer on your iMac

➤ Print a few documents to see how easy it is

One of the great ironies of the computer age is that the computer was supposed to relieve us of most of our paper. The term "paperless office" was (and still is for that matter) thrown around constantly. Nothing could be farther from the truth. The fact is that the computer has made generating hard copies so easy and painless that the amount of paper floating around now is greater than it has ever been. Even email, which is supposed to replace traditional letters and memos, is printed by many people. I am afraid the trees of the world will need to look elsewhere for a savior... the computer is certainly not it.

Ah well. We all need to print...letters, flyers, pictures, certificates, and so on. A printer is a vital component of any iMac system.

Pick a Printer, Any Printer

When it comes to considering a printer for your iMac, there are three basic questions to ask:

➤ Is it iMac compatible?

➤ Does it offer a USB or Ethernet connection?

➤ What kind of imprinting technology does it use?

iCompatibility

When you are looking for a new printer for your iMac, you need to make sure the software that comes with it is Macintosh compatible. This means the printer must be compatible with Mac OS 8.6 or later. If it meets that criteria, the software will work with your iMac. Printer compatibility is always specified on the outside of the box or in the catalog description. If it says it is compatible with the Mac, that is all you need to know. That wasn't so hard was it?

Printing Hardware Is Platform Indifferent

Basic printing hardware is the same, no matter whether it is designed for a Macintosh (which the iMac is based on) or for a Windows PC. The differences come in the printer driver software and the connectors used. Printer driver software developed for Windows PCs will not work on the iMac, and vice-versa. Many Windows PCs can also connect to USB printers, but iMacs cannot use parallel port printers (which is what many Windows PCs use).

Any Port for a Printer

If you have an older iMac (by that I mean a non-DV iMac), your ports will look a little different than those shown in Figure 7.1. And you will have to open the door on the right side of your iMac to see the ports. Don't worry though, the USB and Ethernet ports themselves look just like those in Figure 7.1.

When It Comes to Connecting a Printer to Your iMac, There Are Only Two Options (Really, Three)

You need to somehow connect your iMac to a printer so the iMac can send files to the printer to be printed. There are two basic connection technologies that can be used.

The most likely way that you will connect a printer to your iMac is through the *Universal Serial Bus* (USB) port. This port has an almost flat, rectangular connector that you plug into the USB port on your iMac (see Figure 7.1).

You can also connect a printer to your iMac through the *Ethernet* port. Ethernet is used to network computer devices together so they can "talk" to one another. The Ethernet port on your iMac looks like an overgrown telephone connector (see Figure 7.1).

You are not likely to use an Ethernet compatible printer unless you are also setting up a network.

USB Port   Ethernet Port

Figure 7.1

USB printers are the most likely type you will use with your iMac; the USB port is where you connect the printer to your iMac.

Crossover Cables and You

Although you usually connect a printer to the Ethernet port via a network that includes a hub, other computers, and sometimes additional printers, you can connect an Ethernet printer directly to your iMac through a special Ethernet cable called a *crossover cable*. This cable lets two Ethernet devices network with each other with nothing in-between them.

Beware of Old Serial Printers

The Macintosh family (of which the iMac is a part) started using USB ports relatively recently. Previously, printers could be connected to a Mac through its serial port (also called the Printer port). With the advent of USB, this port is no longer part of the Macintosh architecture. However, there are still serial printers around. You can get a USB-to-serial adapter that enables you to connect a serial printer to your iMac. The problem is that you also have to find a printer driver that recognizes the printer when it is connected in this way. It is possible, but I wouldn't recommend it. With the low cost and high quality of today's printers, you are better off getting a USB printer.

Printing and AirPort

If you use an AirPort station to connect your iMac to a network, you can also connect to any network printers on that network. This means you can print wirelessly too. Cool, eh?

Because Ethernet printers are primarily intended to be used on networks, they tend to be considerably more expensive than USB printers. For most iMac users, a USB printer is the way to go.

On Lasers, Ink, and Other Odd Things

There are four basic types (based on the technology that a particular printer uses to imprint the paper) of printers you may use:

➤ **Inkjet**—Inkjet printers spray small dots of ink on the paper to form images and text. Almost all inkjet printers now sold can print in color. Inkjet printers produce excellent quality text and good-to-excellent quality graphics. For personal printers or those that are shared by only a few people, inkjets are hard to beat. A good quality inkjet printer is an excellent value at less than $300. Epson and Hewlett-Packard make inkjets that are compatible with your iMac

➤ **Laser**—Laser printers produce superb quality for both text and graphics. They are also fast and the best choice for network printing. Lower-end laser printers are affordable enough to also be a good choice for a personal printer. Unfortunately, all reasonably-priced (for home or home office use) laser printers are black-and-white only.

➤ **Color laser**—Color laser printers produce excellent text and graphics and also have color capability. Unfortunately, color laser printers are very, very expensive, and are not likely to be an option for you unless high-quality color printing and network support is required and you have a business that can justify the expense.

➤ **Other printers**—Above color laser printers are dye-sublimation and other higher-quality printers that are used in graphic design and other high-end businesses.

So, Which Printer Is Right for Me?

Most iMac users will find that a USB inkjet printer can do everything they need it to do and then some. Printers are continually getting less expensive and higher quality, so anything you buy tomorrow will be better than what was sold yesterday. Most printers are adequate to excellent depending on what they are being used for. Some are slightly faster than others, or perhaps they do a little better job with full-color graphics, such as photos. In general, I wouldn't worry about the particular models so much—there are too many to keep track of anyway. Simply decide how much you can afford to spend and then get the highest model you can for that amount of money. The bottom line is that any of the Epson or HP USB inkjet printers will probably work just fine for you.

For the remainder of this chapter, I will be showing you how to work with a typical USB inkjet printer. In my case, it is an Epson Stylus 740i, but all inkjet printers work in a similar fashion. In fact, except for the port you use to connect them, working with Ethernet printers isn't different either. The specific dialog boxes may look a little different from printer to printer, but the general tasks will be the same.

Take an iLook

One Printer, Multiple Ports

Some printers have multiple ports. For example, the Epson Stylus 740i has three ports. In addition to the USB port, it has a serial port for older Macintoshes and a parallel port for Windows computers.

Connecting a Printer Is Easy...

After you unpack everything, read all the instruction manuals (right!), plug the power cable in, and install the ink cartridges, the hard work is behind you. Connecting a USB printer to your iMac is as easy as 1-2.

Hot Swappable

One of the great things about USB is that it is *hot-swappable*. This means you can plug in and unplug devices while your computer is turned on or off. Other technologies require that the computer be turned off before you plug devices in.

OK, this is going to be real challenge. Take the USB cable that came with your printer or that you bought separately. Plug the large flat end into the USB port on your iMac (that's 1). Plug the other end into the printer (that's 2). Now take a break because that was really tough work.

...and So Is Installing the Printer Software

Your printer driver determines the features you will be able to use from the Print dialog box in any application. Some of the features you may be able to choose include the following:

➤ **Background printing**—If your printer is capable of background printing (most printers are), the printing process happens in the background while you can work in the foreground.

Desktop Printing

Desktop printing is a nice feature, but unless you use an Apple printer, or a printer that can use an Apple printer driver, you can't use it.

➤ **Desktop printing**—If you use a printer that can use the Apple LaserWriter driver, you can use desktop printing. With desktop printing, an icon of your printer is installed on your desktop. When you want to print a document with that printer, you can drop the document on the printer's icon to print it. You can also open the printer to manage the documents in the print queue; for example, you can remove a document from the queue or reorder documents that are being printed.

➤ **Print quality**—Some printers enable you to choose print quality to conserve toner or ink during draft printing.

➤ **Print in grayscale**—If you are using a color printer that has a black cartridge (in addition to the color cartridge), you can choose to print it in grayscale to save your color ink.

➤ **Print back to front**—When you print a document, it typically prints with the first pages coming out first. This usually results in the document being backward when you pick it up. If you choose the back to front option, the printer starts from the back of the document so that when you pick up your print job, it is in the proper order.

➤ **Print Preview**—Print Preview enables you to see your document as it will be printed. This is useful if your application does not have a Print Preview mode.

➤ **ColorSync settings**—If you are using a color printer, you can choose which color matching technology you want to use—for example, ColorSync or the color-matching technology that is part of your printer's driver.

The Mario Andretti of Printer Drivers

If you use a laser printer, even if it isn't made by Apple, you might be able to use Apple's LaserWriter driver with it (it's installed on your iMac by default). The LaserWriter driver is an advanced driver that provides a lot of excellent features, and Apple is continuously updating it.

What Is ColorSync?

As you work with your iMac, you may see items relating to ColorSync. Although I don't have room to explain ColorSync here, you should know that it is a technology designed to enable you to print with the same colors as you see on your screen. In effect, ColorSync is supposed to put all your components (monitor, printer, and scanner) on the same color page so that what you see is really what you get.

After the printer is set up and hooked up to your iMac, insert the CD that came with your printer and run the installer. Follow any onscreen instructions. After the installation software has done its job, you will have to restart your computer.

Be aware that many printers come with extra goodies on their installation CDs, such as imaging applications, Web page tools, and so on. Take a few moments to explore your printer CD before you put it away in a safe place. (You will need it again someday; trust me on this one.)

Printing Is a No-Brainer

After the driver software is installed and the printer is connected, you are ready to choose the Print command and start spitting out paper, right? Well, almost. First you have to tell your iMac what printer you are going to use and do a bit more configuration of your printer. For that, allow me to introduce the Chooser.

Choosy iMac Users Use the Chooser

The Chooser is that part of the operating system that enables you to "choose" devices to work with, including servers and printers. A bit of clever naming by Apple, eh?

Open the **Apple** menu, and choose **Chooser**. You will see the Chooser window, which has two panes (see Figure 7.2). In the left pane, the device drivers that are installed on your computer are shown. When you select one of these devices, the currently connected devices appear in the right pane. In that pane, you can click a device to use it.

Figure 7.2

In my Chooser, I have selected the SC 740 driver in the left pane (it's highlighted) and the USB port in the right pane.

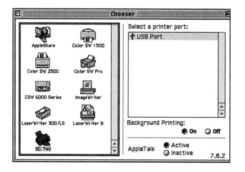

Ethernet

If you are printing to a network, make sure AppleTalk is turned on and that you are connected to the network. When you choose a printer driver, your iMac will search the network for available printers and you will see a list of them in the right pane of the Chooser window.

Find the driver for the printer you just installed and click it in the left pane. Your iMac searches for devices and asks you to select a printer port. In the case of the iMac, you are using the USB port, so click it if it isn't already selected.

If you have an option for background printing, turn it on by clicking the **Background Printing: On** radio button. Close the Chooser and a message appears telling you that you have changed your current printer. Just click **OK** to dismiss the dialog box.

That's it. You are now ready to print.

The Dialog Box Has Changed to Protect the Driver

Try printing a few documents to make sure everything is working. For starters, open the Ride Flyer document you created in the last chapter. From the **File** menu, choose **Print** (or press ⌘+P). You will see the Print dialog box for your printer as supported by AppleWorks (see Figure 7.3). Set the options you want (such as number of pages, whether to use color or black and white, and so on). When you have selected all the options, click **Print**. Because you are using Background Printing, the print status disappears almost immediately and you can go back to your work. In a few moments, your masterpiece appears in the printer's out tray.

Be aware that you won't see the same printer options in the Print dialog box in all applications. Applications can implement their own features in the Print dialog box. For example, you may not see all the options in SimpleText's Print dialog box that you will in AppleWorks' Print dialog box.

The last thing you need to understand about the print driver is the following: When an application creates a page of a document, it determines the dimensions of that page from the print driver that is currently selected in the Chooser. That is why you see the warning about selecting Page Setup in all open applications when you change printer drivers. By opening Page Setup, you force the application to reformat its pages according to the dimensions set by the printer driver.

Changing Printers

If you have access to more than one printer, you can change printers with the Chooser. Open the Chooser, select the driver you want to use in the left pane, and pick the port in the right pane (or printer if you are printing to a network). The next time you print, you will use the new printer.

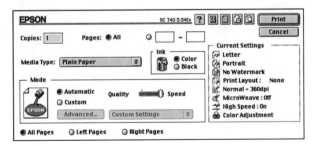

Figure 7.3

The Epson Print dialog box offers a lot of options, as you can see.

The Least You Need to Know

➤ Don't worry about which particular printer to get; just choose a good quality inkjet that is USB compatible.

➤ Any of the newer printers from Epson or HP will work just fine for you.

➤ If you want to have the absolute best quality printer, you will need to spend many thousands of dollars on a high-end dye-sublimation or color laser printer; barring that, your only other realistic choice (for most iMac users) is a black-and-white Laser printer.

➤ If you get a printer that is Ethernet compatible, you can add it to a network and everyone on the network will be able to print to it.

➤ To install and use a printer, set up the printer, connect it to your iMac, run the printer driver installer, and then (after restarting your iMac), choose your new printer in the Chooser.

➤ Use the Print command on the File menu to print your documents.

Part 2

The "i" in iMac is for Internet (or Should It Be Called iInternet?)

If you have been wondering why it is called an iMac, the title of this part should remove any doubts from your mind. The iMac was made for the Internet. With everything you need to connect to and use the Internet already included, there is no better choice for your Net surfing. From its built-in 56K modem to all the software you need, the iMac has it all. (Maybe Apple should have called it the iSurfboard?)

In the beginning of this part of the book, you learn how to get set up for the Net and how to get online. By the time you reach the end of this part, you will be emailing and cruising the Web like a pro. Along the way, you also will learn how to use Sherlock to find things on the Web as quickly and easily as the more famous Sherlock solved cases. I bet you are all iexcited! Well, you should be…so turn the page and get igoing!

BEATS ME...

I DUNNO.

Chapter 8

So Why Is There an "i" in iMac?

In This Chapter

➤ Understand why the Internet is not just a lot of hype

➤ Learn how the Internet works and what you need to do to start using it

➤ Understand email and World Wide Web addresses

The Internet is one of the most significant social and economic movements—it is a movement as much as it is technology—in human history. In just a few years, the Internet (or more simply, the Net) has moved from an obscure scientific and government computer network to become a dominant means of global and local communication, commerce, entertainment, and information.

The Net empowers individuals to act on a global basis by interacting with other individuals, as well as governments, businesses, and other organizations. The Net has already become integrated into many people's daily lives; for example, you can hardly read or hear anything without an Internet address connected to it. For many people, the Internet has become the first stop whenever they are looking for information, products, or even relationships. It doesn't take Nostradamus to predict that the Net will continue to be more and more intertwined with our daily lives.

Fortunately for you, the "i" in iMac really does stand for the Internet; the iMac is a great tool that you can use to get the most out of the Internet.

So, What Is So Special About the Internet?

The answer to this question is easy: electronic mail (email) and the World Wide Web (more commonly called the Web).

There Is More to the Net

Just so you know, there is more to the Net than email and the Web. There are newsgroups, chat rooms, Gopher sites, and so on. But, the main things most people use on the Net are the two that I focus on in this book. As you explore the Net on your own, you can learn about the others if you're interested.

Email Rocks

One of the best things about the Internet is electronic mail (email). With email, you can communicate your thoughts, ideas, and feelings just as you do with regular mail. But, unlike regular mail, email is transmitted almost instantly.

Email has several other advantages that make it an indispensable part of the Internet. For example, through email you can send all sorts of files directly from one computer to another, regardless of the distance between them. Plus, it's more convenient than regular mail (and cheaper!). You can send email from your computer with a single click for a lot less than the price of a stamp. And the Internet is always open. So there's no worrying about holidays or mail delivery times.

You can also send multiple messages as easily as you can send one. Want to send a message to your whole project team? Write one message and send it to everyone at the same time.

You access email through an email program that enables you to create, send, read, and organize your email. Your iMac includes Microsoft's Outlook Express as its default email program (see Figure 8.1). Outlook Express has a lot of great features (you will learn how to use Outlook Express in Chapter 11, "Goodbye Post Office—We Won't Miss You!").

What About Newsgroups?

Newsgroups are electronic discussions among Internet users on any topic under the sun (and some that are better left in the dark). Newsgroups are similar to a radio talk show—you can be a participant or merely an eavesdropper. These newsgroups include discussions about politics, religion, news events, entertainment, music, education, computers, and much more. In fact, there are literally tens of thousands of active newsgroups! (To learn about newsgroups, check out the Outlook Express help system.)

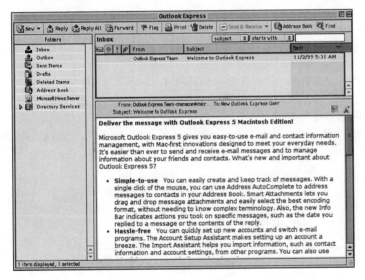

Figure 8.1

Outlook Express is an excellent email program—it's included with your iMac at no extra charge!

As Cool as Email Is, the Web Is Even Better

The World Wide Web is the biggest and fastest growing part of the Internet. It is the most difficult to describe—although it is also the easiest to use. The Web enables you to access seemingly unlimited information in a variety of formats, including text, graphics, sound, and video. This information is all linked together so you can move easily from one point to another via a web-like structure (thus the name).

The best part is that all you have to do to move around is click on well-marked links. For example, while you are reading something or looking at an image, you may come across an underlined word. Click on that word, and you are taken to a different place on the same site, or to another Web site entirely, that has information related to the item you clicked on (by the way, this is called a *hyperlink*). Of course, you can also move directly to specific sites if you want to.

A few examples of the types of Web sites you can find are the following:

➤ **Company Web sites**—Find out what is happening with specific companies, place orders, get help, and so forth.

➤ **Government Web sites**—Access information gathered by the government (using your tax dollars, of course). Some of the best of these are NASA sites where you can see all kinds of fantastic images from space.

➤ **Educational Web sites**—Get information from some of the largest and most well-known academic and scientific institutions in the world.

➤ **Magazines**—Access articles and exhibits online.

➤ **Topical Web sites**—Explore a variety of topics, such as aviation, history, biology, and much more.

➤ **Personal Web pages**—Read and enjoy these sites, which are created by people like you who have something they want to say to the world.

This list only scratches the surface of the Web, but hopefully you get the idea.

You cruise the Web with a Web browser application—your iMac comes with Microsoft's Internet Explorer as its default Web browser (see Figure 8.2). Internet Explorer is a full-featured browser that offers a number of powerful features to make your Web browsing a great experience.

FTP Will Be Very, Very Good to You

FTP (*File Transfer Protocol*) may be one of the most compelling reasons to be on the Net; FTP is the electronic transfer of computer files over the Internet. There are thousands of FTP sites around the world you can access on the Web that enable you to access millions of files that you can download (transfer) to your computer and then use. You can use Internet Explorer to use FTP sites.

In Chapter 12, "Your iMac Makes an Excellent Surfboard," I will show you how to find, download, and use files.

No Regulation Is a Two-Edged Sword

You need to know that, for now at least, the Internet is not regulated. Just like many things in life, that's good and that's bad. It's good because no one can tell you what you can see, say, or do on the Net. That's also bad because there are a lot of things that aren't worth the electrons they use. Fortunately, it's easy to avoid the things in which you don't want to participate. If you stumble onto a site you don't like, simply don't go there again.

For adults this is not a big problem, assuming that we can control ourselves. There is some danger for children, however, so please be careful about giving your kids unmonitored access to the Net. Just like television or movies or any other material, it's up to us to protect our kids as we see fit.

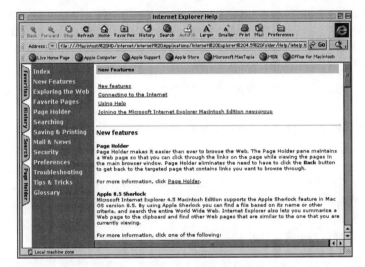

Figure 8.2

Microsoft's Internet Explorer is a full-featured Web browser that also comes with your iMac.

Your iMac can help you in this area as well. It includes an application called EdView Internet Safety Kit. This package consists of two parts. The first is a Web site that contains lists of family-safe Web sites. The second is a filter that allows your Web browser to visit only sites that are approved (they are listed on the Web site).

If you want to install and use this software, insert your iMac Software Install CD-ROM. Open the Internet folder and then open the EdView Internet Safety Kit folder. Read the ReadMe files and then run the EdView installer. You can read the manual that is included in this folder to learn how to use it. (I recommend you read Chapters 9 through 12 before you install and use this package.)

Welcome to the Browser Wars

Internet Explorer is not the only Web browser for the Macintosh. The other major browser is called Netscape Navigator. Both come preinstalled on your iMac but Internet Explorer is installed as the default, so you have to manually activate Netscape Navigator if you want to try it.

If you want to give it a shot, here's a hint: open your hard drive, then open the **Internet** folder, and then open the **Internet applications** folder. Scroll down in the window and you will see an alias to Netscape Communicator (Navigator is one component of the Communicator package).

How Does the Internet Work?

Although you don't need to understand the technical aspects of the Net to use it, you do need to have a grasp of the basic processes involved. Think of using the Internet as driving a car; you don't need to understand the inner workings of the engine, but you do need to know how to put the key in the ignition to start it.

Your iMac Has a Built-in Modem, So Use It!

To access the Internet, you need a computer and a modem. Because you have an iMac, you already have both.

Networking with the Net

You can also connect to the Internet through a network that is connected to the Net. Because you have an iMac, I'm betting that you are using a modem to connect to the Net. If you have access to a network that is connected to the Internet, see your network administrator for help getting connected to the Internet.

The only real thing you need to think about when it comes to modems is how fast they are, or more importantly, how fast yours is. Speed is an essential factor in your enjoyment of the Internet, particularly when you are using the Web. If you have to wait a long time between activities, you aren't likely to enjoy it very much. Your iMac comes with an internal 56K modem (short for 56,600 bits per second). This is as fast as traditional modems come, so you are in great shape to browse at top speed.

Modem?

The modem—MOdulator DEModulator, just in case you were wondering—acts like a translator between your iMac and the telephone line. Your iMac doesn't speak "telephonelinese," which is an analog signal. Your telephone line doesn't speak "computerese," which is digital. The modem helps your computer speak "telephonelinese" and your telephone line speak "computerese."

If you received an AirPort card with your iMac, it can communicate with the modem that is inside the AirPort Base Station. This is cool because it means you can be connected to the Net while using your iMac in different locations—all you need is an electrical outlet and you're all set. You will learn how to set up the AirPort card and Base Station in Chapter 10, "Making Your Connection at the AirPort."

Internet Service Providers Are Our Friends

The Internet is big. Millions of computers located all over the planet. You would think with something this big, it would be easy to get to it, right? Wrong. There are only certain points through which you can enter the Internet; you have to get on the Internet through specific kinds of hardware and software.

Fortunately, there are many *Internet Service Providers* (ISPs) around. An ISP provides a place for you to connect to the Internet. This makes it possible for you to connect via your iMac and modem instead of having to be directly connected to the Internet.

To access the Net, you need an account with an ISP. You, and you alone, connect through this account. In exchange for this service, you must pay the ISP a fee of one sort or another—usually a monthly fee for a certain number of hours of connect time or perhaps for unlimited access time. It can be complicated to find an ISP and get an account. But your iMac contains software that will help you find a provider if you don't have one already.

Username and Password

Your Internet account is controlled by a username and password. The username is your identification while you are on the Internet. The password is a code that makes it much more difficult for someone other than you to access your account through your username.

Connecting to the Net

After you have an account with your ISP, you need software that calls your provider and logs in to your account. Think of this step as the connecting wire between your telephone and the jack in the wall. After this is connected, you can use the phone. In this case, the phone is your computer/modem, the wall jack is the ISP, and the wire is the connecting software.

Jargon Ho!

By the way (commonly abbreviated BTW on the Internet), you've probably noticed there is some jargon associated with the Internet. Many of these terms, such as BTW, are easy to understand. Others are more confusing. Don't worry, however; you'll catch on quickly.

The software you need is built into the Mac OS. It is called Open Transport, and you use the Remote Access control panel and Remote Access Status to connect to and disconnect from the Net.

After you make the connection, you can use Outlook Express for email and Internet Explorer to browse the Web (or other programs if you prefer them).

This all sounds more complicated than it is—your iMac will handle most of the details for you. And in Chapter 9, "Setting Up Your Own iAccount," I will walk you through the steps you need to follow to get connected.

You Can Speak in Net'ese Too!

No doubt you have seen all sorts of weird Internet related stuff on TV, in the newspapers, on boxes, and everywhere else you look. To use the Net, you need to have a good grasp of what all this gobbledygook means (and then you too can run around saying stuff like, "Email me at myname at myprovider dot net").

What Is All This At and Dot Stuff Anyway?

Understanding email addresses is not hard, and you need to be able to have some idea about them to use email. Internet email addresses look something like *username@someplace.xyz*.

The first part of the address, the *username*, is an identifier for the person to whom the mail is being sent. It may be some part or parts of the person's name. (You choose your own username when you sign up for your ISP account.) Each username must be unique within a specific Internet access provider; however, usernames are not unique outside of particular providers. For example, there can be a *johns@nowhere.com* and a *johns@somewhere.net*, but there cannot be two *johns@nowhere.com*.

The next item, the @ symbol, is translated as "at." It separates the username from the location of that user, and says, "Look for this person *at* this location."

The *someplace* identifies where on the Internet the electronic mailbox is located; this is usually the ISP. Other times, it is a company name.

Finally, the *xyz* is a code that represents the type of organization or location that *someplace* is. Common codes include *.com* for a commercial organization, *.edu* for an educational institution, *.net* for an ISP, and *.gov* for government. You may also see a two-letter country code at the end of an address, such as *.us* (USA) or *.ca* (Canada).

When you see an address, it may have more than three parts or fewer than three parts, but each part will be separated by either a period or the @.

Saying Your Address the Net Way

Your email address will be something like *username@someplace.xyz*, where *username* is the username that you selected. For example, my email address is *bradm@iquest.net*. When giving your address verbally, you should follow certain conventions that make your address easier to understand. Pronounce the @ as "at." Pronounce the period as "dot." So, I say that my email address is, "brad m at iquest dot net." Of course, if you have an unusual word, or an unusual spelling of a normal word, be sure to spell out your address.

Now How About the Web?

URLs (*Uniform Resource Locators*) are fundamental to exploring the Web; URLs are a standardized way of identifying places on the Internet. They function just like street addresses do—they tell your browser where to look for a certain place on the Web. URLs also tell your Web browser what kind of Internet service you will be accessing when you move to that URL.

URLs look like the following:

```
servicecode://abc.somewhere.xyz/document
```

Each of the elements of a URL are explained in the following list:

➤ **The service code**—This is the type of Internet service you will be using when you move to the URL (see Table 8.1) .

➤ **The domain or site name**—The next part of the URL is the address of the server hosting the Web site. For example, *abc.somewhere.xyz* stands for a particular Internet service on a specific computer somewhere on the Net. The domain *abc.somewhere.xyz* can refer to many different kinds of machines located all over the world, everything from large computers at major universities to a PC in someone's home. Usually, the *abc* is the service code you are using—*www* for the World Wide Web, *ftp* for file transfer protocol, and so on. The *somewhere.com* identifies the particular computer; it is the computer's Internet name. This part is similar to everything after the @ in an email address.

**Table 8.1   URL Service Codes and the
Services They Represent**

Service Code	Service	Comment
http	World Wide Web	The http code indicates a World Wide Web site. You'll use URLs with this code frequently.
https	World Wide Web	The https indicates a secure Web site; when you transmit data to and from an http site, it is encrypted for security purposes.
ftp	File Transfer Protocol	You'll use ftp URLs when downloading files from the Internet.
mailto	Email	You'll use mailto when sending email via a Web browser and some email programs.
news	Usenet News	You'll see news URLs when reading Usenet News.
file	A file	This code indicates you are looking at a file on your iMac.

> ➤ **The document**—The last part, *document*, is the specific item to which you're moving; it can represent anything from a Web page to a file that you want to download, to a newsgroup message, and so on. However, *document* won't be part of every URL you see. Sometimes, you'll see a URL to a specific server rather than a document. In this case, the URL will end with *abc.somewhere.xyz/*.

Mostly, you don't have to worry about these details as you'll either be entering URLs as you find them or just clicking a link to indicate where you want to go. When you do type a URL, just type it exactly as shown and you'll be fine.

That Was All Very Interesting, But What Do I Need to Do to Get Going?

Because your iMac comes with everything you need to get connected to and use the Internet, here are the few steps you need to follow to join in the Internet age:

1. Run the Internet Setup Assistant to set up your modem and obtain (if you don't have one already) and configure your Internet account (you will do this in Chapter 9).

2. Set up your AirPort card and Base Station for a wireless connection to the Internet (Chapter 10).

3. Start emailing everyone you know (Chapter 11).

4. See the world through the Web (Chapter 12).

5. Use Sherlock to find things (Chapter 13, "Sleuthing Around the World with Sherlock").

The Least You Need to Know

➤ Lots of things on the Internet are great, but the best parts are email and the World Wide Web.

➤ To get on the Internet for yourself, get an account with an ISP, configure your Net applications, and get surfing.

➤ Fortunately, your iMac comes with everything you need; this book and the iMac's Internet Setup Assistant will help you all the way.

➤ Some of the terminology and shorthand of the Internet may confuse you at first; things like @, www, http, and so on may not make sense to you right now; these get you to specific people or places on the Net.

➤ Email addresses for people or organizations look something like yourname@someplace.com, while Web URLs usually look something like www.agreatplacetovisit.com.

➤ After you understand what Net addresses represent, they make sense—and usually you don't even have to type them (thankfully); you can simply click on a link or an address to use them.

Chapter 9

Setting Up Your Own iAccount

In This Chapter

➤ Get your own Internet account

➤ Use the Internet Setup Assistant to configure your iMac to connect to the Net

➤ Try connecting and disconnecting to make sure it works

➤ Get some troubleshooting help if you can't connect (you probably won't need it)

In Chapter 8, "So Why Is There an "i" in iMac?," I told you that your iMac helps you set up an Internet account, and I wasn't kidding. The Internet Setup Assistant is a great little piece of software that holds your hand and leads you through the sometimes confusing world of setting up an Internet account (see Figure 9.1).

Figure 9.1

The Internet Setup Assistant is your personal guide on the road to the Internet.

What makes this a bit more confusing is that your iMac may come with two Internet assistants. One is a fancy multimedia version called Setup Assistant and the other is a plain but effective text-based version called Internet Setup Assistant. Depending on which version of the Mac OS your iMac had when it came to you, the Setup Assistant may have started when you turned your iMac on for the first time. If you worked through the Setup Assistant the first time you turned on your iMac, you don't need to read much of this chapter, so skip to the section called, "Finish the Job." I used the Internet Setup Assistant in this chapter—I prefer it because it avoids the "fluff" of the fancy version. They work in a similar way, but if you use the Setup Assistant, the steps you follow will be slightly different than those I show in this chapter. The general concepts and tasks are exactly the same, though. You can start either one at any time by opening the Assistants folder and double-clicking its icon.

As I mentioned in Chapter 8, a modem is not the only way to connect to the Internet. You may use a network to connect, a cable modem, an Integrated Digital Services Line (IDSL), or other more cutting-edge technology to get on the Net. In this chapter, I've assumed you will be using the iMac's internal modem to connect. If you are using another connection device, much of the information in this chapter will still help you configure your iMac, but there will be some differences for you. If you have problems, contact your system administrator for a network connection or the provider of your service (such as a cable modem) for help.

When it comes to connecting your iMac to the Internet, there are two possibilities. One is that you have never had your own Internet account so you need to find an Internet service provider (ISP) to obtain one. If this is your situation, continue to the next section, which is called, "If You Don't Have an Internet Account, Start Here." The other possibility is that you already have an account and simply need to configure your iMac to use it. If this is your situation, skip to the section called, "If You Have an Existing Internet Account, Start Here."

If You Don't Have an Internet Account, Start Here

If you don't already have an Internet access account, you need to get one before you can connect to the Net. You have two basic choices. One is to go ahead and find an account on your own and then use the Internet Setup Assistant to help you configure it. The other option is to let EarthLink's TotalAccess software (which is integrated into the Internet Setup Assistant) obtain and configure an account with the ISP named EarthLink. EarthLink is a major ISP based in California, but provides local access points all over the country. I have been associated with EarthLink for many years and have found it to be an excellent provider. Its fees are reasonable and the technical support is excellent.

Take an iLook

America Online

You can try accessing the Internet through America Online (AOL) for free, so if you think you may be interested, check it out. To set up an AOL account and begin using it, open the **Internet** folder on your hard drive. Open the **Internet Applications** folder, and then open the **America Online** folder. Double-click the **AOL** application and follow the onscreen instructions to create and configure your AOL account. I don't particularly recommend AOL because it costs more than EarthLink. If you choose AOL, skip the rest of this chapter because it will not apply to you.

The benefit of finding your own account is that you can shop around and look for the "best" provider for your area. Another advantage is that you will understand what you are doing a bit better than you might if you use TotalAccess (because TotalAccess spares you from the details of the process). The disadvantage to finding your own provider is that it can be confusing and is quite a bit more work than using TotalAccess to set up an account.

Frankly, you aren't likely to find a provider that offers better service or lower cost than EarthLink anyway, so I recommend you use TotalAccess to get your account. If you want to do so, skip ahead to the section called, "I Want My EarthLink Account—Now!."

However, if you feel confident about selecting a provider, go ahead and find your own provider. It really isn't hard, and you will find a few tips to help you do so in the next section.

I Don't Want to Take the Easy Way; I Want to Find My Own ISP

If you decide to work with a local ISP or with a national ISP other than EarthLink, you need to get an account with that ISP. The following are some tips to help you find your own ISP:

➤ The people you already know are one of the best sources of information about local Internet service providers. There are probably several people in your immediate circle who have Internet access through a local provider. You should ask these folks if they are happy with their providers. You can also find out whether the provider gives good technical support, how much the service costs, and so on. Using your personal network is an excellent way to find a provider.

➤ Another way to find a local provider is to check out the local news broadcasts in your area. Almost all local TV stations have Web sites that are maintained by a local ISP. At the end of the broadcast, you will see a credits screen saying that Internet services are provided by XYZ Company. XYZ Company might be a good choice for you to check out.

➤ One of the most important things to look for is an account that offers you unlimited access (or at least a large number of hours per month). This means you pay the same amount whether you are on the Net one hour or 100. That is good. If you pay on some sort of time basis (such as so many dollars per hour), you will spend all of your time worrying about how much time you have spent online instead of enjoying the Net. Fortunately, it isn't hard to find an unlimited account these days. This wasn't always the case.

➤ A reasonable fee for unlimited Internet service is about $20–$25 per month. You may have to pay more if you live in a remote area, or you may pay less if you live in an area with a lot of competition.

➤ If the company you work for has a Web site that is administered by an outside ISP or an outside ISP provides Net access for your company, check with that ISP to see if it offers a discount for employees of your company (this means you). Often, an ISP provides inexpensive Internet access to the employees of a company to which it provides service. I have heard of some cases where the ISP offers rates as low as $8 per month for unlimited access. So it is worth a few minutes to see if your company has such a relationship with an ISP.

➤ If you have some access to the Net, perhaps through a friend, a library, or at work, use the Web to locate a provider. Go to `http://the list.com/`, which enables you to find local access providers for just about every location in the world.

After you have an account, skip ahead to the section called, "If You Have an Existing Internet Account, Start Here" to configure your iMac to use that account.

I Want My EarthLink Account—Now!

I can tell you are excited about getting on the Net and don't want to spend a lot of time looking for a provider. Using EarthLink is an excellent way to get started, and with the TotalAccess software, getting an account and configuring your iMac to use it is very easy.

Open the **Assistants** folder on your hard drive. Open the **Internet Setup Assistant**. When you are asked if you want to set up your iMac to use the Internet, answer **Yes**. When you are asked if you already have an Internet account, answer **No**. The TotalAccess software opens and you hear a message explaining the license agreement. Yes, you will hear it. The TotalAccess software uses narration to guide you through the sign-on process. Pretty neat, huh?

Read the agreement and then click **I Agree** (assuming you do of course). To get started setting up your account, click the **Setup** button (see Figure 9.2). The Setup New Account dialog box appears. You hear an explanation of what you will configure with the first screen, which is your username and password. Listen to the explanation and then choose a username and password. Notice your email address and home page URL appear at the bottom of the screen.

These buttons control the narration.   Get help with this button.

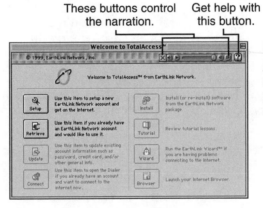

Figure 9.2

EarthLink's TotalAccess software is the easiest way to get your own Internet account.

Continue following the onscreen directions. With the narration, each item is explained to you as you go. After you have completed the basic information, TotalAccess dials an 800 number to find local phone numbers for you to use to set up your account. It also checks the username you selected. If the one you chose is being used by someone on EarthLink, you will have to choose another one.

Eventually, a Product Info screen appears that shows you some of the services you may want. When I wrote this, you could get an unlimited access account for only $19.95 per month. I told you EarthLink is inexpensive! Plus you can try the service for 30 days for no charge.

Please Repeat That

By the way, if you want to have the narration on a screen repeated, click the right-facing black triangle, which is the **Play** button, that is located at the top of the dialog box next to the slider.

Choose the service you want, and then click **Next**. You move to the credit card screen. Enter your information and move on. Continue to follow the instructions and enter information as it is requested. Your iMac dials an 800 number again; if you have entered valid information, you see an Order Accepted window. This means you have successfully obtained an Internet account.

The TotalAccess software begins the process of configuring your iMac to use that account. It starts by asking you to choose a local access number. Choose a number you can dial with no toll charges if possible. (Remember to click the **Play** button if you need to hear the narration.)

When you see the list of local phone numbers, make sure the phone number for your area is toll free for you to dial—this usually means you do not have to dial an area code with the number. If you use a number for which you have to pay tolls, you will spend a lot of money in phone charges while you are on the Internet.

If you can't find a toll-free number for EarthLink on the list of local numbers (usually one for which you do not need to dial an area code to call), cancel the TotalAccess setup and find a local provider or use AOL instead. You don't want to have to worry about phone charges while you are using the Net.

When you get to the Installation dialog box, click the **Install** button. TotalAccess configures your iMac so your EarthLink account information is entered in the appropriate places.

Whoops, I Lost My Net Setup!

If at some point in the future something causes your Net account configuration to be messed up (perhaps you have to re-install your System software), never fear. TotalAccess is able to retrieve your information and re-configure your account for you.

To do so, open the following folders: **Internet**, then **Internet Applications**, and then **EarthLink TotalAccess**. Now double-click **Registration & Utilities**. You will see the Welcome to TotalAccess screen again. This time, click the **Retrieve** button instead of the Setup button. TotalAccess sets up your account for you again.

Make sure you take some time to explore the TotalAccess software. It provides many useful options, including tutorials, a troubleshooting utility, and more. I told you EarthLink is a good company!

That's it! You now have your very own Internet account! Now skip ahead to the section called, "Finish the Job."

If You Have an Existing Internet Account, Start Here

You already have an account or perhaps you got a new account from a local provider. In either case, setting up your iMac to use this account is the same.

Gather Your Information

When you signed up for your Internet access account, your ISP provided you with configuration information for your account; you might have used this information to set up your account on another machine. Gather this configuration information so you can easily refer to it during the configuration process. You need to have the following data ready:

➤ **Domain Name Server**—A Domain Name Server (DNS) is a computer that simply (it isn't really so simple) translates the numbers the computers really use as addresses into English that we humans can usually understand. The DNS makes it possible for you to use an address such as www.companyname.com rather than having to deal with a series of numbers such as 233.453.22.345. The DNS number you need from your provider will be something that looks like 234.45.234.563.

TCP/IP

You may have seen the term *TCP/IP*, which stands for Transmission Control Protocol/ Internet Protocol. All you really need to know is that this is the "language" a computer must be able to speak to be on the Internet.

➤ **Type of configuration**—This information tells your computer what protocol to use to connect to the Net. If you are using a modem, this is likely to be either Point-to-Point (PPP) or Serial Line Interface Protocol (SLIP).

➤ **Your IP address, subnet mask, and router addresses**—These numbers help the machine that you connect to when you call your ISP identify you to the rest of the Internet while you are connected. Most modem-based connections use dynamic IP addressing, which simply means your Mac will have an IP address assigned each time it connects rather than having a static address. Should you think any more about this? No. Just get the numbers you need and know you will be using dynamic addressing.

➤ **Phone number**—You need to have the phone number to dial to reach your ISP. Some ISPs offer different numbers for different modem speeds, so make sure you get the phone number for your modem's speed. (In your case, make sure you get the 56K number so you can connect at the fastest possible speed.) Also make sure you use the connection phone number and not the one for technical support.

➤ **Username and password**—These are the two pieces of information that will uniquely identify you and enable you to access your account. You probably chose your own username when you established your account. Your password may or may not have been assigned by the ISP.

You may have more than one username or password. Sometimes, your ISP will give you one username and password that enables you to connect to the Net and another set (or maybe just one of the them) to let you use your email account. Make sure you know which is which and use the right ones in the right setting fields.

➤ **PPP Connection scripts**—If your provider requires you to use a PPP connection script, make sure you get a copy of it from your provider. Most providers don't require you to use a PPP connection script, so you probably won't need one.

➤ **Email addresses**—You will be given your email address (probably something like username@isp.net). You will also need an address for the server that receives your mail (often has a "pop" in it, such as in pop.isp.net). The third piece of information you need is the address of the server that sends your mail (usually has "smtp" in it, such as `smtp.isp.net`).

➤ **News server**—You should also be provided with a newsgroup server (enables you to read newsgroups). It might look something like, `news.isp.net`.

Now Configure Your iMac to Use Your Account

After you have all the information handy, you are ready to configure your account. Open the **Assistants** folder on your hard drive. Open the **Internet Setup Assistant** and answer **Yes** to the question asking whether you want to set up your iMac to use the Internet. Answer **Yes** to the question asking whether you already have an account. You'll see a screen that tells you what information you need. Because I already provided the list to you, click the right-facing triangle to move to the next screen.

Viva La Difference!

Remember, you can also use the "other" setup utility called Setup Assistant to configure your iMac for the Internet. (It may have opened the first time you started your iMac.) You do exactly the same things that I describe for the Internet Setup Assistant but with slightly different screens.

From this point on, simply fill in the blanks with your account information you gathered. When you complete a screen, click the right-facing triangle to move to the next screen. Most of the screens are self-explanatory. The following are some comments on the more confusing items:

➤ **Phone number**—Make sure you can dial this number for free. If you need to dial any special codes before you dial your ISP's phone number, such as an access code (usually 9), you must use the DialAssist control panel to configure the way your modem will dial before you can successfully connect to the Net. Or, you can simply enter the phone number in exactly the same way you would to dial it with a telephone (use a comma for a pause). You also need to disable call waiting if you have it before you dial up your Internet account.

➤ **Username and password**—Make sure that if your account has more than one username and password, you use the correct username and password to connect to the Net—don't use your email username and password here if it's different from your connect username and password.

➤ **Email password**—If you enter your email password, you will not have to enter it when you check your email. This means anyone who can access your iMac can access your email. Only enter your password on this screen if you keep control of your iMac:.

When you are finished, you see the Conclusion screen. When you are ready to connect, click **Go Ahead**. The Assistant finishes the configuration and begins dialing. In a few moments, you should hear the modems talking. If your iMac is able to connect, the Assistant window goes away and your desktop becomes visible. Look in the upper-left corner and you'll see a flashing Mac/telephone pole icon; this means you are connected to the Net. Congratulations!

If there was a problem and you weren't able to connect for some reason, see the section called, "If You Have Trouble Connecting, Read This—If Not, Skip It" later in this chapter.

Finish the Job

There are just a few more steps you need to do to double-check and finish off your configuration. To do these steps, you will use the Internet and Remote Access control panels.

Double-Check Your Settings with the Internet Control Panel

You should double-check your settings to make sure everything is ready when it comes time to email and surf the Web. Open the **Apple** menu, choose **Control Panels**, and then choose **Internet**. You will see the Internet control panel window (see Figure 9.3).

Figure 9.3

The Internet control panel enables you to configure all of your Internet applications in one place.

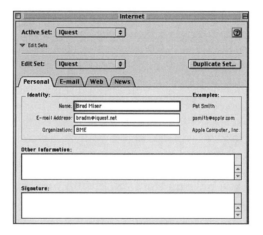

The Internet Control Panel

Configuring the Internet control panel means that Internet applications, such as Outlook Express and Internet Explorer, will be able to access your configuration and you won't have to enter it within each application.

Click the **Personal** tab; check that your name and email address are correct. Enter your company name if you want to. If you want to use a signature on your email, enter it in the **Signature** text box.

Click the **E-mail** tab. All the account information should be entered already. If not, enter it. Using the check boxes, choose an action that should happen when you receive new mail (for example, a sound, flashing icon, a dialog box, or any combination of the three). Also make sure the default email application is set to Outlook Express.

Click the **Web** tab. Click the **Select** button, choose the **Desktop** from the pop-up menu at the top of the Select a Folder dialog box, click **New,** type Downloaded Files, and click **Create**. Then click **Select** again when you move back into the Select a Folder dialog box (make sure **Downloaded Files** is still selected). This step creates a folder into which the files you download are placed. Having a single folder makes it easy to find all the files you download from the Web. Make sure Microsoft Internet Explorer appears in the Default Web Browser pop-up menu.

Click the **Close** box to close the Internet application, making sure you save your changes.

Take an iLook

Reconstructing the Net

If you ever need to adjust the settings for one of your Internet applications, come back to the Internet control panel to do so.

Fine Tune Your Settings with Remote Access

The Remote Access control panel and Remote Access Status application are the two pieces of software that make your Internet connection. There are some details you need to set to make everything work a little bit better.

Open the **Apple** menu, choose **Control Panels**, and then choose **Remote Access**. The Remote Access control panel appears (see Figure 9.4). Click **Options**, and then click the **Redialing** tab. Choose **Redial main number only** from the pop-up menu. Enter a number in the **Redial times** box; this is the number of times your iMac will redial the number in case it is busy the first time it tries. Type 5 to have your iMac redial the number up to five times. Leave the time between retries at 5 seconds.

Figure 9.4

The Remote Access control panel makes your connection to the Net.

No Setup Details?

If you don't see a Remote Access screen similar to the one in the figure, click the triangle next to the word "Setup" to see the details.

Why Have One Net Account When You Can Have Two?

You can set up multiple Net accounts on one iMac. You have to set up each account—just name them differently in the Internet Setup Assistant and then choose the account from the pop-up menus you see in the Internet and Remote Access control panels.

Click the **Connection** tab. In this window, check the **Flash icon in menu bar while connected** check box. This flashes the telephone pole icon in the upper-left corner of your screen while you are connected to the Net. Check the **Disconnect if idle for** check box and enter 10. This causes your connection to be disconnected if no data has been transferred for at least 10 minutes. This is a good idea so you don't tie up your phone line in case you forget to disconnect.

Click the **Protocol** tab. Make sure the **Connect automatically when starting TCP/IP applications** option is checked so your Internet applications can automatically connect to the Net when they need to. Click **OK**.

Close the Remote Access control panel and save your changes.

Your iMac is now fully Net-ready!

Now Practice Connecting and Disconnecting

Using the Internet is always a three-step process. First, connect to the Internet. Second, after your connection is established, run the programs for the services you want to use (for example, Internet Explorer for browsing the Web, Outlook Express for email, and so on). Third, when you are finished, disconnect from the Net.

You will learn how to use Internet applications in the following chapters. For now, practice connecting and disconnecting from your Net account. From the **Apple** menu, choose **Remote Access Status**. The Remote Access status window appears.

Click **Connect.** You will hear your modem dialing out, and you can watch the progress of your connection in the Remote Access window. When the connection is complete, the Remote Access window enables you to monitor the activity of your connection (see Figure 9.5). Watch the Send and Receive meters to see when data is coming from your iMac or coming to it. At this point, you can launch an application to get your email or browse the Web.

Figure 9.5

You can use Remote Access status to connect and disconnect from the Net; when you are connected, it also provides statistics on your connection.

More Than One Way to Connect

You may have noticed the Remote Access control panel also has a Connect button. You can connect and disconnect using the Remote Access control panel the same way you use the Remote Access status window.

You can also use the Remote Access button on the Control Strip (you'll learn about the Control Strip in Chapter 20, "Get a Grip with the Control Strip").

Use whichever way you prefer. They all do the same thing.

Click **Disconnect** to close your connection. The Remote Access window returns to the Idle state. Close the window.

After you are sure your connection works properly, you really don't have to connect manually if you checked the **Connect automatically when starting TCP/IP applications** check box in the Remote Access control panel. With this box checked, your Net applications can connect when they need to.

If this process worked, you have successfully configured your iMac for the Net, and you are ready to start experiencing the Net for yourself (and you can skip the rest of this chapter).

Quiet Modem

The sounds your modem makes as it connects are kind of annoying. After you know everything is set up and working properly, you can mute your modem by opening the Modem control panel and clicking the **Sound Off** radio button. Close the control panel and save your changes. From now on, your modem won't make a peep.

If You Have Trouble Connecting, Read This—If Not, Skip It

You don't need to read this section if everything went well, and you are able to connect and disconnect from the Net. If you are having trouble, read on for some help.

Unfortunately, troubleshooting connection problems can be difficult because there are so many variables involved. These include your modem, your configurations, the phone lines, your ISP's system, and so on. Although I can't list every problem you may have, this section gives you some ideas of the most common problems. Unless you find a simple error, such as incorrect data in the configuration, you will probably have to call your ISP for help. But work through these ideas before you do. Even if they don't solve your problem, they will save you time with your ISP when you do call.

The following sections include the typical problems you may be experiencing. After each problem, you will see the general things you can try to solve your problems.

You Don't Hear or See Any Activity with Your Modem When You Try to Connect

The problem may lie with your modem setup.

Check the Modem and DialAssist control panels to make sure you have installed and configured your modem properly. Test the modem with another application (such as a commercial online service or by connecting to a BBS). If the modem works with another application, you know the problem is related to your configuration. If your modem still doesn't work at all, open Mac Help or see the manual that came with your iMac for troubleshooting help.

Make sure the modem selected during your Net configuration is the right one—it should be the Apple Internal 56K modem.

You Hear the Modem Dialing, but You Never Hear the Call Being Answered

This can happen when your ISP is offline for some reason or it may be simply overloaded. It can also happen if your configuration is not properly set. Open the Remote Access control panel. Check the phone number to make sure it's the right one for your ISP.

Make sure any codes you need to dial before a phone call are reflected in the number. For example, if you need to dial a "9" before making phone calls, make sure there is a "9" before your ISP's phone number.

Try again. Sometimes the phone lines are just busy.

If you still can't get the ISP to answer your iMac's attempts, call your ISP for help.

You Hear the Modem Dialing and You Hear Your ISP's Phone Answering, but You Never Connect

You may see various error messages in the Remote Access Status window, such as, "`Authentication failed.`" This is probably the result of an incorrect configuration.

Open the Remote Access control panel. Make sure your username, password, and the phone number are correct. If not, correct them and try again. From the **RemoteAccess** menu, choose **Modem**. In the Modem control panel, verify that the correct modem is chosen in the pop-up menu. Close the control panel.

From the **Remote Access** menu, choose **TCP/IP**. Make sure PPP is selected in the **Connect via** pop-up menu, **Using PPP Server** is selected in the **Configure** pop-up menu, the **name server addr** block contains the DNS from your ISP, and the search domain is the right one for your ISP. Close the control panel.

Activity Log

By the way, you can choose **Activity Log** from the **Remote Access** menu to see a log of your recent Remote Access activity. This log is sometimes helpful. Have it ready when you call for help.

Try working through the configuration steps again. Give the account another name and make sure you enter the correct information.

If all the information is correct, but you still can't connect, call you ISP for help.

Troubleshooting connection problems can be tough, and fortunately the odds are that you will connect just fine. If not, the problem is most likely incorrect configuration information you can fix in the Remote Access control panel or by redoing the configuration with the Internet Setup Assistant. Your ISP will also be able to help you. After you get your connection working and start using the Net, you will find that your work getting on-line was worthwhile.

The Least You Need to Know

➤ Your iMac has all the hardware and software you need to connect to the Net; all you need to provide is a phone line and an Internet account with an Internet service provider.

➤ If you don't already have an Internet account, consider using EarthLink as your Internet provider; the TotalAccess software installed on your iMac makes obtaining and configuring an account extremely straightforward.

➤ If EarthLink doesn't work for you (perhaps there is no toll-free phone number for your area), you can find a local or other national ISP; you can also use AOL to connect to the Internet.

➤ Use the Internet Setup Assistant to guide you through the process.

➤ You can connect to and disconnect from the Net using the Remote Access control panel, the Remote Access status application, or the Remote Access button on the Control Strip.

➤ With the correct setting in the Remote Access control panel, Internet applications will automatically connect to the Net when they need to.

Chapter 10

Making Your Connection at the AirPort

In This Chapter

➤ Understand AirPort hardware and software components

➤ Install and configure AirPort components

➤ Use AirPort to connect to the Internet, networks, and other AirPort-equipped computers

---

Using an AirPort card and Base station, your iMac can wirelessly connect to the Internet, Ethernet networks, and even to other iMacs or any Mac equipped with an AirPort card. This means you don't need to be tied down by a cable; you are free to roam while you are roaming the world with the iMac. This also makes it extremely easy to share files and play network games with other AirPort-equipped computers. You can also share a single Internet connection among several AirPort-equipped computers.

Learning to Fly

AirPort is an amazing technology that makes wireless communication affordable enough and simple enough for regular people like you and me. The AirPort functionality is provided through the following components:

➤ **iMac**—Your iMac has built-in antennas that are used to transmit and receive signals to and from other computers and the AirPort Base Station.

➤ **AirPort Card**—To use AirPort, your iMac must have an AirPort card installed in it.

➤ **AirPort Software**—The AirPort software is necessary for computers to communicate through the AirPort hardware. Configuration of the software is easy because of the AirPort Setup Assistant that walks you through each step. After the AirPort software is installed, an AirPort Control Strip module is added to your Control Strip.

➤ **AirPort Base Station**—The AirPort Base Station contains access points for a modem and an Ethernet network. When you use it for a dialup connection to the Internet, for example, the AirPort Base Station's modem is used to connect to the Net. Your iMac communicates to the Base Station through the AirPort card and built-in antenna. A single AirPort Base Station can support multiple computers. (You can still use AirPort to connect to other computers that have AirPort cards installed without an AirPort Base Station.)

Prepping the Runway

Before you can use your AirPort, you have to do a little preparation work. You need to install the AirPort card in your iMac, set up the Base Station (if you are using one), and then configure the AirPort software.

Installing the AirPort Card

If you ordered an AirPort card to be installed when you ordered your iMac, you can skip this section. If you obtained the AirPort card separately, you need to install it in the AirPort card slot located at the rear of the iMac under the removable cover. This is not a hard installation to do, so don't sweat it.

Using the iMac installation pamphlet that was included with the AirPort card to guide you, install the AirPort card in your iMac. This pamphlet has excellent instructions that guide you through the six-step process.

Installing the Base Station

There isn't much to installing the AirPort Base Station. Simply attach its power adapter to the station and plug it into a wall outlet. Attach the modem port to a phone jack if you are connecting through a telephone line or to another line if you are using DSL, a cable modem, and so on.

If you are going to connect the Base Station to an Ethernet network, attach an Ethernet cable to the Ethernet port. If you want to use the Base Station to network your iMac with a single computer, you can connect the Ethernet port on the other computer to the Base Station with an Ethernet crossover cable. Otherwise, attach a standard Ethernet cable to your Base Station and to the Ethernet hub.

Installing the AirPort Software

Open the **Assistants** folder on your hard drive. If you see an AirPort Setup Assistant, you don't need to install the software. Skip to the next section. If you don't see the AirPort Setup Assistant, insert the AirPort Software CD into your iMac. Run the installer to install the software.

Apple Terminology

By the way, Apple also calls the AirPort Base Station the Hardware Access Point. The two terms refer to the same thing.

Configuring the AirPort Software to Work with a Base Station

The AirPort includes a helpful assistant that will walk you through the configuration of the AirPort. If you had to install new AirPort software, the Assistant opens the first time you restart your iMac after you install the software. If not, open the **Assistants** folder and double-click the **AirPort Setup Assistant** icon. You will see the AirPort Setup Assistant (see Figure 10.1). Because you have used two other assistants (the Mac OS Setup Assistant and the Internet Setup Assistant), you won't have any trouble with this one.

Figure 10.1

The helpful AirPort Setup Assistant guides you in configuring your iMac and the Base Station.

To set up your AirPort to work with a Base Station, click the **Set up an AirPort Base Station** radio button and then click the right-facing arrow at the bottom of the dialog box. Work through the Assistant by reading the text, entering the appropriate information, and then clicking the right-facing arrow to move to the next screen. The Assistant will set up the Base Station by transferring your Internet setup from the iMac to the Base Station. When the Assistant has finished its work, you will see the Conclusion screen. Your Base Station is now setup to use both the Internet and an Ethernet network.

Got a Connection?

Obviously, you have to have an Internet account set up on your iMac for the Assistant to transfer it to the Base Station. If you don't, go back to Chapter 9, "Setting Up Your Own iAccount," to set up your iMac for the Net.

As soon as the Assistant is done, launch an Internet application that needs to access the Net. (Use Internet Explorer; see Chapter 12, "Your iMac Makes an Excellent Surfboard," for help.) It may give you an error. If so, quit the application and try again. It may take a time or two for the AirPort Base Station to be able to connect, but it should work, and you will be able to wirelessly connect to the Net.

Configuring the AirPort Software to Work with an Existing Wireless Network

If you want to connect to an existing wireless network, open the AirPort Setup Assistant and click the **Set up your computer to join an existing wireless network** radio button and then click the right-facing arrow. Your iMac searches for a network to join. When it finds one, you will have to enter that network's password to configure your AirPort to use it. Do so, and then click the right-facing arrow. When it appears, click the **Go Ahead** button to set up your iMac to use the wireless network. When it has finished, you will be able to access that network (to connect to the Internet for example).

Taking Off

After AirPort is installed and configured, you can use it in the following ways:

➤ **Connecting to the Net with a Base Station**—When you connect to the Net through the Base Station, you can move your iMac around and still be connected. You can travel as far as 150 feet from the Base Station. Because AirPort uses radio waves to communicate, even walls won't stop you.

➤ **Connecting to a Network with AirPort**—You can connect your AirPort to your own or another's Ethernet network that is attached to a Base Station. Use the AirPort Control Strip module to switch between networks. See Chapter 22, "Don't Be Stingy—Share Your iMac and Its Files," to learn how to use a network.

➤ **Connecting to Other AirPort-Equipped Computers**—You can directly network two AirPort-equipped computers together. As long as the computers are set up to use the AirPort connection, they can communicate with each other up to 150 feet apart. This has great application for multiplayer games because there is no need to bother trying to physically link the computers. Simply be within 150 feet of each other, and you can immediately play games over the wireless AirPort network. (To do this, you need to choose **Computer to Computer** on the AirPort module on the Control Strip on each machine.)

Look Ma! No Wires

Using your AirPort Base Station to connect to the Net is literally a no-brainer. Simply open an Internet application that needs to connect to the Net and your Base Station connects to the Net for you. You can then use it just as if you were connected with wire (bleech!).

You can also connect to the Net through someone else's Base Station. Simply configure your iMac's AirPort setup to use that Base Station, and you can access the Net.

What this means is that up to 10 AirPort-equipped Macs can share a single Internet connection. This is really cool.

Connecting to a Local Network with AirPort

Connecting to a local network through the AirPort is just like using wires (without the wires of course). Simply use the Chooser and Network Browser to sign on to network resources. See Chapter 22 for help with this.

Rolling Your Own Network with AirPort

You don't even need a Base Station to use an AirPort network. Use the AirPort Control Strip button (you'll learn about that in the next section) to change the AirPort connection from Base Station to Computer to Computer. You iMac will look for any other AirPort-equipped computers and will connect to them. That is all there is to it. You can have an instant network within a few seconds.

Cruising Through the AirPort

When you install AirPort on your iMac, an AirPort Control Strip module is added to your Control Strip and the AirPort application is added to your Apple menu.

When Is an iMac Like an AirPort Base Station?

Using the AirPort Software Access Point software, you can use another AirPort-equipped computer (such as an iBook, DV iMac, or G4) as a Base Station. In this mode, your iMac uses the modem in the other computer instead of its own internal modem. You need to get this software from Apple to be able to do this.

Sometimes Things Are Slow

Sometimes when you try to connect to a Web site via an AirPort Base Station, it generates an error message and nothing seems to happen. This is because your AirPort Base Station has not had a chance to connect to the Net before Internet Explorer gets impatient and gives up. Wait a moment or two and try again. It will probably work the second time.

Controlling the AirPort from the Strip

The AirPort module on the Control Strip provides you with complete control over your AirPort and the connections you are making with it (see Figure 10.2).

Figure 10.2

The AirPort Control Strip module enables you to control the AirPort.

On the module, you will see the following commands:

➤ **AirPort On (or Off)**—At the top of the module, you will see the current status of AirPort, either On or Off.

➤ **Open AirPort**—This one opens the AirPort application (which you will learn about in the next section).

➤ **Computer to Computer**—Use this command to switch from a Base Station mode to a Computer-to-Computer mode.

➤ **List of available Base Stations**—You will see a list of Base Stations for which your AirPort has been configured. Select a Base Station from the list to use that network.

➤ Turn **AirPort On (or Off)**—This command does just what you think. It turns the AirPort On if it is off and Off it is on. You need to have the AirPort turned on to be able to use the wireless network.

Controlling the AirPort from the AirPort Application

You can open the AirPort application from either the Control Strip module or the Apple menu. When you do, you will see the AirPort application window (see Figure 10.3).

Figure 10.3

The AirPort application lets you manage your own AirPort.

The top part of the application window enables you to see the current status of the AirPort network as well as turn it off or on. You will also see your AirPort ID. If you click the Show Details button, in the lower section of the window, you will see information about the Base Station you are using, such as the strength of the signal you are receiving from it and whether its modem is connected to the Internet.

You can choose the wireless network to connect to from the **Network** pop-up menu.

You can move to the AirPort's Help Center using the **Help** button.

AirPort Utility—Use It if You Need To

The AirPort Utility application enables you to manually configure a Base Station. This application is located in the AirPort folder that is in the Apple Extras folder. I just wanted you to know about it in case you should ever need to use it, but you probably won't. Most likely you'll only use it to increase the amount of idle time before your Base Station drops off the Internet. (The default is 10 minutes, which will probably be just fine.) If you do want to change it, launch the AirPort Utility, choose the Base Station you want to configure, click **Configure** (you have to enter a password for that Base Station), click the **Internet** tab, and enter a new time in the **Disconnect if idle** field. Close the application and save your changes.

Leaving the AirPort

You may have to go back to using wires to connect to a network or to the Internet, but hey, life can't always be perfect.

To switch back to wired operation, turn the AirPort off using the Control Strip module or the AirPort application.

If you are connecting to an Ethernet network, open the AppleTalk control panel and choose **Ethernet built-in** from the pop-up menu. Close the control panel and save your changes.

To switch back to using the iMac's built-in modem, open the TCP/IP control panel. From the **Connect via** pop-up menu, choose **PPP**. From the **Configure** pop-up menu, choose **Using PPP Server** (assuming you are connecting via the most common kind of dial-up account—if not, choose the option that is applicable for your type of account). Close the control panel and save your changes. You will be able to connect through your built-in modem application.

Restart your iMac and all should be as it was before AirPort.

The Least You Need to Know

➤ AirPort consists of the following components: an AirPort-capable computer (such as the iMac, iBook, or G4 Mac), an AirPort card, the AirPort software, and an AirPort Base Station. (You can use AirPort to connect to other computers without a Base Station.)

➤ To set up the AirPort, install the card in your iMac. Then install the AirPort Base Station if you are using one. Finally, run the AirPort Setup Assistant to configure it for you.

➤ To connect to the Internet, open an Internet application; the Base Station will connect to the Net and you can use the application.

➤ Use the AirPort module on the Control Strip or the AirPort application to switch between connection options and Base Stations depending on what you are trying to do (connect to a network, connect to other AirPort-equipped computers, and so on).

Chapter 11

Goodbye Post Office—We Won't Miss You!

In This Chapter

➤ Learn how Outlook Express can handle all of your email needs

➤ Learn to read and write (emails that *is*)

➤ Set up your own electronic address book

➤ Understand how you can keep your email organized

➤ Learn how to send and receive files via email

Email has become the communication medium of choice for many people. Using email, you can communicate with anyone or any organization in the world that has access to any email service. Not only can you reach out and touch these people, but email is also easy, convenient, fast, and inexpensive. It's also more interactive than regular mail (also known as snail mail) because you can get a reaction to your email almost immediately.

Email also enables you to send just about anything you can store on your iMac. You can send files (text, images, sounds, movies, or whatever) as attachments to your email messages. For example, you can send a text file to a colleague for her review. The possibilities are almost endless.

Why Are There Servers in My Mailboxes?

You will also see some name and newsgroup servers in your list of mailboxes. That is because Outlook Express is also a full-featured newsgroup reader. Want to learn more? Open the **Help** menu and choose **Outlook Express Help**. Search for help with newsgroups.

Touring Microsoft's Outlook Express

Outlook Express is a full-featured email program that has many useful tools you can use to make the most of email.

Experiencing Outlook Express— A Quick Look

Outlook Express uses a three-pane window (see Figure 11.1). The left pane contains all of the email folders you set up, as well as standard folders Outlook Express provides for you. The Inbox is where all the mail you receive is deposited (unless you set up a filter to send it to another folder). The Outbox is used to hold mail you've created (until you send it). The Sent Mail folder contains all the messages you have sent. The Drafts folder is a folder for drafts of email messages on which you are working that aren't ready to send yet.

Figure 11.1

Outlook Express is a full-featured email client—it uses a three-pane window to make it easy to get to various functions and tools.

Email folders   Tool buttons   Email box pane   Reading pane

Folder and server pane

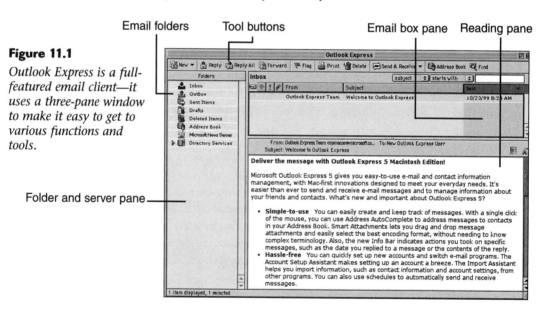

Across the top of the window, there are buttons for tasks you do frequently; for example, New for creating a new message and Delete for deleting messages or folders.

The top pane on the right side of the window contains a list of all the messages in the folder selected in the left pane. To view the contents of a message, click it in the top pane and the message body appears in the lower pane, which is where you will read the text of your messages.

A Double-Click Will Do You

You can also read a message by double-clicking it. When you do, the message opens in its own document window.

Didn't I Already Configure Outlook Express?

Yes, you did. You configured most of the important stuff for Outlook Express when you set up your Internet account in Chapter 9, "Setting Up Your Own iAccount." Outlook Express is now set to do the basic tasks, such as retrieving your email. But that is not good enough for us, is it? Well, is it? Of course not. We aren't idiots, after all.

There are a few minor tweaks you need to do to make Outlook Express function at its best for you. Besides, making these minor changes will also show you how to change any preferences you may need to change in the future.

Versions, Versions, Everywhere

In this chapter, I show you how to use version 5 of Outlook Express. When most iMacs first shipped, version 4.5 was installed. Because I'm not psychic, I don't know which version came on your iMac. They work similarly, but the interface is a bit different. If you are using version 4.5, I recommend you update it to version 5 so the information in this chapter matches what you will see on your screen (and it is generally better to use the newest versions of most applications). You can tell whether you are using version 4.5 by the splash screen when it opens or by opening the **Apple** menu and then choosing **About Outlook Express**. You will see the version number in the resulting window.

To upgrade to version 5—it's free to do so— you need to use your Web browser to go to www.microsoft.com/mac/download and download it. Read Chapter 12, "Your iMac Makes an Excellent Surfboard," to learn how to download and use files from the Web.

Open the **Internet** folder and double-click the **Microsoft Outlook Express** icon. When Outlook Express opens, you may see the Outlook Express Setup Assistant. (This is most likely to happen if you are upgrading from version 4.5.) You use the Setup Assistant the first time Outlook Express opens after you upgrade. You should choose the **I already have an email account** radio button and click the right triangle. In the next screen, click the current email program you are using (for example, Outlook Express) and then click the right triangle. Each of the screens should have your information on them because you have already configured your account. If so, simply verify the information and move to the next screen. If not, enter the information before you move to the next screen. When you are finished, you will end up in the Outlook Express window.

If you don't see the Outlook Express Setup Assistant window, don't worry. Your settings were entered back in Chapter 9 when you configured your Internet account. In this case, you will end up in the Outlook Express window without seeing the Outlook Express Setup Assistant.

From the **Edit** menu, choose **Preferences** to open the Preferences window (see Figure 11.2). Across the top of the window, you will see various tabs. You use these tabs to set your preferences for various tasks, such as reading or composing email.

Figure 11.2

You configure Outlook Express in the Preferences window.

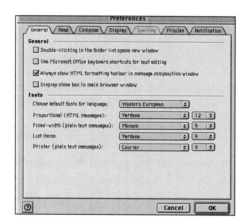

Some of the settings I'm going to ask you to set may not make sense to you now, but please make them anyway. I'll explain why you made them later. Trust me on this, okay?

Click the **General** tab (it may already be selected) and review the options you can set here. Take a good look to get an idea of what you can change. The general settings you are most likely to use are to set the fonts Outlook Express uses. For now, uncheck the **Always Show HTML formatting toolbar in message composition window** check box.

Click the **Compose** tab. Make sure Plain Text appears in the **Mail format** pop-up menu. Uncheck the **Reply to messages in the format in which they were sent** check box.

Why Plain Text?

Outlook Express has the capability to work with formatted text. So why do I tell you to turn it off? Mostly because you aren't likely to bother formatting your email. Email is all about speed, so who wants to spend a lot of time applying formatting to messages? Besides, how the formatting is seen depends on the program used to read it. Not everyone uses Outlook Express, so you don't know whether your recipients will even be able to see your formatting. Finally, replies are much more clear with plain-text messages. If you want to experiment with formatting your email, you can always turn it back on again.

Click **OK** to close the Preferences window.

Now double-check your account configuration to make sure you are good to go. From the **Tools** menu, choose **Accounts**. Double-click your email account. In the resulting window, check the settings to make sure everything is as you set it when you first configured your iMac for the Net. If something is not right, correct it. When you are done, click **OK** and close the Accounts window.

Spelling Preferences?

If you have Microsoft Office 98 installed on your iMac, Outlook Express can use the Office spell checker to check the spelling in your emails. If this is the case for you, you can use the Spelling tab preferences to determine how the spell check works on Outlook Express. For example, you can have Outlook Express check your text for spelling errors as you type.

You've Got to Write 'Em to Get 'Em!

I'll bet you are excited about sending your first email message. Who should you send it to? If you know someone's address, go ahead and send it to her—just replace the address, subject, and text I'm using in the following paragraphs with information that is appropriate for your recipient. If you don't know any email addresses of your friends or family, try writing to me just so you get the hang of using Outlook Express. (You can tell me what you think about this book at the same time!)

Take an iLook

Auto Connections to the Net

By default, your iMac automatically connects to the Net when an application needs to do so. For example, when you tell Outlook Express to send and receive your email, it automatically connects to your account to get your email.

This option is set using the Remote Access control panel. If you choose not to configure the automatic connection feature, you will need to connect to the Net yourself before sending or receiving email. (You learned how to do this in Chapter 9.)

Be an iMac Wizard

Write Your Email Offline

It's usually a good idea to write your emails while your computer isn't connected to the Net. That way you don't tie up your phone line. When you are ready to send your messages, you can connect to the Net, send them, and then log off again.

Write Your Email

To get started in the wonderful world of email, click the **New Message** icon at the top of the window (or press ⌘+**N**). You will see the new message window, ready for you to create your masterpiece. You move into the addressing dialog box because you need to tell Outlook Express who you are sending mail to (see Figure 11.3).

The cursor is in the To box, so type the email address of the person to whom you want to send email. (If you want to send a message to me, use bradm@iquest.net.) If you want to send the same message to more than one person, press **Tab** and enter another address. If you want to Cc someone on the message, click the **Cc** tab and enter the addresses for the Cc recipients. You should Cc someone on a message if you want them to have a copy of it, but it is only for their information. In other words, you don't expect the Cc'd person to do anything with the information in the message; you just want them to be aware of it. Do the same thing for any Bcc recipients. The difference between the Cc and Bcc recipients is that in the emails the recipients receive, the Bcc recipients will not appear in the list of people to whom the message was sent. Keep going until all the addresses are in. Press **Return** to close the addressing dialog box.

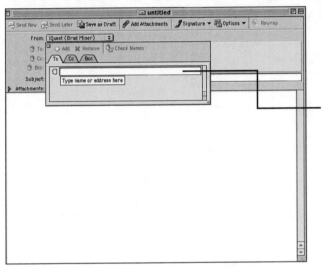

Figure 11.3

When you create a new message, you will see a new window like this one.

Enter the address of the recipient here.

Now enter a subject for the email. Try to use meaningful subjects when you send email so the recipient has a good idea of what the message is about. For example, if you write to me, use something like "Feedback on Your iMac Book."

Press **Tab**, and you move into the body of the message. Type your message (see Figure 11.4).

Use good writing practices when you are creating your emails. Remember, someone has to read your message, so don't waste his time.

Take an iLook

Saving Email You Send

By default, Outlook Express saves a copy of each message you send in your Sent Mail folder.

Try to use the three c's of writing: conciseness, clarity, and completeness. When you finish typing your message, edit it. Check for spelling errors, poor sentences, and so on. Fix any problems you find.

Figure 11.4

Don't make emailing yourself a habit!

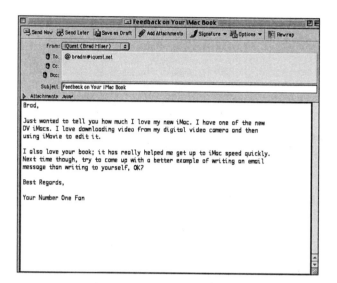

Brad,

Just wanted to tell you how much I love my new iMac. I have one of the new DV iMacs. I love downloading video from my digital video camera and then using iMovie to edit it.

I also love your book; it has really helped me get up to iMac speed quickly. Next time though, try to come up with a better example of writing an email message than writing to yourself, OK?

Best Regards,

Your Number One Fan

Take an iLook

Please Don't Yell!

Don't type your messages in all capital letters. IT LOOKS LIKE YOU ARE YELLING AT THE RECIPIENT OF YOUR MESSAGE. I am assuming you don't want to yell, of course. If you do, NEVER MIND!

Click the **Send Later** icon. Your message moves into the Outbox, which becomes highlighted to show you it contains a message. Follow the same steps to create other messages you want to send.

Now Send Your Email

When you are ready to send your messages, click the **Send & Receive** button (or open the **Tools** menu, choose **Send & Receive** and then choose **Send All** from the hierarchical menu). Your iMac connects to the Internet, and your email is sent.

Congratulations! You've just sent your first email message! Easy, wasn't it?

Read 'Em If You've Got 'Em

Sending email is fun, but receiving it is even better! In fact, you will probably get all excited when you check your email the first few times. And that's okay because receiving email is one of life's simple pleasures (and it isn't even fattening!).

Retrieving and Reading Your Email

Now it's time to see who is sending email to you!

Click the **Send & Receive** button. If your iMac is not already connected to the Net, it connects and begins to download your email. If you did not have Outlook Express save your password, you are prompted to enter your password. Do so, and click **OK**. If you receive email, you hear a sound and your email is downloaded to your Inbox. You see the new messages in bold because you have not opened them yet.

Click a new message in the Inbox window (it is highlighted to show it's selected), and it will appear in the message window (see Figure 11.5). Read the message. (Scroll if you need to.)

If you want to delete a message after you have read it, click the **Delete** button (the trash can icon) while you have the message open or selected. When you want to move to the next message in your Inbox, click it or

Spell Checking Emails

If you don't have Office 98, you should get a spell checking utility to use on your email. An excellent choice is Casady & Greene's Spell Catcher. It provides a spell checker for all your applications, including Outlook Express.

press the down or up arrows key (which you use depends on whether the message you want to read is below or above the current one). Its contents appear in the lower pane of the window. Continue reading until you have read all your messages.

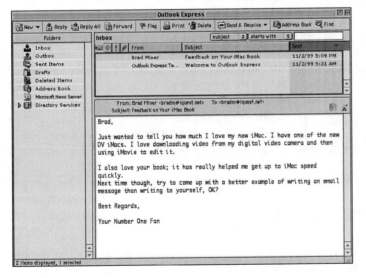

Figure 11.5

I hope the email you receive is more worthwhile than this one!

When you delete a message, it is moved into the Deleted Items folder. If you want to retrieve a message you deleted, click the **Deleted Items** folder, select the message you want to undelete, and drag it to your Inbox. The message then appears in your Inbox again.

Send Now!

If you click the **Send Now** button when you are finished with a message, Outlook Express immediately connects to the Net and sends the message instead of moving it into your Outbox.

By default, deleted messages remain in the Deleted Messages folder until you empty the folder. To empty the Deleted Items folder, open the **Tools** menu, choose **Run Schedules**, and then choose **Empty "Deleted Items" Folder**.

Sending an Email Message Can Be as Easy as Hitting Reply

One of the great things about email is that you can carry on extended conversations by replying to email messages. When you reply to a message, Outlook Express creates a new message for you and automatically addresses it to the person from whom it came. The subject is also modified by the addition of "Re:" to the front of it. After you send your reply, the recipient can reply to your reply and so on.

Checking Your Email in a Hurry

To quickly send and receive all your email, press ⌘+M.

Before you learn how to do this, however, you need to understand one of the most important things about replying to email: quoting.

When you reply to email, it's a good idea to quote the message to which you are replying. Quoting means you paste the relevant part of the original message into your reply so your reply can be understood in the context of the original message. This enables the recipient to better understand your reply. For example, pretend you just received a long message about the latest developments in the Mac OS saga. You are all excited about the fact that the Mac OS comes with a new Corvette. (Just kidding of course, it only comes with a Yugo.) So you fire off a reply that says, "That's great." If that is all that is in your reply, the recipient may have no idea what you think is great. But if you quote the part about the Corvette, the recipient of your reply will understand exactly what you are talking about.

When you reply to a message, Outlook Express automatically copies all of the original message into your reply. To differentiate the original message from your reply, Outlook Express attaches the > symbol to the text from the original message. If the person you sent the reply to replies to your reply, the original message is marked with two symbols like this: >>. Your reply will be marked with one >. And so it goes. By the way, this is one of the reasons I suggest you use plain-text messages. Quoting is much easier to do in plain-text messages than in formatted messages.

Scheduling Your Email

With Outlook Express's scheduling feature, you can have it automatically do all sorts of things, such as sending and receiving your email and emptying the deleted items folder. For example, it is often convenient to have Outlook Express check for email every hour or two so you don't have to remember to check it yourself. To set up schedules, open the **Tools** menu and choose **Schedules**. You can use the schedule tools to define when specific actions happen.

Quoting is essential, but you should be selective about what you quote. Outlook Express automatically pastes the entire message into your reply. If you are only replying to a portion of the original message, delete everything but the portion to which you are replying. If you don't, your reply will be longer and less clear.

Click on a message you have received (in any mailbox). You will see the text in the lower right pane of the Outlook Express window. Click the **Reply** button or choose **Reply to Sender** from the **Message** menu. The message opens in a new message window. The text from the previous message has been pasted into the window and the reply is already addressed. The quoted message text is marked with the quote character, >.

Now type your reply, editing the quoted material as necessary so any replies you make to specific items are clear. A reply should look much like a conversation, because that is basically what it is (see Figure 11.6).

And Replies to All...

You will also see a Reply All button. Use this when the message you are replying to had more than one recipient and you want your reply to go to all of those recipients. Reply only goes to the original sender. Reply All goes to every one on the distribution list—remember that, because replying to all can be embarrassing if you don't intend to do so.

Figure 11.6

This is a reply to a message; notice how the original message text has been pasted in and marked with the quote symbol >.

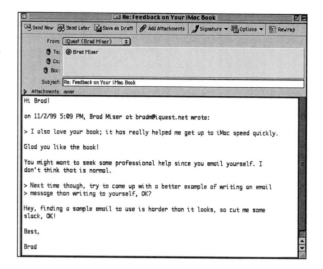

When you are done with your reply, click the **Send Later** icon. You reply is placed in your Outbox and sent the next time you send and receive your email.

Making Your Own Electronic Black Book

Email addresses are not fun to type. Plus, it is easy to make mistakes when you type them—one mistake in an address and your email will not be delivered. (It bounces right back to you.) Fortunately, the Outlook Express Address Book feature enables you to store email addresses so you can easily address your messages.

Creating Your Address Book

To get started creating your own list of contacts, click the **Address Book** button. You will see the Address Book window. Click the **New** button, and you will see a new Contact window containing many fields for all sorts of data. Enter information for your contact. At the least, enter a first name, press **Tab**, and enter a last name. You can enter as much or as little other information as you like. When you are done entering this information, press **Enter**.

Because this Address Book is for email, you will definitely want to enter an email address. Click in the e-mail addresses window. In the pop-up window, enter the email address and press **Enter.** When you return to the information window for your new contact, you will see the information you have entered (see Figure 11.7).

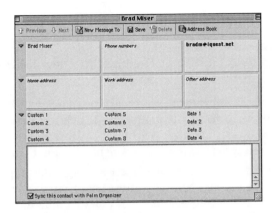

Figure 11.7

Is this contact really necessary?

There are many fields in which you can store a lot of information. Fill them as you need to. When you are done, click **Save** to store the data. Close the window and you will see your new entry in the Address Book window.

Creating a Contact Without Typing

The easiest way to create a contact for someone is to use an email you receive from them. With the message selected, open the **Tools** menu and choose **Add to Address Book**. Outlook Express extracts the email address and creates a new contact containing that address. It also does its best to extract a first and last name if it can, but this sometimes does not work.

You can edit a contact (to correct the name Outlook Express botched for example) by opening the Address Book window, selecting the contact you want to edit, and clicking the Open button. You will see an edit window for that contact; you can then change any information for that person. Click the **Save** button and then close the window when you are done.

Using Your Address Book

Of course, the purpose of creating a contact is to be able to easily address a message. There are several ways to add the contact's address to a new message, as you can see in the following list:

➤ Click the **Address Book** button. In the Address Book window, select the contact to which you want to send an email, and click the **New Message To** button. A new email message window with that address appears. Type the subject and then your message. That is a lot easier than typing the address, isn't it!

➤ In the To, Cc, or Bcc blocks of a new email message, start typing the name of your contact. As you type, Outlook Express tries to match what you are typing with someone in your Address Book. As it makes a match, it fills in the name; if you have several Address Book entries with the same first name, you may have to type into the last name for Outlook Express to find the right match. When you see the name you intend to send the email to, press **Enter**. Your email is correctly addressed.

➤ In the Address Book window, select the name of the person to whom you are sending an email. Hold down the **Control** key and click the mouse button. From the pop-up menu, choose **New Message To**. A new blank message with that email address is created for you.

Grouping Your Favorite People

There are often situations in which you want to regularly send emails to a certain group of people. For example, you might be sending status updates to all the people on your project team. With the mailing list feature of Outlook Express, you can make addressing such emails a one drag operation.

First, you need to create a mailing list, which is simply a collection of email addresses under one name. In the Address Book window, click **New Group**. A new, untitled mailing group is created. Name the group; its name is highlighted already (try something like Project Team) so just type the name and click **Add**.

Now add the people to the mailing list. Click the **Address Book** button that is at the top of the group window. Your Address Book opens. Drag a name from the list onto the mailing list and release the mouse button. Drag the next name over and continue until all of the people are in the group. In the group's window, click **Save Group** to save it. Then close the window.

Using a group to address a message works just like using a "regular" contact. You can type its name, drag it from the Address Book window, or click it and use the contextual menu to address a new message. Your email will be sent to everyone in the group.

Organizing Your Email

As you start sending and receiving a lot of mail, keeping it all in the Inbox will become a pain as you scroll through tons of messages looking for the one you want. Fortunately, Outlook Express provides you with tools to keep your email nice and tidy. The most important tool is the capability to create folders in which you can store your email.

You can add your own folders to Outlook Express, and it is easy to move messages from one folder to another. The following are a few pointers on how Outlook Express folders work:

> ➤ New folders can be created by opening the **File** menu, choosing **New**, and then **Folder**. When the folder is created, its name is selected and you can name it whatever you like.

> ➤ Folders in Outlook Express work just like folders in the Finder. (For example, you can rename them by selecting the folder's name, pressing **Enter**, and then typing the name.)

> ➤ Subfolders within folders can be created by selecting a folder, choosing **File**, then **New**, and then **Subfolder**. Name the subfolder and it appears within the selected folder.

> ➤ The contents of a folder can be expanded or collapsed by clicking the expansion triangle next to its name—just like the List view on the desktop.

> ➤ Messages can be moved from one folder to another by dragging and dropping them. Select the mail message you want to move and drag it onto the folder in which you want it stored. When the folder becomes highlighted, release the button and the message is moved into that folder.

The Point of No Return

The Outbox is the point of no return for email. If a message is still in the Outbox, you can open and change it. If it's no longer in the Outbox and you have sent your mail, it's too late to make any changes.

Sent Mail Folder

If you do have Outlook Express save all the mail you send (which it's set to do by default), you should open up the Sent Mail folder every so often and delete any messages you no longer need. Otherwise, this folder can grow very large.

Using Email to Send and Receive Files

One of the best features of email is that you can send and receive files with your email. This makes email one of the most convenient ways to transfer files to other people. Files sent via email are known as *attachments*.

Before you get to receiving and sending files, however, you need to have some understanding of file encoding and file compression.

To transmit files over the Internet, they have to be encoded in certain ways so they will be useable when they arrive. Unfortunately, not all computers use the same encoding schemes to send files. This is not a problem when you receive files because Outlook Express automatically decodes most files types for you, but you do need to be aware of encoding when you send files.

Because files can be quite large and thus take a long time to send, file compression techniques have been developed to make files small in order to send them over the Net. When they reach you, you must uncompress them to use them. Your iMac comes with the utility you need to work with compressed files. This is covered in the next chapter because you are most likely to need to deal with compressed files when you download them from the Web. However, you may receive compress files via email as well.

Receiving and Using Attached Files

When you receive an email message that has a file attached to it, you will see a paper-clip icon next to the Subject of the message. Click the message to select it. Read the text. To see the files that are attached to it, click the Expansion triangle next to the word **Attachments**. You will see a list of files that are attached to the message (see Figure 11.8).

Figure 11.8

Email is a great way to transfer files—the paper-clip icon tells you a file is attached to this message.

This message has a file attached to it.

Click here to see a list of the attached files.

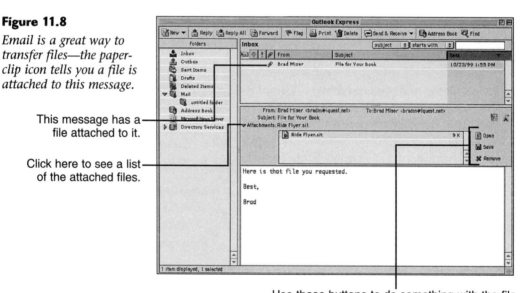

Use these buttons to do something with the file.

You use file attachments in two ways. One is to view the contents of the files while in Outlook Express. To open a file, select it and click **Open**. The file is opened in the appropriate application).

The other way is to download the file from the email message to store it on your hard drive. Then you can open it with an application just as you would any other file. To download a file instead of viewing it, select the file and click the **Save** button. Use the **Save Enclosure** dialog box to name the file (if you want to change its name) and to tell your iMac where you want the file saved. When you are done entering this information, click **Save** to save it).

Attaching Files to Your Email

To send a file to someone else, you need to attach it to an email message. Attaching a file to an email message is quite simple. Create your message as you normally do. From the **Message** menu, choose **Add Attachments**. Using the Choose Object dialog box, maneuver to the file you want to send. Select it, and click the **Choose** button. Continue to add as many files as you need to send.

When you return to the message window, you will see the names of the files you have attached listed next to the word **Attachments**. Click the Expansion triangle to show the details of the attachments to your message (see Figure 11.9).

Here is where the only tricky part comes in. You need to set the encoding and compression options for that attached file. To do this properly, you should know what kind of computer the person to whom you are sending the file uses: a Macintosh or a Windows PC. If you don't know what kind of computer the recipient uses, assume they use a PC because that is the lowest common denominator (and PC encoding will work fine for most files you send).

Compressed Files

If the file you choose to open is compressed, it opens with the uncompression utility, StuffIt Expander. After the file has been uncompressed, you can work with it just like any other file.

Don't Delete That Message!

If you receive an email with files attached, make sure you save those files to your hard drive *before* you delete the message. After Outlook Express removes the message from the Deleted Messages folder, the attachments will be gone too.

Adding Files Is a Drag

An easier way to attach files to a message is to drag them from the desktop onto the message window. When you do, they will be attached to the message.

Figure 11.9

This email has a file attached to it, and you can see the details about that attachment in the attachments window.

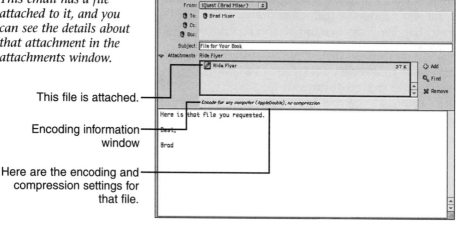

This file is attached.

Encoding information window

Here are the encoding and compression settings for that file.

Select the attached file and examine the encoding and compression options set for it. (They appear directly above the message body.) If they are okay, you don't need to do anything. If not, click the settings to pop up a dialog box (see Figure 11.10).

Figure 11.10

You use the dialog box shown in this figure to set encoding and compression options for an attached file.

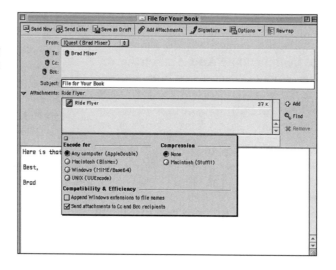

If all the recipients use Macintosh computers, check the **Any computer (AppleDouble)** or **Macintosh (BinHex)** radio button. Either will work fine. The **AppleDouble** setting works for most other computers, so that is your best bet. (It is also the default encoding.) Also click the **Macintosh** compression radio button so the files will be compressed before they are sent. (They will be a lot smaller and will take less time to send.)

144

If any or all the recipients use Windows computers, use the default encoding (AppleDouble), and check the **Append Windows extensions to file names** check box. This ensures the file will be easier to use for the recipients. Do not use any compression because most Windows PCs can't deal with files that have been compressed by StuffIt (the Macintosh compression format).

When you are done setting options, click outside the dialog box to close it. You will see the options you have chosen in the encoding information window. Click **Send Later** to move the message to your Outbox. When the recipient receives your email, he will also get the file you attached. Cool, isn't it!

The Least You Need to Know

➤ To use email, you must have an Internet account, an email account, and an email application. Assuming you worked through Chapter 9, you have all three.

➤ Outlook Express is an excellent email application that is included with your iMac.

➤ In addition to the basic email reading and writing tools, use the Address Book to save email addresses so you don't have to type them.

➤ Use folders to keep your email organized.

➤ Use file attachments to receive and send files.

Chapter 12

Your iMac Makes an Excellent Surfboard

In This Chapter

➤ Use Internet Explorer to cruise the Web

➤ Set your own Home Page

➤ Use Favorites to make life easier

➤ Search the Net for everything from Apples to Zinc

➤ Download files to your iMac—as easy as clicking the mouse button

➤ Visit way cool Web sites

You are about to experience a revolutionary form of communication, which also happens to be a revolutionary form of entertainment, commerce, the arts, and education. The World Wide Web is evolving into a phenomenon the likes of which has never been seen before.

The World Wide Web enables you to virtually explore the world from your iMac. And the world is only as big as your imagination. Just imagine being able to tap into some of the finest university libraries in the world to research a paper. It's possible. But there's more. You can buy and sell goods and services, watch movie clips of upcoming feature films, hear fantastic sounds, visit art galleries, experience different types of imagery, and read about any topic under the sun. Are you a news junkie? The Web enables you to browse through newspapers and magazines from all over the world.

The good news is that your iMac is the perfect tool with which to travel the world through the Web.

Walking the World Wide Web

All Web pages share a certain basic structure (see Figure 12.1). The Web page itself is within the inside borders of the browser window. Everything else you see is part of Internet Explorer, which is the default Web browser on your iMac. Within Web pages, you will see text, graphics, and links. The text and graphics you'll no doubt understand. Links are the only thing that really makes a Web page different from many other documents you view. Links are simply pointers to someplace else. That place may be another Web page, a different part of the current Web page, a larger view of a graphic, a file, and so on. Most links are shown by underlined text, but many graphics also contain links. Using a link is simple—click a link and you move to wherever it points.

Figure 12.1

This isn't the prettiest Web page you will see, but this Home Page makes a good starting point for your Web explorations.

Favorites toolbar   Address bar   Tool buttons   Sherlock button

Favorites tab
History tab
Search tab
Page Holder tab

Take an iLook

Have You Been Framed?

Some Web sites use frames, which simply divide the page into different sectors. Usually the frame on the left side of the window contains a live list of contents of the site. To move to a particular area, you simply click it in the left frame. Sometimes, you can resize frames and sometimes you can't. It depends on how the page is designed.

As with email, there are two basic steps to get you on the Web:

1. Connect to the Internet (if you allow it to, your iMac will handle this step for you).
2. Launch Internet Explorer and browse the Web.

Addressing Your Request

You will see URLs for Web sites all over the place, including television, newspapers, magazines, advertisements, and so on. How do you visit a site when you have its URL? I'm glad you asked.

From the **Apple** menu, choose **Remote Access Status**. When the window appears, click **Connect** (or press **Return**). Your iMac works its way onto the Net. When your status becomes connected, open your hard drive, then open the **Internet** folder, and then double-click the **Microsoft Internet Explorer** icon. Internet Explorer opens and you move to your Home Page (more about that in a bit). That is all there is to it; you are on the Web!

To move to a specific site, use its URL. Open the **File** menu and choose **Open Location**. In the Open Internet Address dialog box, type the URL

Letting Internet Explorer Do the Work for You

If you have Remote Access configured to allow automatic connections, you can just open Internet Explorer and it connects to the Net for you. Unless you have changed this, your iMac is configured to allow this by default.

of the site you want to visit. Because you like Apple, start there. Type `www.apple.com` and click **Open.** You move to Apple Computer's Web site (see Figure 12.2).

Figure 12.2

Apple Computer's Web site has a lot of great resources for you.

Type Less

There are some shortcuts you can use when you type URLs. If the server address for a site is www.something.com, you can just type the something (for example, to move to Apple's Web site at http://www.apple.com, just type apple). If you have visited the site before, Internet Explorer fills in most of the address for you.

Instead of using the Open Location command, you can enter the URL directly in the Address bar just below the toolbar. You can even modify the URL already in the box—this may save you some typing. When you have the URL the way you want it, press **Return** (or click the **Go** button) to move there.

Although entering URLs is easy enough, they can be long and are a pain to type. Fortunately, you probably won't type them very often, and using Favorites (which you will learn about later in this chapter), you should only have to type a URL once.

Browsing Around

The method that really makes the Web "the Web" involves moving by using hypertext links. These links are gateways to other sites. You can spot links by looking for underlined words, different colored text, and graphics. Each of these links can indicate a link to another site. You simply activate the link and move to the site it links with by clicking on the link. Go ahead and try it.

When you move over something on a Web page and the pointer turns into a hand with a pointing finger, you are over a link. Click the mouse button and you will move to the site at which the link points.

While you are looking at the Apple Web site, scroll around until you see a link—move over some of the graphics and look for the hand cursor. Click the link to move to that area. That is all there is to browsing with links. Click on more links and explore.

Notice that the links you have followed change color to indicate you have followed those links.

Look for the URL

Another way for you to tell that your cursor is over a link is to watch the lower left part of the screen. When you are over a link, you'll see the URL of the site to which the link points. If you are not over a link, you won't see a URL there.

(You can set the colors that are used to track links in Internet Explorer's Preferences window.) This can be useful when you are really roaming far and wide because you can avoid going places you've already been.

Amazing isn't it? The Web is one of the few things in life that does live up to its media hype. How can something this cool be so easy to use?

Using Internet Explorer's Tools

Just under Internet Explorer's menu bar is the toolbar. You can activate these buttons by clicking on them. Not much explanation is required, but just in case they don't make sense to you instantly, here's the *Reader's Digest* version of what each one does:

➤ **Back and Forward**—These buttons take you either back to the last page you visited or forward to the next page in the list of sites you have visited.

➤ **Stop**—This one stops everything Internet Explorer is doing. If you try to move to a site and it is taking forever and a day, click on this to make Internet Explorer stop what it is doing. You will probably use this button quite a bit.

➤ **Refresh**—This button refreshes the current page, which makes Internet Explorer go get the page again. Occasionally, a page will have problems when you try to load it to your machine. Other times, such as with weather maps or stock quotes, the data on the page may have changed. This button tells Internet Explorer to reload the page to clear any errors and get any new data.

➤ **Home**—This button takes you back to your Home Page. You will learn about this in a later section.

➤ **Favorites**—This one opens the Favorites window, in which you can organize your favorite Web sites.

➤ **History**—This button opens the History tab.

➤ **Search**—The Search button opens the Search tab and takes you to your default search site.

➤ **AutoFill**—As you use the Web, particularly when you shop on it, you will often have to complete forms. Internet Explorer's AutoFill feature automatically completes standard information for you. After you provide AutoFill with the information it needs, you can complete many forms by simply clicking the **AutoFill** button. (To use AutoFill, you need to tell Internet Explorer your information. To do so, click the **AutoFill** button. Answer **Yes** to the question about moving into the AutoFill Preferences window. When you get to the window, fill in all your information and click **OK**.)

➤ **Larger and Smaller buttons**—These buttons increase or decrease the size of the fonts used to display a Web page.

➤ **Print**—I bet you know what this one does.

➤ **Mail**—This button opens your default email program, which should be Outlook Express.

➤ **Preferences**—This one opens the Preferences window you use to configure Internet Explorer.

151

Making Yourself a Home on the Web

In Web-speak, your Home Page is the term used for the page your Web browser automatically goes to when you launch it. You can set your Home Page to be any page you want it to be. Internet Explorer is preconfigured to use a personal Home Page on Excite.

Internet Control Panel

You can also use the Internet control panel to set your Home Page. (Open the control panel, click **Web,** and enter the URL for your new Home Page.) Setting it there causes all your Web browsers to use it. Configuring it within Internet Explorer causes that Home Page to be used only in Internet Explorer.

But the Home Page you choose is up to you. To change your Home Page, move to the site you want it to be (enter the URL via the **Open Location** command or type it in the Address bar and press **Return**). When the new page has loaded, click in the address bar, select the URL, and choose **Copy** from the **Edit** menu (or press ⌘+**C**).

Click the **Preferences** button on the toolbar. In the Preferences window, click **Home/Search**. You will see the preferences window for those settings. Select the Address in the Home Page area and press ⌘+**V** to paste your URL in the box. Uncheck the **Automatically go to this Home Page when opening a new window** check box (see Figure 12.3). Click **OK**.

Figure 12.3

Because I like to keep up with the latest news, I set my Home Page to be CNN's Web site.

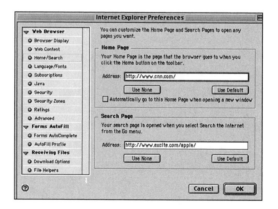

Whenever you open Internet Explorer, it moves to your new Home Page. You can move there yourself at any time by clicking the **Home** button..

Playing Favorites

On the Web, not only is it okay to play favorites, it is expected behavior. Favorites are an easy way to store URLs to which you may want to return; they make going back to sites extremely easy. All you have to do is select a favorite from a menu or click a button to quickly move back to that site.

Using Favorites

Using Favorites is as easy as can be, and your iMac already has a number of useful Favorites set for you. Open the **Favorites** menu, and choose a Favorite from the menu. Some Favorites are actually folders that contain Favorites grouped together. When you select a folder, a hierarchical menu displays the Favorites in that folder. You will move to that site—no typing required.

Dropping CyberCrumbs

Using the predefined Favorites is great, but it isn't likely you will find Favorites for all the sites you want to visit. Fortunately, it is quite simple to create your own Favorites.

Move to a site you will want to come back to. When you have moved to that site, open the **Favorites** menu and choose **Add Page to Favorites**. A Favorite for that site is created and appears at the bottom of the **Favorites** menu.

To visit that site again, select it from the **Favorites** menu.

Adding Favorites with Speed

You can quickly add any sites to your Favorites by pressing ⌘+**D** when you are visiting the site.

Cleaning Up Your Crumbs

Adding and using Favorites is so easy that you are bound to pile up a lot of them as you move about the Web. Internet Explorer provides tools you can use to keep your favorites organized so they will remain easy to use.

Open the **Favorites** menu and choose **Organize Favorites**. You will see the Favorites window (see Figure 12.4). You can use this window to manage and organize your favorites. The left column shows the name of the Favorite and the URL is shown in the right column. Folders look and work just like they do on the desktop. (For example, to expand a folder, click its Expansion triangle.)

You can reorganize your Favorites by dragging them up and down in the window, which changes the order in which they are displayed on the Favorites menu.

Keeping Up with Microsoft

Microsoft is continually updating and improving Internet Explorer. You should periodically check Internet Explorer's Web site at www.microsoft.com/mac/ie/ for updates and support.

153

Figure 12.4

With this Favorites window, you can keep all your favorite Web sites as close as a click.

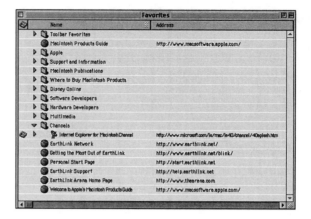

You can create new folders for your Favorites by opening the **Favorites** menu and choosing **New Folder**. To put a Favorite in a folder, drag it onto the folder.

You can see that it is simple to keep your favorites organized. Here are a few more tips you can use to work with favorites:

➤ You can add a divider between favorites or between Favorite folders by using the **New Divider** command on the **Favorites** menu. The divider is added below the folder that is selected when you choose the command.

➤ You can sort favorites items by clicking the newspaper icon in the upper-left corner of the Favorites window. The favorites are sorted according to item name.

➤ You can use the **New Favorite** command to manually add favorites by typing the site's URL.

Using the Favorites Toolbar

In the Favorites window, you will see a folder called Toolbar Favorites. When you place a Favorite in this folder, it appears as a button on the Favorites toolbar, which is just below the Address bar. To use a Favorite on the toolbar, simply click it.

Internet Explorer is preconfigured with several Favorites on the toolbar. If you don't want to use these, you can remove them by dragging them out of the Toolbar Favorites folder. You can also replace them with your own Favorites so you can access them easily.

Using the Favorites Tab

If you click the Favorites tab that is along the left side of the Internet Explorer window, you will see the Favorites area (see Figure 12.5).

154

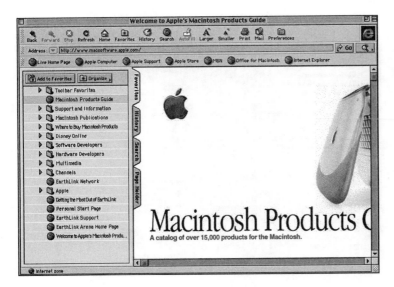

Figure 12.5

You can manage all your Favorites using the Favorites tab.

In the Favorites area, you can do most of what you can with the other Favorites tools, and this area can be a more convenient way to use and manage Favorites. You can do the following tasks:

➤ Click a Favorite to move there.

➤ Use a Favorite that is in a folder by expanding the folder and clicking the Favorite.

➤ Organize your Favorites by dragging them up and down in the window, placing them in folders, and so on.

➤ Add a Favorite by clicking the **Add to Favorites** button.

➤ Access the other Favorites tools by clicking the **Organize** button.

Revisiting History

As you travel the Net, Internet Explorer diligently makes a list of each site you visit. This list makes it easy to get back to any site that is still on the History list.

Click the **History** tab and you will see a list of all the sites you have visited recently (see Figure 12.6). To move back to a site, click it in the History area. Click the **History** tab again to close it.

Be an iMac Wizard

Changing History

To set the number of sites Internet Explorer remembers that you have visited, choose the Advanced pane of the Internet Explorer Preferences window. Change the amount shown in the **Remember the last __ sites visited** field. The default value *is* 300.

Figure 12.6

Using the History tab, you can quickly move back to any site you have recently visited.

You can also return to a site you have previously visited by opening the **Go** menu and choosing the site from the menu.

Internet Explorer creates folders into which it places the sites you have visited on previous days. To move back to a site you visited on a particular day, open the folder with that day's date and click the site.

If you want to clear the History list, set the number of sites Internet Explorer remembers to zero. After you click **OK**, Internet Explorer forgets its past. You can reset the number it remembers if you want to create another History list.

Finding a Needle in the Cyberhaystack

Although the Web is a great thing, it does have its problems. One of them is that there is so much information of every conceivable kind that the Web appears to be a jumbled mess of pages and links going back and forth with no overall organization or order. And you know what? That's exactly what it is. The power of the Web is that anyone—assuming he cares to learn how—can put his own page on the Web, and any Web page can be linked to any other Web page. Combined with the millions of Web sites available—with thousands being added each week—this makes for quite a jumbled morass of information.

This arrangement is fine if all you want to do is click around and follow the links provided on various pages. It also works if you have specific URLs to visit.

Often, however, you may want to find Web pages relating to specific topics or even certain keywords. Fortunately, there are resources available (called *search engines*) on the Web to help you sort through the tangled web of Web pages and find what you are looking for.

Searching with Yahoo!

This site wins the award for having the best name *and* for being one of the most useful areas from which to search for information on particular topics. After you use it, you'll agree that its name is appropriate.

The Yahoo! site enables you to find Net resources related to a wide variety of topics (see Figure 12.7). These topics run the gamut from art to society to culture.

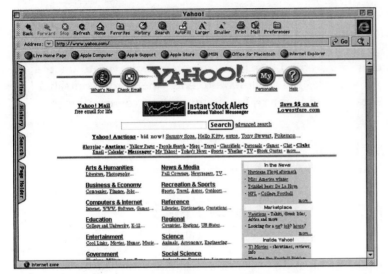

Figure 12.7

Yahoo!—a site by any other name would not be half as good.

Not only is the Yahoo! site powerful, but it's as easy to use as the Web itself. Want to see more about some topic? Just click on it. As you continue to click through the links, you will move farther down into the Yahoo! hierarchy until you start moving to individual Web pages that contain the information for which you are looking.

By the way, the numbers in parentheses after a topic are the number of site links within that topic.

You can also search for specific information with Yahoo!. Move to the Yahoo! page at www.yahoo.com, and enter the text for which you want to search in the field next to the **Search** button. Click **Search**. Yahoo! searches for sites that contain your search text. When it finishes, you see the results window that contains the matches with your text.

To move to a site to see whether it has the information for which you are looking, click its link. Click **Back** to move back to the Yahoo! results page or use your history list to move back. You can continue to explore the links Yahoo! found until you find the information for which you are looking.

Boolean Expressions

When you use a word in your search such as *and, or, not,* and so on, you are using a Boolean expression. Most search engines enable you to use Boolean expressions in your searches, but not all of them do it in the same way. Although Yahoo! provides radio buttons for advanced searches, some sites require you to use the words themselves; for example, you might have to enter the words "contextual" *and* "menu" in the search field to search for information on contextual menus.

There's more to Yahoo!, but this is enough to keep you busy. If you need more information about Yahoo!, just click the Help link on the Yahoo! Home Page.

Using the Search Tab to Search the Web

The Search tab provides a nice tool you can use to search the Web. Click the **Search** tab. You will see the search area. Choose the search engine you want to use from the **Choose provider** pop-up menu at the top of the area. Enter the text for which you want to search and then click **Find It**, **Search**, or whatever term the particular engine you have chosen uses. The engine performs your search. When the search is complete, you see a list of links in the Search area. Click one of these links, and you will see the page in the right part of the window (see Figure 12.8).

Figure 12.8

Internet Explorer's Search tab is nice to use because you can set your search in the tab window and see the results in the right part of the window.

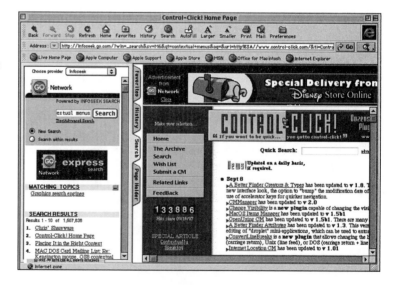

The Search tab is a great way to search because you can see the results of the search without leaving the search page. You can quickly check the results of your search by clicking the links in the search area and looking in the right part of the window. This prevents you from having to use the Back button to constantly return to the search page.

When you are done with your search, click the **Search** tab to close it.

Searching with Sherlock

I've saved the best for last. You can use the Mac's powerful Sherlock feature to search the Net. In fact, Sherlock is so useful that I devoted the entire next chapter to it.

Take an iLook

Expanding the Tab Windows

You can make any of the tab windows larger by clicking in the area between the tab area and the browser window. When the pointer changes to two vertical lines, drag the border to change the width of the tab window.

Holding Your Pages

When you are looking at a page, you will probably want to follow a lot of the links on it. Some pages are primarily link holders and don't contain much information. Internet Explorer's Page Holder enables you to move the linking page to the Page Holder area. Then you can click the links and see the results in the right part of the window. This prevents you from having to move back and forth among the pages.

Move to a page with a lot of links on it—try a news page, such as www.cnn.com. Click the **Page Holder** tab to open it. Click the **Add to Page Holder** button. (It's in the upper-right corner of the area, it looks like a window with a large arrow pointing to the left.) This moves the page into the Page Holder area. Click a link in the Page Holder area and you will see the resulting page in the right part of the window.

To make the right area larger so you can see more of the linked page you are reading, close the Page Holder tab by clicking it. When you want to move to another page, click the tab to open the Page Holder area, click a link, and read the page. (Close the tab to make the page larger.)

Using the Page Holder makes browsing a lot of links more enjoyable because you can lay off the Back button.

Finding Files in All the Right Places

One of the best things about the Web is that you can download files from it. These files may be applications, graphics, text files, updates, or whatever. Downloading files is simple after you get the hang of it.

Downloading Files from the Web

First you must move to the file you want to download. There are lots of great sites for Mac files; one of the best is `www.macdownload.com`. Use Internet Explorer to move to this site. (You should add a Favorite for this site because you will be back.)

Search for a file. Just for fun, enter `system sounds` in the text box and click **Search**. The search is performed and you see the results in a new window.

When you want to download a file, click on it. You move to a page containing additional information on the file. When you want to download the file, click the **Download Now** button. The file is downloaded to your iMac and you see the Download Manager window (see Figure 12.9). When the file has been downloaded, you see Complete next to its name in the Download Manager window.

Figure 12.9

Internet Explorer uses the Download Manager window to provide information on the files you are downloading.

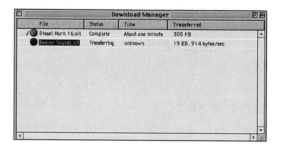

Multiple Downloads

You can download multiple files at the same time. Click the download links for each file you want to download. They will each be moved into the Download Manager and will begin to download. Be aware, however, that each file consumes some of the data stream coming into your computer, so each file will download more slowly than it would if you downloaded one at a time.

You can also continue to browse the Web while your files are downloading. The speed decreases a bit, but at least you can do something while the files are downloading.

That is really all there is to downloading files—simply click on the files you want to download to your iMac, and Internet Explorer does the rest.

Using Files You Have Downloaded

Most files stored on the Web are encoded and compressed; these are the same processes that are applied to email attachments. Most Mac files are compressed using the StuffIt format. Your iMac comes with the tools you need to expand the compressed files you download—these files have the .sit suffix on their filenames.

StuffIt!

StuffIt Expander, which uncompresses compressed files, is freeware that comes with your iMac. (It's located in the Aladdin folder that is in the Internet folder.) Your iMac also comes with DropStuff, which you can use to compress files (when you want to email them to someone, for example). DropStuff is not freeware. If you use it for more than 30 days, you need to register it—the fee is $30.

Internet Explorer handles the decoding for you, and it automatically unstuffs files in the .sit format.

If for some reason a file does not get uncompressed automatically, double-click the .sit file. A dialog box appears that tells you the application StuffIt cannot be found. In the window, select **StuffIt Expander** and click **Open**. The file is unstuffed using StuffIt Expander and then you can use its contents.

When it finishes, you will see both the compressed and uncompressed versions of the file. You can work with the uncompressed version and throw the compressed version away.

Exploring the Best Mac Sites

After you have used the Web for awhile, you will develop quite a list of sites you use regularly. Until then, you can explore some of the sites listed in Table 12.1. They provide a good starting point for your Web adventure.

Table 12.   Good Web Sites for Mac Users

URL	Description	Comments
Mac Sites		
www.apple.com	Apple Computer's Web site	You can shop in the Apple Store as well as get support and read the latest Apple and Mac news.
macworld.zdnet.com	*Macworld* magazine's Web site	You can read the latest Mac news as well as search for information on specific topics .
www.macaddict.com	Web page of *MacAddict* magazine	More Mac news from a very pro-Mac site
www.machome.com	Web home of *MacHome* magazine	Read the magazine, download files, and more.
www.macintouch.com	Ric Ford's MacInTouch site	An outstanding source of Mac news, especially for troubleshooting and updates
www.macfixit.com	Ted Landau's MacFixIt site	Another excellent site for help with Mac problems
www.maccentral.com	Home of MacCentral Online	More Mac news
www.outpost.com	Home of Cyberian Outpost	Cyberian Outpost is an excellent source for all Mac software and hardware.
www.macdownload.com	ZDNet's site for Mac software	Good source from which to download shareware and freeware
Other Sites		
www.mcp.com	Home of Macmillan Computer Publishing	Get lots of great information on computer books.
www.cnn.com	CNN Interactive	An excellent news site
www.weather.com	Home of The Weather Channel	All the weather information you would ever need

URL	Description	Comments
www.loc.gov	U.S. Library of Congress Web site	An amazing collection of important documents, all available on the Web
www.reel.com	Home of Reel.com	An excellent source for videos and DVDs; if it is available, reel.com will have it. (You can also rent videos.)
www.netflix.com	Home of Net Flix	You can buy or rent DVDs here.
www.amazon.com	Home of Amazon.com	This is the ultimate book store.

This list is relatively small compared to the list you will build on your own. Still, it gives you some great sites to visit. Between these and your preconfigured favorites, you have a lot of sites you can visit already!

The Least You Need to Know

➤ To surf the Web, you need a computer, a modem, a Web browser, and an Internet account...your iMac has the first three, and if you worked through Chapter 9, you have the last one too.

➤ Using the Web is easy; after your iMac is set up to use the Net, launch Internet Explorer and enter URLs in the Address bar or simply click links to move around.

➤ Use Favorites to make it easy to revisit sites you find valuable.

➤ You can use search engines, such as Yahoo!, or you can use the iMac's powerful search tool, Sherlock, to find specific information on the Web.

➤ Ranking the great things about the Web is tough, but being able to download files from it has to rank near the top.

➤ Download files by clicking their links; files are downloaded to your iMac where you can use them.

Chapter 13

THE GAME'S A FOOT!

Sleuthing Around the World with Sherlock

In This Chapter

➤ Search the Internet the Mac way using Sherlock

➤ Create your own search channels and add search sites

➤ Master Sherlock by using neat Sherlock tricks

➤ Find files on your hard disk (and any other disk you use for that matter)

Cruising around the Net is great, but more often than not, you need to find something specific. Perhaps you want information on the latest developments related to iMacs. Or maybe you need to keep up with your favorite TV shows. Or you might need to find a specific piece of software to download and use.

In the last chapter, I showed you how to use a Web search engine to search the Internet—Web search engines are great and you will use them regularly. In that chapter, I also promised to show you a better way. Now is when I fulfill that promise. Get ready to be amazed.

The Mac OS includes a search utility called Sherlock. Why is it called Sherlock? Probably because it can find things as well as the legendary detective after which it is named. Sherlock can search the Internet, your iMac files, and even your documents. Sherlock is one of the most powerful parts of the Mac.

Searching the Net—the Sherlock Way

You already learned how to use a search engine, so you may be wondering why Sherlock is such a great thing. There are many things you can do with Sherlock, including the following:

➤ **Search multiple sites at one time**—Using Sherlock, you can search multiple locations using one search, and you can control exactly which sites are searched. You can also create your own sets of sites (called channels in Sherlock-lingo) to search.

➤ **Save your searches**—You can save your search criteria so you can re-run a search by double-clicking a file. Try that with a Web search engine!

➤ **Create shortcuts to Web sites you find**—When you drag a Web site from Sherlock to your desktop, a shortcut is created. You can return to that site by simply double-clicking that shortcut.

➤ **Limit your searches to the type of information for which you are looking**—You can use channels to choose the sort of information for which you are looking. For example, you can ask Sherlock to search only news-related sites.

Searching Is More Fun (and Productive) with Sherlock

There are several ways to get to Sherlock. For now, open the **Apple** menu and choose **Sherlock 2**. You will see the Sherlock window. Click the icon that has a drawing of the Earth—this is actually the Internet channel (see Figure 13.1).

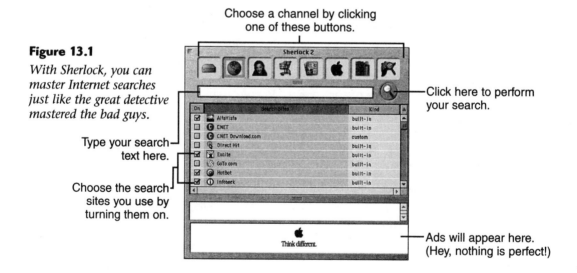

Figure 13.1

With Sherlock, you can master Internet searches just like the great detective mastered the bad guys.

What Happened to Sherlock 1?

Sherlock was introduced to the Mac in Mac OS 8.5. Since then, Sherlock has undergone major improvements and the result is Sherlock 2. Sherlock 2 adds many features and a totally new interface to the application. If you've never used Sherlock, you will just have to trust me that Sherlock 2 is a major improvement in what was already a great tool. (Actually, Sherlock 2 is version 3, but that is another story....)

Plugging It In

Sherlock searches sites through *plug-ins*. Plug-ins are small pieces of software Sherlock uses to connect to the search site. Sherlock comes equipped with many plug-ins for many Web sites, and you can download and add plug-ins for many other Web sites that offer them.

Using a plug-in, also called a *search site*, is simple. If the plug-in's check box is checked, it is searched. If not, it's not searched.

Most of the Channel Icons Are Self-Explanatory...

For the channel icons that aren't self-explanatory, point to the icon and wait a moment. The channel's name appears in a pop-up box.

Channeling the Net

Channels are collections of related search sites. For example, Sherlock comes with several channels, including the following:

➤ **Internet**—These sites are general Internet search sites.

➤ **People**—You use this channel to find individual people.

➤ **Shopping**—Use this one when you simply have to buy something—now!

➤ **News**—I am sure you get the idea.

You can change channels for specific searches so the results are more likely to be what you are looking for.

Other Paths to Sherlock

You can also open Sherlock by double-clicking its icon on the desktop. You can also open the **File** menu and choose **Search Internet**. If you want to do it the hard way, you can also open the **System** folder, then the **Apple Menu Items** folder, and then double-click the **Sherlock 2** icon.

Searching the Net

Now that you know the basics of Sherlock, try using it to search. For this example, pretend you want to see if the iMac has appeared in the news lately. Sherlock can help.

Open Sherlock 2 if it isn't already open. When the window opens, click the **News** channel (the icon looks like a newspaper). In the text box, enter iMac. Choose the sites you want to search by checking the check box next to each site. Uncheck the sites you don't want to search. Click the **Search** button. If you aren't connected to the Internet, your iMac connects itself. Then Sherlock moves onto the Net and performs your search. You can see its progress by watching the Searching progress bar.

By the way, turning off sites you don't want to search is good because your search will be finished faster and there is less likely to be a lot of duplication in the results.

When Sherlock has finished, the list of search sites is replaced by the list of matches to your search text. For each item that meets your criteria, you will see the name of the page, its relevance to your search (sometimes), the date of the page, and the site on which the page is located (see Figure 13.2.)

Figure 13.2

Sherlock has found that the iMac is in the news.

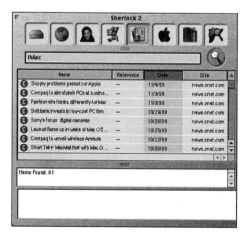

You may notice Sherlock's results window looks a lot like folder windows in the List view. This similarity is more than skin-deep. The results window works just like a folder window too. For example, to sort the results, click the column heading by which you want to sort the list. You can also resize the columns, reverse the sort order, and so on.

You can also resize the entire Sherlock window by using its **Size** box.

Scan through the results of your search. When you find a site that looks interesting, click on it. You will see a summary of that site in the summary window; the summary window starts off pretty small, so make it larger by dragging on the resize handle, which is located in the center of the window just above the summary area (see Figure 13.3). The summary usually shows you the first couple of lines from the page.

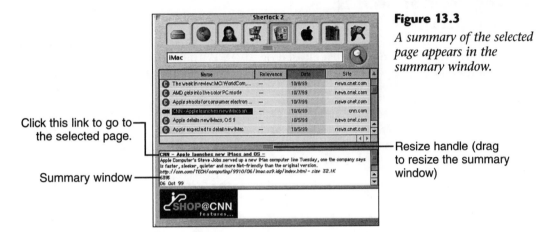

Click this link to go to the selected page.

Summary window

Figure 13.3

A summary of the selected page appears in the summary window.

Resize handle (drag to resize the summary window)

If you find a summary that looks promising, click its link in the summary window. Internet Explorer opens and takes you to that site. When you are done reading, switch back to Sherlock and choose the next results page in which you are interested. Continue visiting the results sites until you find everything you need).

When you enter your search criteria, you don't have to limit yourself to a single word or phrase. You can use certain words to make your search more specific. For example, if you want to find information on a particular movie on DVD, you could type the name of the movie, then the word **and**, and then **DVD.** That search would look for instances of the movie title and DVD. You can also use **or** to conduct searches (which means find this "or" that). These words are examples of Boolean expressions.

If you want to find an exact phrase, enclose it in quotation marks.

Experiment to see which sort of search expressions work best for you. One of the great things about Sherlock is that it's relatively insensitive to how you type your search text.

The following example illustrates all the steps you need to use Sherlock for your own searches.

1. Open Sherlock.
2. Click on the channel you want to use for your search.
3. Type the text for which you want to search.
4. Choose the search sites in the selected channel you want to search.

5. Click the **Search** button.

6. Read the summaries for any sites that look promising.

7. Click the links in the summary window for those summaries that look like they provide the information for which you are looking).

Saving Your Searches

There may be certain searches you want to run regularly. Perhaps you like to keep up with all the news about your favorite computer company, or perhaps you want to find out when a good movie is released on DVD. With Sherlock, you can save the criteria for any search you run. When you want to run the search again, simply open the criteria file and run the search.

Open Sherlock and perform a search—pick one you will want to run again in the future. When you are done with the search, open the **File** menu and choose **Save Search Criteria**. In the Save dialog box, name the search, choose a location in which to save it, and click **Save**. Your search is saved.

To run a saved search, open Sherlock and from the **File** menu, choose **Open Search Criteria.** Move to the search you want to run, select it, and click **Open**. Sherlock restores everything about your search, including the channel, the search sites, and the search phrase. Then it conducts your search. Cool, huh?

Run a Search with a Double-Click

You can also run a search by double-clicking its icon.

Creating Your Own Channels

Sherlock comes with a number of channels, but the predefined channels do not include all the search sites that are available. Not to worry—you can create your own custom channels and add Sherlock plug-ins for your favorite search sites.

To create your own channel, open Sherlock and from the **Channel** menu, click **New Channel**. In the New Channel dialog box, type the name for your channel. Choose an icon for your channel using the up and down arrows. Choose your channel's type from the **Channel type** pop-up menu; choose the type that reflects the search sites you will add to it. For example, if you want to add a shopping site, choose **Shopping** from the pop-up menu. For general searches, choose **Searching**. Type a description in the **Description** box if you want to. Then click **OK**.

When you return to the window, you won't see anything different. Did you mess up? Nope. You can't see your channel because Sherlock fills up the first row of channels. Drag on the Resize handle just below the Channel window (it's a group of horizontal lines) until you see the next line of channels. And there your new channel will be (see Figure 13.4).

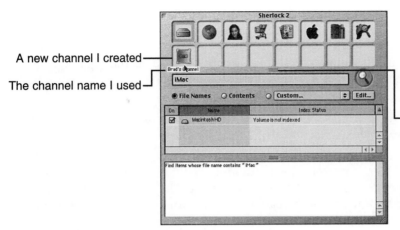

A new channel I created—

The channel name I used—

Figure 13.4

I created a new channel (cleverly called Brad's Channel) in which to store new search sites.

Resizing handle (drag to expose or hide channels)

If you click your new channel, the search window will be empty. Not too useful yet, is it! It will be after you add some search sites.

As you travel around the Web, you will see many sites that offer Sherlock plug-ins. You can add these sites to your channels so you will be able to use Sherlock to search them. To see how this works, I'll add a plug-in for the Dictionary.com Web site so I can search for information to help me write better.

Go to the Sherlock Plug-in Directory Site at www.apple.com/sherlock/plugins.html. Click on the plug-in you want to add; in this case, I clicked on the Dictionary.com link to move to the Dictionary.com Web site. Once there, I went to the Help page, asked for help with searching with Sherlock and clicked the plug-in to download it to my iMac. Move to the downloaded file. (If you set a folder into which to download all your files, open that folder.) Drag the .src file that you downloaded onto the search site window for your channel. After a moment, you will see the search site in the channel.

You use plug-ins that you add just like the search sites Sherlock comes with. Turn them on by checking the check box next to them, and they will be used for your search.

Take an iLook

Presumptuous, Isn't It!

Sherlock assumes you will want your own channel and has an empty channel for you already. It is called "My Channel" and has the Deerstalker cap for its icon. You can add search sites to this channel as well as to any you create.

Take an iLook

Choosing Channels

You can also select a channel by choosing it from the **Channels** menu.

Using Cool Sherlock Net Tricks

Now you know the basics of Sherlock. The following are three neat Sherlock tricks:

➤ When you select a result site, press ⌘+**B** to open that site in a new browser window. This is useful when you want to keep several of the results pages open at the same time.

➤ Open a results page by dragging it from the results window onto a browser window. That page will be opened in the browser.

➤ To create a shortcut to a page, drag it from the results window onto your desktop (or into a folder). An icon appears. To move to that site, double-click the icon. Your browser opens and takes you to that site. This is a good way to store pages you need for a temporary research purpose (rather than creating Favorites to them in Internet Explorer).

Answering the All-Too-Common Question, "Where Is That File?"

Sherlock is great for finding things all across the globe. It's equally adept at searching your relatively puny hard drive to help you find files you have "misplaced."

Finding Files the Easy Way

Pretend (I know it's a stretch) you ignored what I told you about creating a special folder into which to download files. Then pretend you downloaded a Sherlock plug-in to the Dictionary.com! site, but have no idea where you put it. You can use Sherlock to find it.

Take an iLook

Easy Open

You can work with the icons in the results and summary windows just like you can in a folder window. Double-click an icon to open it. Drag it from the windows to the Trash to delete it. Get the idea?

Open Sherlock. This time, click the hard disk icon. (It's name is Files.) The Sherlock window changes into its "local" mode. You use this mode to search your iMac. Click the **File Names** radio button if it isn't already selected. Type the file name you are looking for. (If you were looking for the Dictionary.com plug-in, you could type Dictionary.src.) If you can't remember that whole name, just type in the parts you can remember. Click the disks you want to search—this should seem a bit familiar to you (see Figure 13.5).

Figure 13.5

You can use Sherlock to look for files on your iMac's hard drive. (This search would find files with Mac OS 9 in their name.)

Click the **Search** button. Sherlock begins looking for all the filenames that meet the criteria you typed. When it's done, you'll see the list of files and folders that contain all or part of the text you entered. To see where the file is located, select it in the Results window. The path to it appears in the summary window.

Finding Files the iMac Wizard Way

Unless you have a better memory than I do, there may be times when you simply can't remember the name of a particular file. Do you think this stumps Sherlock? Of course not. You can use Sherlock to search for many different attributes of a file. For example, you can search for any files created or modified on a day, for specific file types, and so on.

Open Sherlock. This time, click on the **Custom** radio button. Click the **Edit** button. You will see the More Search Options dialog box. Check the check boxes next to the criteria

Take an iLook

Mix and Match

You can add as many criteria to the More Search Options dialog box as you like. Sherlock tries to match them all at the same time. Adding more criteria is good because it makes the search more specific.

to use them for your search. Then enter the information you want to use and choose an operator from the pop-up menus. For example, to search for all the files created within a week of 10/15/1999, check the **date created** check box, choose **is within 1 week of** from the pop-up menu, and use the date controls to set the date to 10/15/1999. Click **OK**. Then click the **Search** button. Sherlock locates any files or folders that meet the criteria you chose.

Searching Inside Documents

Just as you can use Sherlock to search for the attributes of files, you can also use it to search for files by their content. This works okay, but I haven't run into many people who actually use this feature. That doesn't mean it won't be useful to you, of course.

Be an iMac Wizard

Use a Schedule

If you are going to regularly search for files by their contents, set up a schedule for the index and choose an index time when you won't be using your iMac.

Open Sherlock and click the **Contents** radio button.

Before you can do any content searches, you must index any drives you want to search. From Sherlock's **Find** menu, choose **Index volumes**. Select the drive you want to index and click **Create Index**. You will see a warning that indexing takes a long time—your iMac is not kidding either! Click **Create**.

When the indexing is finished, enter the text for which you want to search. Click the **Search** button. The documents that contain your search text appear in the results window.

The Least You Need to Know

➤ To use Sherlock to search the Web, open the **Apple** menu and choose **Sherlock 2**; when Sherlock opens, choose a channel, choose the search sites you want to use, enter your search text, and click the **Search** button.

➤ Click a result to see a summary of the page in the summary window; to move to that page, click its link in the summary window.

➤ Create your own Sherlock channels and add search sites to them to create custom search tools.

➤ Select a site in the results window and then press ⌘+B to open that site in a new browser window.

➤ Drag a site from the results window to your desktop to create a shortcut to that site; double-click the shortcut to go to the site.

➤ Sherlock can find files on your local disks too; you can search by filename, attributes, or even contents.

Part 3

iMac Equals iFun

Until now, I have focused on the rather utilitarian aspects of your iMac, such as how to work with folders, how to create documents, how to use email and the Web, and so on. These are all great topics and you need to know them, but you probably didn't yell, "Whoohoo!" when you learned about them.

In this part, you learn how to do some things purely for the fun of it. None of the chapters in this part are necessary for you to communicate, do your work, and all the other mundane aspects of life. However, I bet you will really enjoy doing what they teach. So grab some soda, coffee, or whatever beverage you are partial to, and get to the fun. Who knows, you might even yell, "Whoohoo!" (Okay, probably not, but you get the idea.)

Chapter 14

Giving Your iMac an iMakeover

In This Chapter

➤ Tweak your iMac's appearance to give it a unique personality

➤ Use themes so you can quickly hide your "I gotta be me" look when you need to look like you are serious

➤ Understand why and how to use the Monitors control panel

One of the best things about an iMac is that it is way cool looking. There is no other computer that even comes close to being as unique—on the outside at least. When you first get your iMac, however, its desktop looks pretty much like every other desktop on every other Macintosh. It's okay to look at, but you have to be you, right? Why not make your iMac desktop a place where you feel comfortable and that suits your personality?

You May Not Be a Plastic Surgeon, But You Can Change Your iMac's Appearance

Your iMac uses colors everywhere. Some are subtle and you barely notice. Others jump out at you. Some even serve an important purpose. You can make these colors what you want them to be. How, you ask? Your magical makeover tool is the wonderful Appearance control panel.

Open the **Apple** menu, choose **Control Panels**, and then choose **Appearance**. You will see the Appearance control panel. It has several different tabs you can use to customize different aspects of your iMac. Click the **Appearance** tab (see Figure 14.1).

Figure 14.1

With the Appearance tab of the Appearance control panel, you can change the colors your iMac uses to get your attention.

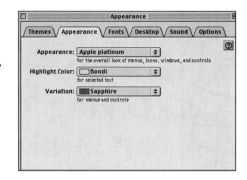

This tab has three pop-up menus. Each menu controls a different aspect of the interface you see.

The Appearance pop-up menu controls the general look of menus, windows, icons, and other standard elements of the Mac operating system. Apple may provide other choices besides Apple platinum some day, but for now, you can't do anything with this one.

The Highlight color pop-up menu is the most functional of all the Appearance settings you will use. The highlight color is the color your iMac uses to tell you that something has been selected and is ready to move, edit, and so on. You should use a color that grabs your attention most easily, because that's the whole point. From the pop-up menu, choose a color that you want to try. No need to close the control panel, simply click the desktop to move back to it. Select a folder and wait a second or two. The highlight color appears. Like it? If not, click back in the Appearance control panel and keep trying until you find "your" color.

What Color Is "Other"?

In some of the pop-up menus for colors, you will see the choice Other. If you select Other, you move into the Mac's Color Picker. This utility enables you to design your own colors. There are six variations on how you can do this—my favorite is the Crayon Picker. Click on the variation you want and play with the color controls until you have a color that interests you. When you return to the control panel, your custom color is applied.

The Variation pop-up menu controls the color of menus and window controls, the most noticeable of which is the color of the scroll boxes. It works the same way the Highlight pop-up menu does. Choose a color, click in a desktop window (make sure it is one with visible scroll boxes), and see if you like it. If not, pick another color.

Fonts, Fonts, Everywhere Fonts

In many ways, the Mac was built on fonts. It was the first computer on which you could control the fonts. The Fonts tab of the Appearance control panel enables you to tell your iMac what fonts it should use.

Click the **Fonts** tab of the Appearance control panel, and you will see three more pop-up menus (see Figure 14.2). Use the Large System font menu to choose the font family used on menus. Use the Small System Font pop-up menu to set the font family used on smaller text elements such as labels (as of this writing, you can only use Geneva so there really is no choice). Use the Views Font pop-up menu to set the font family used in folder views for icon names; you can use the **Size** menu to choose a default font size for these items as well.

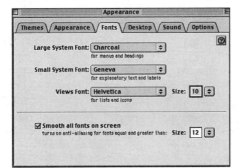

Figure 14.2

Fonts built the Mac; you can use the Appearance control panel to tell your iMac which fonts you like.

The last option on this tab is Smooth All Fonts On Screen. This makes large size fonts appear less blocky than they normally would. The downside is that it requires more computing power to display smoothed fonts. If you want to see the difference this feature makes (it's on by default), turn it off by unchecking the check box. If you find the appearance of large fonts to be acceptable, you can leave it off. If not, turn it back on.

You Don't Have to Be an Interior Designer to Decorate Your iMac

I admit it...the first couple of appearance items you learned about are not very exciting. That is about to change; this is where the really good stuff is. One of the most fun things to play around with is the appearance of your desktop. You can fill your desktop with either desktop patterns or desktop pictures. Desktop patterns use color and shapes to fill your desktop with (hopefully) pleasing textures and colors. Desktop pictures are photographs that appear on your desktop. If you feel very artistic, you also can combine the two.

Playing with Patterns

Desktop patterns are somewhat simpler than desktop pictures because they usually involve basic shapes and colors rather than a full-blown image. Desktop patterns consist of smaller "squares" of patterns that are repeated to fill up the entire desktop, much like a quilt is made of "squares" of material. These squares are usually either 16×16 pixels or 128×128 pixels "big." Your iMac comes with a large variety of desktop patterns you can use, or you can create your own patterns to use.

Open the Appearance control panel and click the **Desktop** tab. You will see the Desktop Settings window (see Figure 14.3). The window has two panes. In the left pane, you'll see a preview of the pattern that is selected from the list in the right pane. Just below the preview, you'll see the name of the pattern, its size in pixels, and its file size.

Figure 14.3

You can have hours of fun playing with your desktop's patterns and pictures!

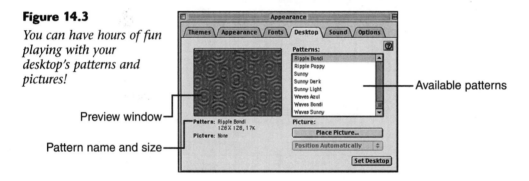

Available patterns

Preview window

Pattern name and size

Use the scrollbar to scroll through available patterns in the right pane. Select a pattern to preview it in the left pane. When you find one you like, click the **Set Desktop** button. When you see your desktop, it will have the pattern you just selected.

If you are the artistic type (which I am definitely not), you can create and use your own desktop patterns.

Use a graphics program to create a 16×16 pixel block (or 128×128—as long as it is square, it doesn't matter which). Save the file as a common picture format, such as PICT. Drag the file you created onto the preview window in the Appearance control panel. You will see your pattern in the preview window. If you like it, click the **Set Desktop** button to fill your desktop with your new creation.

Desktop Pattern Tips

When selecting or creating a desktop pattern, keep the following points in mind. Keep the pattern simple. Complexæ patterns can interfere with your ability to see things on your desktop. Use only a few colors. Again, too many colors can make your desktop distracting rather than pleasing. Avoid lots of medium-sized graphics in a pattern. If you use a graphic that is about the same size as an icon, you will have an even harder time finding the real icons. Keep the "pattern" graphic significantly smaller or larger than the icon size that you use. You can also use a photo or a part of a photo as a pattern.

Painting Your Screen with Beautiful Pictures

Desktop pictures are even more fun than desktop patterns. You can make your desktop into anything you can picture (literally). Photographs of scenery make excellent desktop photos as do photos from special occasions or even special people.

Open the Appearance control panel and click the **Desktop** tab. Click the **Place Picture** button. In the Choose a File dialog box, maneuver to the file that you want to use as a desktop photo. For starters, open the Photos folder that is within the Desktop Pictures folder. Select a photo, and click the **Show Preview** button. You will see a small version of the photo on the right side of the window. If don't you like that photo, select another

Cut and Paste a Pattern

You can also select a pattern in your graphics program, copy it, and then paste it in the preview window of the Appearance control panel to apply it. When you do this, your new pattern won't have a name. Choose **Pattern Name** from the Appearance control panel's **Edit** menu to give it one.

one and try again. After you find a photo you want to use, click **Choose**. You will move back to the preview window, but now you will see a preview of your photo. To use it, click **Set Desktop**. Check out your desktop now (see Figure 14.4).

Figure 14.4

This desktop now sports a nice photo of a Poppy flower.

Free Photos

Your iMac comes with a number of pictures that you can apply to your desktop. These are stored in the Desktop Pictures folder in the Appearance folder that is in the System Folder. You will find many more photos to use in the Additional Desktop Pictures folder that is in the CD Extras folder on the Software Install CD-ROM. Drag the photos you want to use into the Desktop Pictures folder on your hard drive to be able to use them on your desktop.

To try another photo, you have to remove the current one first. To do that, click the **Remove Picture** button. (This does nothing to the actual photo file; it just takes it off your desktop.)

182

You will really like using a desktop photo and are probably wondering where you can get more. The following are some ideas for you:

Drag and Drop

You can also drag a picture file onto the preview window, just as you can do with a pattern.

➤ There are lots of images on the Internet that you can download and use on your desktop (almost any photo or graphic will work). As long as you use it for strictly personal use, you don't have to worry about copyright issues either. But if the image is part of a shareware collection, make sure you pay the shareware fee!

➤ You can also have your photos developed on CD-ROM and then use the digital versions from the CD-ROM as desktop pictures.

➤ If you have a digital camera or a scanner, you can create desktop pictures from your own photos. For example, I use a digital camera to take photos during bike tours and use these as my desktop pictures. They are a nice reminder of the life that exists away from the keyboard (which is needed, especially in the dead of the Indiana winter!).

➤ A picture can also be a drawing, painting, or even a frame that you capture from video. If you can capture something in an image file, it can be a desktop picture.

➤ You can use just about any standard graphic file format as a desktop picture. The formats you can use as desktop pictures include PICT, JPEG, TIFF, GIF, and so on. Although you can't use formats that are proprietary to a graphics or image-editing application, most of these applications enable you to save files in one of the "standard" graphic file formats.

The size of the photo you use and the size of your desktop affects how that image appears. For example, if you use a 640×480-sized image on an 800×600-sized desktop, it won't fill the screen using the default settings. You can use the **Position Automatically** pop-up menu to fit the picture to the desktop. Using this pop-up menu, you have the following choices:

➤ **Position Automatically**—Under this setting, your iMac does what it thinks best.

➤ **Fill Screen**—This one fills your desktop with the image, but keeps the image to scale.

➤ **Scale to Screen**—This scales the photo as needed to fill the desktop.

➤ **Center on screen**—This one places one copy of the image in the center of the desktop. If the image is smaller than the desktop, you see the selected pattern filling the space between the photo and the edge of the desktop for a nice framing effect.

➤ **Tile on Screen**—Your iMac fills the screen with as many copies of the photo as are needed to fill the desktop.

183

Be an iMac Wizard

Picture Combos

You can also use an image-editing program to combine multiple photos into a single desktop image. For example, if you have individual photos of your favorite landmarks, you can paste them all into one image and use that to see all of them at once.

To apply one of these treatments, choose it from the pop-up menu.

No matter how nice the photo you use is, who wants to look at the same image day after day? Wouldn't it be neat if a different photo was used each time your turned on your iMac? Of course it would be, and of course you can. You can have your iMac randomly select and display different desktop pictures so that each time it starts, you see a different image.

Instead of moving a single photo onto the preview window in the Desktop tab of the Appearance control panel, drag a folder containing photos onto it. Your iMac will randomly choose an image from this folder and display it in the window. Set the desktop picture. Each time you start your iMac, it will select another photo from this folder and display that photo on your desktop. This is really cool!

Themes, Themes, Themes, La Da Da Da, Themes, Themes, Themes...

Themes enable you to store all your appearance customizations (appearance of menus, fonts, desktop pictures, and so on) in a single place. You can then switch between sets of customizations (themes) by simply changing the theme you are using. Themes enable you to quickly change many aspects of your desktop because you don't have to change all the individual settings. You can use the themes that came with your iMac, and you can create your own themes by creating and saving your own customized appearance settings.

Pick a Theme, Any Theme

Choosing a theme is simple. Open the Appearance control panel and click the **Themes** tab (see Figure 14.5).

Scroll through the list of available themes. When you see one you want to try, click it. Your desktop changes to reflect that theme. Experiment until you find one you like. When you're done, close the control panel.

184

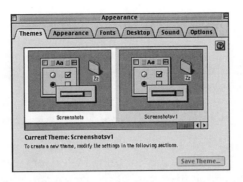

Figure 14.5

Themes are great because you can change many settings with a single click.

Rolling Your Own Themes

Although there are several themes that come with your iMac, you can also create your own themes to use. Open the Appearance control panel, and adjust any settings (**Appearance, Fonts, Desktop, Sounds,** and **Options**) to your taste. When you are through tweaking the interface, click **Save Theme**. Name the Theme and click **OK**. It is now part of the list of available themes. You can switch back to your theme at any time by clicking it.

You can remove a theme from the list by selecting it and pressing **Delete**.

Gonna Have a Resolution, You Know...

Lastly, you can change some of the functional aspects of your screen's appearance. You do this in the Monitors control panel (see Figure 14.6).

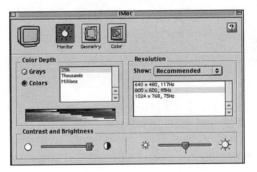

Figure 14.6

The Monitors control panel enables you to control how your screen looks.

185

It's Two Control Panels in One

If you are using Mac OS 8.6, you won't find a Monitors control panel; however, you will find a Monitors & Sound control panel. Prior to Mac OS 9, the Monitor and Sound control panels were part of the same control panel. The older control panel works similarly to the two newer ones, but the figures and descriptions you will read in this book will not quite match up with what you see onscreen. However, the functions work very similarly so I'm sure you won't have any trouble figuring them out.

I See All the Pretty Colors of the Rainbow

You can use the Color Depth section of this control panel to determine how many colors your iMac displays. The larger number of colors you choose the higher quality the images are, but your machine will have to work harder to display them. To change the number of colors your iMac uses, click the number you want to be used. Your iMac will only be able to display that number of colors.

You can also make your iMac use only 256 shades of gray by clicking the **Grays** radio button.

Size Does Matter

The amount of desktop real estate you have to work with is controlled by the number of pixels it can display (also known as its resolution). The higher number of pixels, the more room you have on the screen, but   the smaller each pixel will look to you (because the screen doesn't actually change size, only its pixels do). Depending on which version of the iMac you have, you may have up to three choices for your screen's resolution: 1024×768, 800×600, or 640×480. Click a resolution to select it. Try them all to see which you prefer. Many people prefer the 800×600 setting, but try the others just to make sure.

It's So Bright It Hurts My Eyes

You can control the contrast and brightness of your screen by using the sliders at the bottom of the Monitors window. Adjust these settings to suit your particular preferences.

This Geometry Is Easier Than the High School Version

If you click the **Geometry** button, you will see controls you can use to control the location, size, and shape of the display area of your screen. The controls are mostly self-explanatory. Click a radio button to choose the item that you want to adjust, and then use the contextual buttons to make your changes.

Color Profiles and You

The Monitors control panel also has a Color button. This button enables you to set the ColorSync profile that your iMac uses. ColorSync is a technology that attempts to make the colors you see consistent across devices (such as your iMac, a scanner, and a printer). You should leave this set to **iMac**.

The Least You Need to Know

➤ You have a lot of control over how your iMac's desktop and interface looks; you can change the fonts, colors, and desktop pattern and picture.

➤ Use the Appearance control panel to make these sorts of changes; each tab controls a different characteristic.

➤ You can easily switch many of the characteristics with a single click by creating and using themes.

➤ You can use the Monitors control panel to set the number of colors your iMac uses as well as your screen's resolution.

Chapter 15

Making Your iMac Laugh, Cry, Talk, and Howl

In This Chapter

➤ Learn to use the sound controls on your iMac

➤ Change the alert sound

➤ Record and use your own alert sounds

➤ Add sounds that you download from the Internet

➤ Make your iMac talk to you

Unlike PCs, sound has always been integrated into the Mac. From the beginning, the Mac could make sounds, and not just simple beeps or dings either. The Mac could quack like a duck, screech like a monkey, and yes, even do a standard computer beep. Your iMac continues in this tradition—sound is an important part of the iMac experience. And as you probably expect, you can do all sorts of fun customization of the sounds your iMac makes.

Turn Down That Sound (or Turn It Up)!

You will hear lots of sounds coming from your iMac. Being an iMac wizard means knowing how to manage all that racket, uh, I mean sound.

Changing the Volume with the Control Strip's Volume Slider

If you've never used a Mac before, you may be puzzled at the lack of a volume control on the outside of the iMac. Many Macs, even those with built-in monitors and speakers, have lacked a hardware volume control. I must admit that I find this annoying, especially given that the new iMacs have such nice built-in speakers that you probably won't even use external speakers. (Most external speakers have volume knobs or sliders.) Ah well, no machine is perfect.

You can control the volume coming from your iMac with the Sound Volume slider (it's the button with the speaker icon on it) on the Control Strip. Click on the **Volume Control** button and drag the slider up to make the volume louder or down to make it quieter. If you drag the slider all the way to the bottom, your iMac becomes muted.

Using the Sound Control Panel Is Useful and Fun

You manage the many sounds of your iMac through the Sound control panel. From the **Apple** menu, choose **Control Panels**, and then **Sound**. The Sound control panel has two panes. In the left pane, you choose the area of sound you want to control and in the right pane, you adjust the controls for that area.

Two Control Panels in One

If you are using Mac OS 8.6, you won't find a Sound control panel, but you will find a Monitors & Sound control panel. Prior to Mac OS 9, the Monitor and Sound control panels were part of the same control panel. The older control panel works similarly to the two newer ones. For example, instead of clicking Alert Sounds, in the Monitors & Sound control panel you click the Alerts button. The figures and descriptions you will read in this book will not quite match up with what you see onscreen; however, the functions work similarly, so I'm sure you won't have any trouble figuring them out.

To adjust your iMac's volume, click **Output** in the left pane of the control panel and you'll see the output controls in the right pane (see Figure 15.1). Drag the volume slider to the right to turn up the volume or left to turn it down. Check the **Mute** check box to mute it.

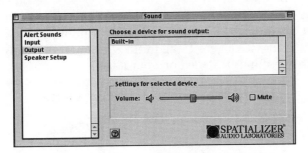

Figure 15.1

You can make your iMac louder, quieter, or even mute with the Sound control panel.

Speaker Improvements

If you have a DV iMac, it has fairly good speakers built in to it. These may satisfy your ears and be all the speakers you ever need. However, if you have one of the earlier iMacs, the speakers built into them are, um, not so good. You may want to add a good pair of external speakers to make the most of music, games, and so on. To use external speakers, plug them into the speaker port on the right side of your machine (behind the door on older iMacs). The iMac's internal speakers become disabled when you do (as they do if you plug in headphones).

You will use the Sound control panel for a lot more than simply changing the volume, but it works similarly for these other tasks as you will see.

Your iMac Is Like a Baby—It Makes Noise to Get Your Attention

When you learned about alert windows, you learned that your iMac makes a warning sound when it displays an alert window. Unless you have just started using your iMac, you have likely heard at least one alert sound already. You can change the alert sound that your iMac uses, and even better, you can create your own alert sounds.

Changing Alert Sounds

You may be familiar with the quack, beep, or other alert sounds your iMac makes when it wants to get your attention. These sounds are fun to play with, and your iMac comes equipped with several from which you can choose.

To change your alert sounds, open the **Sound** control panel. In the left pane of the window, click **Alert Sounds**. In the right pane of the window, you will see controls that affect the alert sounds (see Figure 15.2). In the upper part of the right pane, you will see a list of the alert sounds installed on your iMac.

Figure 15.2

Changing alert sounds is fun!

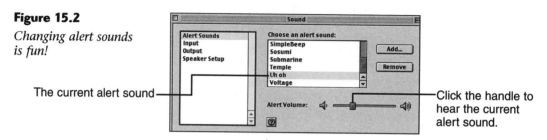

The current alert sound

Click the handle to hear the current alert sound.

To hear the current alert sound, click the handle of the Alert Volume slider. Your iMac plays the alert sound. Adjust the volume of the alert sound by dragging the slider to the left to make the sound quieter and to the right to make it louder. Note that the Alert Volume slider affects only the alert sound and not the general volume level for your iMac. In other words, this slider adjusts the relative volume of the alert sound compared to the general system volume. If you make the alert sound loud and then turn up the system volume too, when the alert sounds, you may jump out of your chair. Generally, you will probably want the alert sound toward the left end of the slider so it gets your attention without being annoying.

To choose a different alert sound, click it in the right pane of the window. When you do, the new alert sound plays. Use the volume slider to set its volume (all alert sounds are definitely not created equal). When you've found the perfect alert sound, close the control panel. When your iMac wants to get your attention, it will play the sound you chose.

Creating Your Own Alert Sound

After a while, you may get tired of using the same old alert sounds. If so, add your own. You can record an alert sound from *any* sound source from which you can record. These include the built-in microphone, audio CDs, QuickTime movies, and so on.

One neat thing to do is extract alert sounds from audio CDs; you can choose any clip from your favorite song to be your alert sound. Find a song you want to take your sound from. It doesn't matter which you use: you can always add more sounds from other songs later.

Open the **Sound** control panel again and click **Alert Sounds**. Insert the CD with the song clip you want to use in the CD drive. After the disc loads, the CD starts playing.

Your iMac comes with AppleCD Audio Player, a nice program you can use to control audio CDs. You need to use it to capture a sound clip from your CD. Open the **Applications** folder, then open the **AppleCD Audio Player** folder, and then double-click the **AppleCD Audio Player** icon to open it. Stop your CD by clicking the **Stop** button (the button with a square on it).

Don't Make a Lawyer's Day

If you use a copyrighted audio CD (which any you use probably are), make sure you do not distribute any sound clips you make from them. Although you aren't violating copyright laws by making clips for your personal use, you would be if you started distributing those sound clips to others.

Using the controls in the AppleCD Audio Player, get to a point about 20 seconds before the part you want to use as your alert sound—you need to give yourself enough time to get back into the Sound control panel and start recording. (The AppleCD Audio Player works just like your stereo's controls.)

While the CD is playing, switch back to the Sound control panel by choosing **Sound** from the **Application** menu. Click the **Add** button and you will see the recording window; you can monitor how loud the CD is being recorded by watching the speaker icon (see Figure 15.3). Just before you get to the part you want to use as an alert sound, click the **Record** button. Click the **Stop** button when you have recorded all the sound you want. (You can only record up to five seconds, which is much longer than you want an alert sound to be anyway.) Click **Save**, name the sound, and click **OK**.

Control your recording with these buttons.

This bar shows how long your recorded sound is.

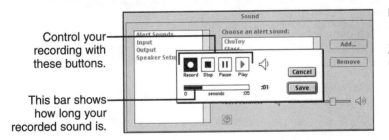

Figure 15.3

With the recording tool, you can record your own alert sounds.

You are returned to the Sound control panel, and you see that your new alert sound is selected. Click the volume slider handle to hear your new sound, and adjust the volume as needed. Close the control panel. Your iMac will play your new sound when it needs your attention.

QuickTime Is Better

You can use QuickTime to extract a specific part of a song rather than having to time it carefully as I describe in this chapter. Using QuickTime is much more precise than using the recording tool. You'll learn about QuickTime in Chapter 16, "Watch Some QuickTime Movies and Then Make Your Own."

A Better Mic

You can also add an external microphone to your iMac by plugging a PlainTalk-compatible microphone into the port located on the right side of your iMac. Note that you can't use any old microphone—it has to be PlainTalk-compatible.

You can add as many sound clips as you want; they all appear in the Alert Sound window, so you can easily switch between them. Remember that each sound clip requires some amount of memory to store, so don't go too crazy with them!

You can also use your iMac's built-in microphone to record your own alert sounds. To do so, open the **Sound** control panel and click **Input** in the left part of the window. Now choose **Built-in Mic** from the **Input Source** pop-up menu. Click **Alert Sounds** and then click **Add**. Start recording and make some noise. (Depending on how you are situated in relation to the microphone, which is located above the screen, you may have to move closer to the mic to get good volume on your recording.) Click **Stop**. Save your sound if you like it.

Finding Cool Sounds on the Internet and Adding Them to Your iMac

As fun as recording your own sounds is, it can be even more fun to use sounds other people have recorded, especially those from you favorite movies or TV shows. You can download all sorts of sounds from the Internet and use them on your iMac.

Adding an Alert Sound from the Net

Finding sounds for your iMac is yet another great use of the Net. In Chapter 13, "Sleuthing Around the World with Sherlock," you learned how to use Sherlock to search for things on the Net. Now use it to search for some great sounds to jazz up your iMac.

Open **Sherlock** and search for Mac and sounds. Your iMac connects to the Net, and Sherlock looks for Web sites that match both Mac and sounds (use the Internet channel). Sherlock will likely find numerous sites that offer Mac-compatible sounds. Click a site and your iMac opens Internet Explorer and takes you there. Download the sound files you want to try on your iMac.

To make sure the file is a valid alert sound, double-click it. (If the file was not uncompressed automatically, use StuffIt Expander to uncompress it first.) If it plays, you can use it. If not, you will need to convert it to a System sound using a sound utility.

Close all open applications. Open the **System** folder and drag your alert sound file onto the System file. Close these folders. Open the **Sound** control panel and click **Alert Sounds**. You will see the sound you downloaded in the Alert Sound list. Click it to use it as your alert sound. Close the control panel.

A Great Sound Application

The application Sound Converter enables you to convert sounds from one format to another.

Giving Your iMac a Cool Startup or Shutdown Sound

How would you like your iMac to greet you each time you start it up with the famous phrase, "Good morning, Vietnam!" from the movie of the same name? Or perhaps you would like your iMac to sound like Hal just before he whacked Dave in *2001: A Space Oddessy*. You can have your iMac play any sound when it starts up or when you shut it down.

Search the Net for some sounds you really like and download them to your machine. Drag the sound file (or files) onto your System Folder, wait for the System Folder to spring open, and then drag the file onto the Startup Items folder (if you want the sound to play when your iMac starts up) or the Shutdown Items folder (if you want it to play when your iMac shuts down).

The Double-Click Test

How do you know which sounds you can have your iMac play at start up or shut down? This is pretty simple actually. Just double-click the sound file. If it plays, you can use it.

If you get tired of hearing those sounds, simply drag them out of the folders in which you put them. You can replace them with other sounds or leave your iMac in silent-running mode for awhile.

Before You Leave the Sound Control Panel...

There are two other areas of the Sound control panel that you probably won't use all that much, but just in case, you should know they are there.

If you recorded your own sound with the iMac's built-in mic, you know that the Input controls determine which sound input source your iMac uses. If you click

Input in the left pane of the Sound control panel, in the upper part of the right pane, you will see the input devices you have. (Unless you have added some external devices, you will see Built-in or Internal CD.) You can choose an input source for sound using the **Input Source** pop-up menu. Whichever source you choose is the one your will hear and record.

The Speaker Setup controls enable you to adjust the balance of stereo sound. These controls enable you to set the relative volume of each speaker.

Your iMac Can Talk to You

Using its Text-to-Speech capabilities, your iMac can read the text in alerts and dialog boxes to you, and it can even read whole documents to you! Your iMac has a number of voices it can use to speak to you. There is just something cool about hearing your iMac speak. Hear it for yourself.

Speaking Dialog Boxes

If you've let some alert dialog boxes sit on your screen for awhile you may have been surprised when your iMac started speaking the words in the dialog box to you. No, your iMac is not possessed by some ancient spirit—it's supposed to do that.

If you haven't heard this yet, open an alert dialog box. Try dragging a file into the Trash, and then open the **Special** menu and choose **Empty Trash**. When the warning dialog box appears, let it sit there for a moment. After a little while, your iMac reads the text in the dialog box to you. Pretty neat, huh?

You can control how your iMac speaks to you, both its voice and what it says. You do this with the Speech control panel. From the **Apple** menu, open **Control Panels**, and then open the **Speech** control panel. From the **Options** pop-up menu, choose **Voice** (see Figure 15.4).

Figure 15.4

Are you hearing voices? (Don't worry, you don't need psychiatric help.)

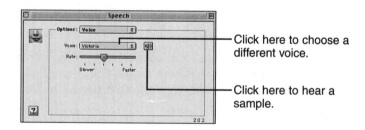

Click here to choose a different voice.

Click here to hear a sample.

Try playing with the voices first. From the **Voice** pop-up menu, choose another voice, for example, **Zarvox**. Click the **speaker** icon, and your new voice speaks a sample phrase for your entertainment. You can change the rate at which the voice speaks by dragging the **Rate** slider.

Now click the **Options** pop-up menu and choose **Talking Alerts**. You will see the Talking Alerts window. Use the **Speak the phrase** pop-up menu to determine the phrase your iMac will speak before it begins reading the dialog box's text. You can also choose to have your iMac speak the various predefined phrases one after the other in the order they are listed or in random order. If you don't want your iMac to speak an alert phrase, uncheck the check box.

If you want the iMac to read the dialog box text to you, check the **Speak the alert text** check box. (It is checked by default.)

If you have both the **Speak the phrase** and **Speak the alert text** check boxes checked, your iMac first reads the phrase and then reads the text in the dialog box.

Finally, set the time delay between when the alert window appears and when the iMac begins to speak the phrase and text. Setting a shorter time reduces the pause between the alert appearing and your iMac speaking. Close the control panel when you are done.

Putting Words in Your iMac's Mouth

If you choose **Edit Phrase List** from the **Speak the phrase** pop-up menu and then choose **Add**, you can type your own phrase for the iMac to speak. Use the **speaker** icon to hear your iMac read the phrase, and if you like it, click **OK**. Your new phrase appears on the **Speak the Phrase** pop-up menu.

Speakable Items?

When you first opened the Speech control panel, you may have seen the Speakable Items option. This feature enables you to speak commands to your iMac. This mostly works, although I have not found it very practical. Usually, choosing commands via menus and the keyboard is faster and more reliable, but you may want to play with this capability. To learn how to use it, use the Help center to search for help on Speakable Items.

Reading Is Fundamental—For Your iMac

Your iMac can also use its voices to read documents to you in applications that support Text-to-Speech (which many do). To see how this works, find a readme file (there are several in the Mac OS Read Me Files folder) and open it. The file opens in the SimpleText application. From the **Sound** menu, choose **Speak All**. Your iMac reads the text of the document to you. Choose **Stop Speaking** to shut your iMac up. You can also choose different voices from the Voices submenu.

Many applications support text-to-speech, so check your favorite application to see if it can read to you.

The Least You Need to Know

➤ There are two ways to adjust the volume level on your iMac: the Volume slider button on the Control Strip and the Volume slider in the Sound control panel.

➤ Your iMac plays an alert sound when it wants to get your attention; use the Sound control panel to change the alert sound your iMac plays.

➤ Use the Recording tool in the Sound control panel to record your own alert sounds (from an audio CD for example).

➤ You can also use sounds you've downloaded from the Internet as alert sounds; any sound file you place in the System file (in the System Folder) can be used for an alert sound.

➤ Your iMac can speak dialog box text to you and it can also read documents to you; use the Speech control panel to adjust the former and text-to-speech compatible applications for the latter.

Chapter 16

Watch Some QuickTime Movies and Then Make Your Own

In This Chapter

➤ Watch QuickTime movies and TV

➤ Explore virtual reality worlds and hear MP3 music

➤ Upgrade to QuickTime Pro so you can...

　➤ Create and edit your own movies

　➤ Make cool alert and startup sounds from QuickTime movie sound tracks

Your iMac is a multimedia powerhouse. With its QuickTime technology, your iMac enables you to watch QuickTime movies and TV, explore virtual worlds, view animations, and do some simple video editing to make your own QuickTime movies.

Watching QuickTime Movies Is Not Like Going to the Theater (But It Is Cool Anyway)

QuickTime is the technology your iMac uses to display time-synchronized data. That sounds rather technical, but it isn't really. Time-synchronized data is any data that consists of multiple parts and have to work together. The easiest example is a movie in which the video and sound elements have to remain synchronized or you end up with a movie that doesn't make a lot of sense.

QuickTime—A Rare, Apple-Developed Standard

Apple's QuickTime has been very successful. So successful, in fact, that it is a standard on Windows computers as well as Macs. QuickTime movies on Windows will play the same way they do on Mac. QuickTime has also been widely adopted on the Web; many videos and animations you find on Web sites are QuickTime files. That's good for you because you can play them.

You will encounter QuickTime movies everywhere, including your hard disk, CD-ROM games, Web sites, and most recently, via QuickTime TV.

Although it's natural to think of QuickTime in terms of video, you should remember QuickTime can be used for sound, animation, and other dynamic data as well. And not all components have to be present at all times; for example, you can have a QuickTime movie that consists only of a soundtrack.

Playing for QuickTime

You can view all kinds of QuickTime movies through the QuickTime Player application. With the QuickTime Pro upgrade of QuickTime Player, you can also do some basic editing of QuickTime movies. (You will learn how to do that in the last part of this chapter.)

QuickTime and File Formats

QuickTime supports file formats that you are likely to encounter on the Internet as well as on CD-ROMs and other sources of multimedia files. (QuickTime Pro supports even more file types than the standard version of QuickTime does.) Some of the more common file types you will use are .mov (QuickTime movie files), .mpg (a video encoding scheme that is used across all platforms), .avi (Windows movie files), and .mid (MIDI music files).

Open the QuickTime Player by double-clicking its icon on the desktop (which is actually
an alias) or by opening the **QuickTime**
folder (which is in the Applications folder)
and then double-clicking its icon. (If you see
messages asking you to upgrade to
QuickTime Pro, just click **Later** for now.)
You will see a blank QuickTime Player
document window.

What you need is a movie to watch.
Although it's certainly not very exciting, the
Sample Movie file will introduce you to the
QuickTime Player's basic features. From
QuickTime Player's **File** menu, choose **Open
Movie**. In the QuickTime folder, you will see
a movie called Sample Movie. (If you have
another QuickTime movie available, by all
means open it instead.) Open **Sample
Movie** and you will see it in the QuickTime
Player window (see Figure 16.1).

What Does Modem Speed Have to Do with This?

You may see a dialog box stating
that QuickTime needs to know at
which speed you connect to the
Internet. This is used for streaming,
which you will learn about in a
moment. For now, click the **56K**
radio button and close the
QuickTime Settings control panel.

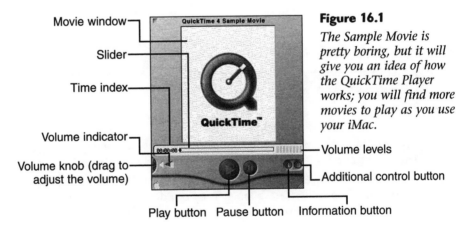

Figure 16.1

*The Sample Movie is
pretty boring, but it will
give you an idea of how
the QuickTime Player
works; you will find more
movies to play as you use
your iMac.*

Movie window
Slider
Time index
Volume indicator
Volume knob (drag to adjust the volume)
Volume levels
Additional control button
Play button   Pause button   Information button

Many applications can play QuickTime movies, and most of them use controls similar
to those that QuickTime Player uses. Some examples include SimpleText, Microsoft
Word, Internet Explorer, and many more.

If you click the **Additional control** button, a panel pops out that has several other
controls you can use (see Figure 16.2).

Figure 16.2

This pop-down panel has additional controls you can use to fine tune your movie experience.

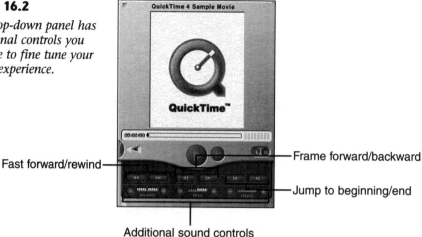

Fast forward/rewind

Additional sound controls

Frame forward/backward

Jump to beginning/end

Most of the controls work just as you would expect them to. For example, to play the movie, click the **Play** button. To pause it, click **Pause**. You can move to any point in the movie by using the fast forward button or you can simply drag the slider to the point at which you want to be.

Updating QuickTime

QuickTime can check for new components, such as upgrades to the QuickTime extensions or new QuickTime TV channels. To check for updates, open the QuickTime Player. From the **Help** menu, choose **Check for QuickTime Updates**. If updates are available, they are downloaded to your iMac and installed. When the installation is complete, you are prompted to restart your iMac so the updated software can be used.

The other commands you should know about are on the Movie menu. These are: Normal Size, which makes your movie the "standard" size for your screen; Double Size, which doubles the size of your movie; and Fill Screen, which makes your movie as large as possible. Use these commands to size the window as you see fit. You can also drag the window's resize handle to change its size; the QuickTime Player ensures that the window remains proportional.

That is about all there is to watching movies with QuickTime Player. Check the Preferences command on the Edit menu for the settings you can adjust.

Movies on the Web

Unless you have used a Mac before, you probably do not have many movies to view. Fortunately, there is literally a whole world of movies to watch on the Web. You will find thousands of movies to watch on every subject and topic under the sun.

Apple maintains several Web pages dedicated to QuickTime. These pages include software and updates that you can download, information on how QuickTime works, links to QuickTime showcases, and so on. The URL to this site is www.apple.com/quicktime. Whenever you have any questions about QuickTime, this should be your first stop.

Open Internet Explorer and go to www.apple.com/quicktime/showcase. This takes you to a site containing a gallery of QuickTime movies you can view.

With QuickTime, movies can be *streamed*. Streaming means files can be viewed while they are being downloaded; this makes QuickTime even more valuable for the Web.

Click the **Movie Trailers** button to move to the QuickTime Movie Trailers page. Click on a trailer and you will see the QuickTime logo with the invitation to click here to play the movie. Do so, and you will see a mini-QuickTime Player window. The trailer begins to download to your iMac. When enough of it has been loaded onto your machine, it begins to play. Sit back and enjoy! You can control the playback using controls that work just like the QuickTime Player controls, although they don't look nearly as nice.

Reality According to QuickTime

QuickTime Virtual Reality (VR) enables you to interact with panoramic, virtual worlds. You can move around within a world, and you can even closely examine objects within that world. QuickTime VR is an amazing technology. QuickTime VR is widely used on the Web, so there is no shortage of VR worlds for you to explore.

Find a QuickTime VR world to explore. If you have never used QuickTime VR before, you may not have any QuickTime VR files on your Mac. If you don't, never fear. There are plenty to view on the Web. Go back to the QuickTime Showcase site. Look for links that describe exploring a world or examining a product. Follow the link until you get to a site that enables you to view something with QuickTime VR (see Figure 16.3).

Figure 16.3

This VR Ferrari is probably about as close as I will ever come to being able to explore one!

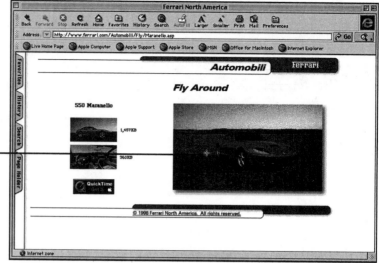

This pointer lets you move around in the image.

Move the pointer over the QuickTime VR movie, and it changes into a gloved hand. This indicates that you're viewing a QuickTime VR movie. To move around the image, simply hold the mouse button down (the cursor changes to a closed hand to show you that you are grabbing the figure) and move your mouse. The image moves accordingly, and you can view the image from many angles.

To zoom in on part of the image, hold down the **Shift** key. To zoom out again, press the **Control** key.

Lastly, you can move the image around by holding the **Option** key down while you drag it around.

QuickTime VR files can also be viewed with the QuickTime Player or the QuickTime plug-in through a Web browser. The difference between a "regular" QuickTime movie and a QuickTime VR movie is in how you control the movie. With a QuickTime VR movie, you can move around in it, while a "regular" QuickTime movie plays in a sequential fashion.

There are a lot of QuickTime VR worlds for you to explore. They are all used similarly, whether they are on the Web or stored on your iMac, and you use the QuickTime Player to view them.

Check Out Some MP3 Tunes

MP3 is a new file format that enables almost-CD-quality music to be stored in fairly small files. This makes distribution of high-quality music over the Web a practical reality. You can go to many different sites and download music from your favorite musicians as well as many more of whom you have never heard. You can download songs and then listen to them as many times as you like.

To get the most out of MP3 music, you should get an MP3 application such as MacAMP. These applications enable you to do all sorts of cool things, such as creating your own playlists. However, the QuickTime Player also plays individual MP3 files. When you find an MP3 file (visit www.mp3.com for a few thousand to try), download it to your iMac. Open QuickTime Player and then open the MP3 file. Click the **Play** button and you will hear the song. With all the available MP3 music, this should keep you busy for a few years....

I Can't Find the MP3 File!

Before you try to open the MP3 file you downloaded, make sure it is named appropriately. Sometimes, Internet Explorer names these files with the .asp extension, which relates to a script file. QuickTime Player won't be able to open the MP3 file if you leave this name on it. Rename the file so it ends with .mp3 and it will open just fine.

I Want My QuickTime TV!

With its streaming capabilities, QuickTime can also be used sort of like your TV. You can see live or recorded content on various channels that make their content available in the QuickTime format. The current list of QuickTime TV providers includes Disney, NPR (which is actually a radio feed), Fox News, and many more. Additional providers are being added all the time. There are two ways you can get to QuickTime TV content.

One is to connect to the Web and go to www.apple.com/quicktime/showcase/live. You will see a selection of channels from which you can choose.

To view a channel, click its link. You will move to a page for that site. You will see two links. One looks like a small QuickTime Player window; click the **Play** button and a QuickTime Player window opens and immediately begins playing the clip or the live broadcast (see Figure 16.4). Clicking the other link, which is the "click here to begin streaming" link, either moves you into the same live QuickTime Player window and begins the broadcast or moves you into a special QuickTime Player window. This window displays a variety of streams you can view. To view a stream, click it and it begins playing on your iMac. How well this works depends on the traffic on the Net. Sometimes the clips will be clear and easily viewable. Sometimes they won't work so well; the audio may drop out or the picture may not be very visible.

Figure 16.4

With QuickTime TV, you can watch live news broadcasts right on your iMac screen!

The second way to get to QuickTime TV is to use the QuickTime Player's Favorites feature. Open **QuickTime Player** and from the **Favorites** menu, choose a channel you want to view. When the channel's window appears, click a stream to view it. It opens in a QuickTime Player window and begins to play.

Making Your Own Favorites

If you choose **Open Favorites Drawer** from the **Favorites** menu, you will see a pop-up menu that has an icon for each favorite. Click an icon to view that channel. You can change the contents of your favorites by choosing **Organize Favorites** from the **Favorites** menu and deleting or renaming the channels that you see. You can also add additional favorites by choosing **Add Favorite** while a channel is being played.

Making Your Own QuickTime Movies For Fun But Probably Not For Profit

Watching QuickTime content is a lot of fun, and occasionally is even educational. But you can have even more fun by creating and editing your own QuickTime content.

Go Pro

The version of QuickTime that comes with your iMac has a basic set of QuickTime capabilities that enable you to view QuickTime movies. If you want more QuickTime capability, you can upgrade to QuickTime Pro. This version, which costs about $30, has significantly more features than does the basic version.

QuickTime Pro provides you with all the capabilities of "regular" QuickTime, plus many more, including the following:

➤ Playing full-screen video

➤ Downloading and saving QuickTime movies that you see on the Web

➤ Exporting QuickTime movies in a variety of formats, including the Digital Video (DV) format. (You will see why this is so cool in the next chapter.)

➤ Viewing files in a wider variety of formats

➤ Editing and saving movies in a variety of formats

➤ Copying and pasting material from a variety of formats into QuickTime movies

➤ Creating slideshows from a series of still images

> **Be a Rookie Before You Go Pro**
>
> I recommend you play with QuickTime awhile before upgrading. If you find that you have no desire to edit QuickTime movies, there is no reason to get QuickTime Pro.

Upgrading to QuickTime Pro requires no new software—all you need is an upgrade code. The upgrade process takes only a few minutes..

There are several ways to upgrade. You may see a prompt suggesting that you upgrade to QuickTime Pro. In that prompt, click **Upgrade Now**. When you do, follow the onscreen instructions to upgrade. You can also upgrade by going to the QuickTime Web site at `www.apple.com\quicktime`. You can also upgrade through the Registration screen in the QuickTime Settings control panel.

To do the latter, open the **QuickTime Settings** control panel, and choose **Registration** from the pop-up menu at the top of the window. Click **Register On-line**.

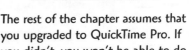

> **No Rookies Allowed**
>
> The rest of the chapter assumes that you upgraded to QuickTime Pro. If you didn't, you won't be able to do the steps I explain. You can still read them to see what you are missing, of course.

You will move onto the QuickTime Pro registration site. Follow the onscreen instructions to order your upgrade. When you are done, an upgrade code will be emailed to you. When you have the code, open the **QuickTime Settings** control panel, choose **Registration** from the pop-up menu, and click **Enter Registration**. Complete the form, and when you return to the QuickTime Settings window, you will see your registration number and that QuickTime is now the Pro Player Edition. Congratulations and welcome to the big leagues.

DV iMacs Rock

If you have a DV iMac, you can do much more sophisticated video editing with the iMovie application that is installed on your hard drive. In addition to editing DV movies that you download from a DV camera, you can also edit QuickTime movies you have exported into the DV format. You will learn how to do this in the next chapter.

Cut and Paste Movies

Editing movies with QuickTime Player Pro is easy because it works just like most other Mac applications. You can select portions of a movie and paste them into other movies, cut them, or duplicate them. Working with QuickTime content is similar to working with regular text or graphics.

Find Your Clips

First, you need to find a couple of clips to work with. Use Sherlock to search your iMac hard drive to see if you have any QuickTime files on your iMac already. (If you don't know how to use Sherlock, see Chapter 13, "Sleuthing Around the World with Sherlock.") Search for files of file type MooV. If you find a couple of clips you want to use, great; if not, you can find some clips on the Web.

Because you now have QuickTime Pro, you can download and save QuickTime movies from the Web. Go to the QuickTime Showcase site (`www.apple.com/quicktime/showcase/`). Play some movies until you find one you want to use in your own creation. After you watch a movie, point to it, hold down the **Control** key, and click the mouse button. You will see a pop-up contextual menu with QuickTime related commands. Choose **Save as QuickTime Movie** and save the QuickTime movie to your iMac. Find another clip and save it to your iMac in the same way.

It's Two Movies in One

One of the easiest movie edits is to paste two movies together to create a new movie. Launch QuickTime Player. From the **File** menu, choose **New Player**. You will see an empty QuickTime movie window. Save your movie by opening the **File** menu and choosing **Save As.** Name your movie file something like **My Movie** and click **Save**.

Open a movie from which you want to copy; use one of the clips you downloaded earlier. To select a portion of the movie, move the selection markers until the shaded area of the play bar contains the segment of the movie you want to copy. As you drag the markers, you will see the frames you are selecting in the movie window (see Figure 16.5). To make choosing the precise segment you want easier, open the **Additional** control window and move through the clip frame-by-frame.

Where Else Can I Get Movies?

Many multimedia CD-ROMs come with QuickTime movies on them. Look for any files that have names that end in .mov.

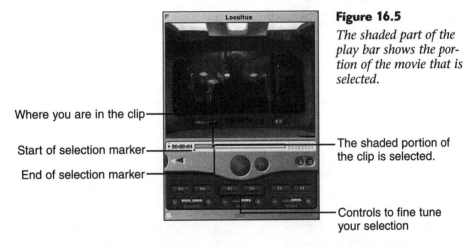

Where you are in the clip

Start of selection marker

End of selection marker

Figure 16.5
The shaded part of the play bar shows the portion of the movie that is selected.

The shaded portion of the clip is selected.

Controls to fine tune your selection

To play your selection before you copy it (to make sure you have what you want), open the **Movie** menu and choose **Play Selection Only**. When you click **Play**, just the portion of the clip you have selected will play. This makes the selection process much easier. To view the whole movie again, choose **Play Selection Only** to turn that command off. When you have the clip you want, choose **Copy** from the **Edit** menu (or press ⌘+**C**) .

From the Window menu, choose **My Movie** (or click on its window) to move back to your movie. Open the **Edit** menu and choose **Paste** (or press ⌘+**V**). Now your movie contains the clip that you copied. Play your movie to view the clip.

To trim your clip, use the selection markers to choose the part you don't want and then open the **Edit** menu and choose **Cut** (or press ⌘+**X**). That part of the clip is eliminated. Press ⌘+**S** to save your movie.

Where Did You Get the Clips You Are Using?

For these steps, I'm using some clips from *Star Trek: The Next Generation* that I digitized from video tape. This is copyrighted material so I only use it for my personal use; never distribute copyrighted material to anyone (unless you own the copyright, of course).

From the **File** menu, choose **New Player** and then **Open Movie**. Now open another clip and select a portion of it. Copy that selection and move back into your movie. Drag the position marker to the location in your movie at which you want to paste the clip. (If you want to move all the way to the end of your clip, click the **end of movie** button, the right-facing triangle with a line attached to its apex.) Paste the second clip.

Play your movie to see it; it moves from one clip to the other. Trim out segments you don't want and save your movie when you are happy with it. You have made your first QuickTime movie!

Transitions

A transition is the means by which one clip moves into the other; there are lots of different types of transitions that are used when creating videos. The most common is the fade, where one scene gradually fades into the next. Unfortunately, you can only do one kind of transition with QuickTime Player: the straight cut (one scene ends and the next begins with no transition effect). If you are careful with the clips you paste together, you can make the transitions work fairly well. To do more sophisticated transitions, you need to use a full-featured, digital video editor, such as iMovie.

This is just the start of what you can do with movie editing, but hopefully you can see how easy it is to create your own movies from other movies. You can do a lot more with the QuickTime Player, but I only have room to show you one more trick. (My editor is already yelling at me about the length of this chapter!) But you should explore on your own and see what other neat things you can do with the QuickTime Player. Don't forget to check the online QuickTime help (choose **On-line QuickTime Player Help** from the **Help** menu).

Create a Cool Alert Sound from A Movie

You already know how to create an alert sound from an audio CD-ROM. Although that was fun, it is kind of frustrating to capture just the right clips for your alert sound. With QuickTime Player, you can capture the precise sound you want to use much more easily.

Find a clip that contains a sound you want to use. (This can be any QuickTime movie or a track from an audio CD.) Open **New Player**, and then open the clip you want to use. Use the selection markers and Play Selection command to choose the segment that contains the sound you want to be your alert sound. Choose **Copy** from the **Edit** menu (or press ⌘+**C**).

Create a new movie by choosing **New Player** from the **File** menu. Open the **Edit** menu and choose **Paste.** The portion of the clip you selected is pasted into the new movie.

Option and the Edit Menu

When you hold down the **Option** key and choose **Edit**, you will see some new options, including Add and Trim. **Add** pastes a new track with the selection on the clipboard that runs in parallel with the portion selected in the play bar, whereas **Paste** adds a selection to the end of the area selected in the play bar. **Trim** removes everything from a movie *except* what is selected.

QuickTime movies are made up of different tracks. For example, the video is contained in a video track, the audio in an audio track, and so on. These tracks can be manipulated independently from one another. Because the alert sound contains only audio information, you need to get rid of the video part of your clip. Open the **Edit** menu and choose **Delete Tracks.** In the Delete Tracks window, select the **Video Track** and click **Delete**.

When you move back into your clip, you won't see any video, but the audio will still be there. Click **Play** to preview it. When it meets with your approval, open the **File** menu, choose **Save**, and click the **Make movie self-contained** button.

Now that you have the sound clip, the next step is to convert it into a system sound that your iMac can play as an alert sound. Open the **File** menu and choose **Export**. From the **Export** pop-up menu, choose **Sound to System 7 Sound** (see Figure 16.6). Name the sound and save it to your desktop. Quit QuickTime Player.

Figure 16.6

This alert sound is Austin Powers saying, "Yeah Baby Yeah!"

Now move back to your desktop and you will see the sound you just created and saved. Double-click it to hear it. Now, drag it onto your hard disk, and when the disk opens, drag it onto your System Folder and release the button. You are asked if you want the file moved into the System file. Click **OK**, and your file is moved into the System file, which is where alert sounds are stored. (If you have open applications, you will have to quit them before doing this.)

From the **Apple** menu, choose **Control Panels** and then **Sound**. In the Sound control panel, click **Alert Sounds**. Select the alert sound you just created. Adjust the volume and then close the control panel. When your iMac needs your attention, it will play your new sound.

The Least You Need to Know

➤ QuickTime is the part of the Mac OS that enables it to handle time-synchronized data, such as video and sound, animation and video, and so on; QuickTime makes multimedia on the iMac possible.

➤ You can watch QuickTime movies (which can be video, QuickTime TV, and QuickTime VR) with the QuickTime Player application.

➤ You can also watch QuickTime movies on the Web because of the QuickTime plug-in that works with Internet Explorer.

➤ If you upgrade to QuickTime Pro, you will be able to edit QuickTime movies, and you can also download and save QuickTime movies you find on the Web.

➤ QuickTime movies are documents, and you can manipulate them just like other documents. (For example, you can cut and paste clips from one movie to another.)

ACTION!!

Chapter 17

Your DV iMac Is a Home Theater System—Only Better!

In This Chapter

➤ Play music CDs and create your own playlists

➤ Watch DVD movies on your iMac

➤ Create and edit your own digital videos with iMovie

DV iMacs come very close to being the ultimate information and entertainment appliance. In addition to cruising the Web, email, QuickTime movies, and all the other great things you have learned about, your DV iMac also enables you to listen to music just like your car or home stereo (only better), show movies like a home theater (only better), and input and edit DV movies just like a digital movie studio (not quite as good, but a whole lot cheaper and easier).

Your iMac Is Alive with the Sound of Music

One of the great things about the DVD drive in your DV iMac (or the CD-ROM drive in a non-DV iMac) is that it can play the same audio CDs that you play in your home or car stereo. You can play an audio CD in the background while you work with any other applications. If you are like me, there is nothing better than listening to your favorite tunes while you work or play. Your iMac comes with a couple of neat tools you can use to listen to your favorite music.

Non-DV iMacs Can Play CDs Too

Any Mac, including non-DV iMacs, with a CD-ROM drive can play audio CDs using the tools described in this section.

Listening While Your Work, Play, or Surf

By default, your iMac automatically plays any audio CD that you insert into it. Give it a try! Insert an audio CD into your iMac and within a few seconds, you will hear beautiful (or not so beautiful, depending on your taste) music coming forth. Adjust the volume and listen to your heart's content.

Controlling the Tunes

Automatic play is neat, but it only plays through the CD sequentially, one track at a time. If you want to exercise some control over your music, the easiest way is to use the **CD Player** control button on the Control Strip. (You'll learn more about the Control Strip in Chapter 20, "Get a Grip with the Control Strip.")

Speakers Count

Your DV iMac comes equipped with pretty good speakers. You can even add a special sub-woofer module to give you better bass (good for music, movies, and games). Non-DV iMacs aren't quite so good. Non-DV iMac speakers are tinny sounding. If you want better sound, consider adding external computer speakers. You can add USB speakers or just plug a "regular" set into the external speaker port.

Insert an audio CD into your iMac's drive and it begins playing. Click the **Play CD** button on the Control Strip (see Figure 17.1). You will see a set of controls you can use to change how your CD is playing. Most of the controls are self-explanatory. For example, to pause a CD, choose **Pause** from the menu. (If no CD is playing, this will say Play instead of Pause.) To make the CD play over and over until you just can't take it anymore, choose **Repeat**. You can jump directly to any track by choosing it from the menu.

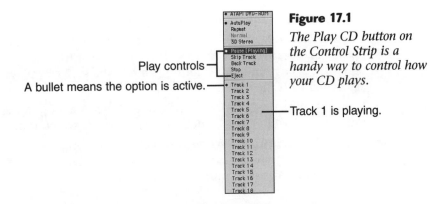

Figure 17.1

The Play CD button on the Control Strip is a handy way to control how your CD plays.

Play controls

A bullet means the option is active.

Track 1 is playing.

Listen to Your Faves with the AppleCD Audio Player

AutoPlay and the Play CD button on the Control Strip are fine for most people, but you demand more from your music. You can't simply listen to the songs in their original order, nor do you want to listen to all the songs on most CDs. You need more!

That is where the AppleCD Audio Player comes in. This application gives you complete control over your audio CDs. Get started by opening the **Applications** folder and then the **AppleCD Audio Player** folder. Double-click the **AppleCD Audio Player** icon. You will see the AppleCD Audio Player window (see Figure 17.2).

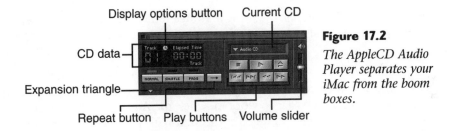

Display options button   Current CD

CD data

Expansion triangle

Figure 17.2

The AppleCD Audio Player separates your iMac from the boom boxes.

Repeat button   Play buttons   Volume slider

The AppleCD Audio Player provides you with the following controls and information:

➤ **CD data**—This area shows the track you are playing, and depending on the options you have selected, it can show a variety of time-related data on the current CD. To change the information, click the **Display Options** button (the little clock) and choose the time data you want from the pop-up menu.

➤ **Current CD**—This window shows you the CD currently mounted on the desktop. Before you label a CD, you will see Audio CD. If you click the CD label, you can jump to any track on the CD. The check mark indicates which track is playing.

➤ **Volume**—This slider controls the output level from the CD. Note that it's not the same as adjusting the system volume with the sound control panel or the sound button on the Control Strip; it adjusts only the relative volume level of the CD.

215

➤ **Play buttons**—These work just like you probably expect them to.

➤ **Normal/Shuffle/Prog**—These buttons control the mode of the AppleCD Audio Player. **Normal** plays the CD from the first track to the last. **Shuffle** plays the CD by randomly shuffling among tracks. **Prog** plays the program associated with the CD.

➤ **Repeat**—When this button is clicked (and shows a loop rather than a straight line), the CD will play continuously, regardless of which mode it is in.

➤ **Expansion triangle**—When you click this, the AppleCD Audio Player window opens to display the labeling and programming area. What you see depends on which mode you are in (normal, shuffle, or program).

Controlling the CD with Your Keyboard

You can use several keys to control an audio CD. The spacebar plays or pauses. The up and down arrow keys control volume. The left and right arrows jump back or ahead.

To use the AppleCD Audio Player, insert an audio CD into the drive and click the buttons to see how they work. If you have used any sort of CD player, you'll get the hang of it right away.

Name That Disc!

Unless you have an odd music collection, I doubt that you have any CDs called Audio CD. Your iMac can't read a disc's label so it calls them all the same thing. You can set your iMac straight by naming each of your CDs; after you name them, your iMac will always remember the name when you insert the CD again. You can also name the tracks. After all, how useful is it to see tracks by their number?

Insert a CD into your drive. Click the Expansion triangle and you will see the track listing window. Drag the resizing box to make the window larger so it's easier to work in. Click the Audio CD text in the middle part of the window to highlight it. Replace this text with the title of your CD. Now press **Tab** and you will move to the Track 1 window where "Track 1" is highlighted. Replace this text with the title of the song that is the first track of the CD. Press **Tab** to move to the second track and type the name of the second song. Keep doing this until you have named all the tracks on the CD. Now the information that AppleCD Audio Player shows is much more meaningful.

Don't Lose This File!

If you regularly label and program your CDs, make sure you back up the CD Remote Programs file, which is located inside the Preferences folder in the System Folder. And make sure you place a copy of this file in the Preferences folder whenever you update or replace your system software. If something happens to this file and you don't have a copy of it, you will lose all your CD customization information, including titles, song names, and any programs you create.

Put another CD in and enter its name and all the song titles it contains. Notice that the AppleCD Audio Player now reflects the new information. Eject that CD, and put the previous one back in. Voila! Your iMac remembers all the information you entered from the previous CD. You only have to enter information for a CD one time. From then on, your iMac recognizes it automatically.

Program Your Own Tunes

If you're like me, some of your CDs have songs you don't like very much, and others have songs you like to hear over and over again. With AppleCD Audio Player, you can create custom programs that play the CD tracks in any order you like. (You can also repeat or skip individual tracks.) Every time you play a CD for which you have created labels or a program, you can use its program. No more wading through a song you hate!

Creating a program is really easy, and it makes you feel like you are your own disc jockey. Insert a CD (use a CD for which you have entered the name and song titles) in your iMac and open the **AppleCD Audio Player**. Click the **Expansion triangle** to reveal the Track window. Click the **Prog** button. The window is divided into two panes.

The pane on the left shows the tracks that are on the CD. The pane on the right contains your custom playlist. To move a song onto the playlist, drag it from the left pane and drop it into a slot on the right pane. Continue doing that until you have all the songs in the playlist that you want to hear. You can rearrange songs in the playlist by dragging them up or down. You can have as many tracks as you want on your playlist—make the window bigger if you need to. When you are done, click the **Play** button and your custom program plays.

This program will always be available when you insert this CD. To play the program, make sure the **Prog** button is selected and click **Play**. To play it in its regular order again, click the **Normal** button.

217

Your iMac Is a Digital Movie Theater

DV iMacs include a DVD drive; the DVD drive can read all CD formats, including CD-ROM discs, audio CDs, and so on. That is good. It can also read DVD-ROM discs, which is better. What is really cool about the DVD drive is that it can play DVD movie discs, so you can watch them right on your iMac screen! Apple includes the Apple DVD Player, which enables you to control your DVD movies. (You can even play them in the background while you "work".)

Sorry, Non-DV iMac Owners

If you have a non-DV iMac, sorry, but you do not have a DVD drive or FireWire ports. The rest of this chapter won't be of any use to you so you might as well skip to the next chapter. Or you may want to read it anyway, but I can't be held responsible if doing so causes you to upgrade to a DV iMac right away!

Going to the iMac Theater

To get started, insert a DVD movie in your iMac. If you don't have any other DVD movies, you can always use the excellent *Bug's Life* DVD that was included with your DV iMac. After a few moments, you will see the DVD mounted on your desktop. Now open the hard drive, then the **Applications** folder, then the **Apple DVD Player** folder, and then the **Apple DVD Player** application. The Apple DVD Player has two windows: the Controller and the Viewer (see Figure 17.3).

Figure 17.3

The Apple DVD Player uses two windows; the Controller window provides the controls you use to watch the movie.

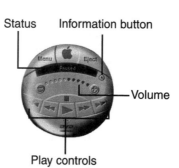

Status   Information button

Volume

Play controls

You can use the Controller to control the playback of your movies. Most of the controls are self-explanatory, such as Play/Pause, Scan Forward/Backward, and Skip to Next Chapter/Previous Chapter. The Menu button takes you to the DVD's main menu, from which you can usually choose the setup (such as captioning and languages) and special features (such as deleted scenes and trailers). You can use your mouse to choose items on the DVD's main menu. (You can also use keyboard commands; see the Apple DVD Player help to find out which keyboard commands are available.)

Apple DVD Player Won't Play

If you have upgraded your DV iMac from Mac OS 8.6 to Mac OS 9, there is some chance the Apple DVD Player will stop working after the upgrade. If this has happened to you, you probably did a "clean" install in which you created a brand-new System Folder for Mac OS 9. To restore your Apple DVD Player, you need to move the following files from the Extensions folder in the Previous System Folder to the Extensions folder in your new System Folder: DVD Decoder Library, DVD Navigation Library, DVD Region Manager, and DVDRuntimeLib. Restart your iMac and the Apple DVD Player should start working again.

The Apple DVD Player assumes you want to play the movie immediately, so the movie begins to play as soon as the Apple DVD Player is open.

Controlling Your Movie Like a Pro

You can do a lot of things to make your movies play the way you want them to. You may not like the Controller taking up screen space. Hide it by opening the **Window** menu and choosing **Hide Controller**. You can control the movie using the commands on the Control menu.

You can also use various keyboard shortcuts to control your movie. For example, the **spacebar** Plays or Pauses a movie. Pressing ⌘+. stops a movie. Pressing the ⌘ key and the right or left arrow scans forward or backward. Pressing the ⌘ key and the up and down arrows changes the volume.

You can also change the size of the Viewer window. To do this, use the **Video** menu. Select among four sizes and Present Video on Screen. To make the Viewer window larger or smaller, choose the size you want from the **Video** menu. (You can also use the ⌘ key while typing **0, 1, 2,** or **3** to choose a size.) The last command on the **Video** menu is **Present Video on Screen**. This clears the rest of the screen so all you see is the contents of the Viewer window. This mode is similar to what you would see on a regular TV. In this mode, you can still activate commands by using the keyboard or by pointing to the menu bar. (When you do, the menu bar becomes visible and you can choose commands on it.)

What's With the Black Area at the Top of the Screen?

Some movies appear in Widescreen (also called the 16×9 format). This is the same format that is used by movie theaters; the screens you see in a movie theater are wider than they are tall. Your iMac screen is closer to being square (like most TV screens are). When you view a movie in Widescreen format on your iMac, the top and bottom of the screen will contain black bars. Why would you want this? In Widescreen format, you see all of the picture as the movie producers intended.

The other format, often called full-screen or Pan & Scan, uses all of the screen. To do this, the movie's image size is increased to fill the height of the screen. Because the screen and movie are of different proportions, you actually lose the edges of the movie. You don't see all of the picture, but what you do see is larger. Some DVDs contain a movie in both formats so you can choose between them.

Maximizing DVD Playback

Showing a movie is a lot of work for your iMac. It has to decode each frame of the movie, play the sound, and keep everything synchronized. Your iMac does this through software (rather than through a dedicated DVD decoder card). This means your iMac will sometimes struggle to keep up with the movie, and you may see the soundtrack get slightly out of synch or you may see some digital artifacts on the screen. If you notice such problems, you may want to create a video-optimized configuration so the DVD application has the resources it needs to display the movie in the best possible way. Complete the following tasks to create your DVD-maximized configuration:

➤ **Give the Apple DVD Player more RAM**—Increase the RAM allocated to the Apple DVD Player. See Chapter 23, "Beating the System," to learn how to do this.

➤ **Use Extensions Manager to shut down all unnecessary system software**—This includes as many extensions and control panels you don't need. Again, see Chapter 23 to learn how to use Extensions Manager.

➤ **Turn off virtual memory**—Use the Memory control panel to turn off Virtual Memory. (You will learn about virtual memory in Chapter 23.)

➤ **Unmount network resources, turn off File Sharing, and turn off AppleTalk**—Being connected to a network can cause activity for your iMac. Drag any mounted network servers to the Trash to disconnect from them. Use the File Sharing module on the Control Strip to turn off File Sharing. Use the AppleTalk module on the Control Strip to make AppleTalk inactive.

Your DV iMac Is a Digital Video Editing Studio

With its FireWire ports and the included iMovie application, your DV iMac enables you to create and edit digital videos. You can acquire video clips by importing them from a DV camera (via FireWire) or by exporting QuickTime movies in the DV format and then importing them into your project. You can then build your own digital videos using iMovie, which is a powerful, but easy-to-use digital video editing application. After it's done, you can export it to DV tape or you can save it as a QuickTime movie.

Gather Your Clips

Before you construct your own digital video, you need to have the video clips you will use in it. There are two basic ways you can acquire digital video clips for your video projects:

➤ **Use a DV camcorder**—You can use a DV camcorder to record video and then copy that video onto your iMac. Most DV cameras include FireWire output (also called IEE 1334 output). To download video from your DV camera to your iMac, connect the FireWire output from the camera to the FireWire ports on your iMac. You can use the controls in iMovie to capture clips.

➤ **Export QuickTime movies into DV format**—If you have upgraded to QuickTime Pro (see Chapter 16, "Watch Some QuickTime Movies and Then Make Your Own"), you can export QuickTime movies into the DV format so you can use them in your DV projects. To create a DV version of a QuickTime clip, open the QuickTime movie in the QuickTime Player application. Open the **File** menu and choose **Export**. In the Save dialog box, choose **Movie to DV Stream** from the **Export** pop-up menu. Choose a location in which to save your movie, name it, and click **Save**.

Plan your movie so you can decide which clips you will need and where you will get them.

Prepare Your Digital Video Project

Open the **Applications** folder, then open the **iMovie** folder, and then open **iMovie**. You should see a prompt asking if you want to open an existing project or create a new one. Choose the **Create new** option and give your project a name.

When you get into iMovie, you will see four general areas (see Figure 17.4). In the preview window, you can view clips of the movie you have created. Its controls work similarly to those in the QuickTime Player. You use the shelf to store the various clips you will use in your project. The effects palette contains tools you can use to add titles, music, transitions, and sounds to your movie. The clip viewer and audio viewer enable you to see the video and audio clips in detail.

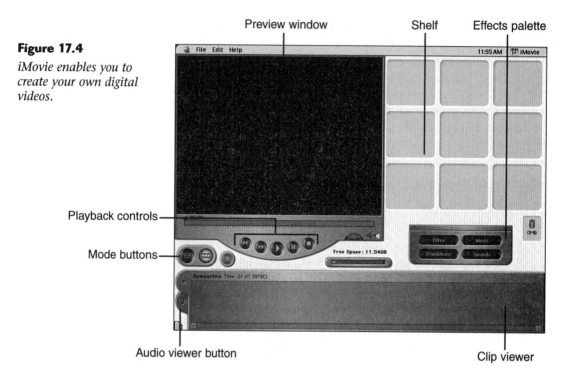

Figure 17.4

iMovie enables you to create your own digital videos.

Import Your Clips

You need to move your clips into iMovie's shelf so you can use them in your movie.

If you will be downloading clips from a DV camera, click the **Camera mode** button (it looks like a camcorder). The preview window changes to the capture window. Play your video and use the **Import** button to capture clips to the shelf.

If you are importing QuickTime movies that you can export into DV versions, quit iMovie. Place the DV movie versions in the Media folder that is your project folder. Open your project. A prompt appears telling you some stray clips were found. Click **OK** and the clips appear on the shelf.

Create the Video Track

Preview a clip by selecting it in the shelf. When you do so, it appears in the preview window. Click **Play** to play the clip. When you find the clip you want to be first in your movie, drag it from the shelf to the clip viewer. Continue previewing clips and placing them on the clip viewer in the order in which you want them to appear. Click **Play** again and your movie plays.

Use the selection markers to trim the clips to get rid of parts you don't want. In the clip viewer window, click the video clip you want to edit. In the preview window, move the playhead to where you want to begin your edits. Press the **Shift** key and selection handles appear. Drag the selection handles to the part of the clip you want to remove. (That part should be highlighted on the scrubber bar.) Open the **Edit** menu and choose **Cut**. The offending video is removed (see Figure 17.5).

Clip on the shelf

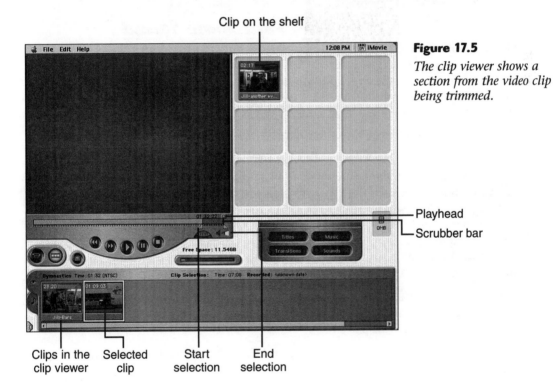

Figure 17.5

The clip viewer shows a section from the video clip being trimmed.

Playhead

Scrubber bar

Clips in the clip viewer   Selected clip   Start selection   End selection

Continue moving and editing clips until all the edited clips are in place.

Add a Transition or Three

You probably want a nice transition from one clip to another rather than the straight cut that is done by default. Click the **Transitions** button on the effects palette to pop up transitions that you can place between clips. You can select any of the transi-

223

Smooth Beginnings (and Endings)

You can also add transitions before and after the clips in the clip viewer so your movie begins and ends with a smooth transition.

tions you see on the list, and the selected transition is previewed for you in the preview window. Use the slider to set the duration of the transition. Click the **Preview** button to see another preview of the transition.

When you find the transition you want to use, drag it from the Transitions palette and place it between the two clips you want to transition between. The transition appears in the clip viewer window just like your clips do.

Continue adding transitions until the video track is complete.

Now Add Some Sound

iMovie enables you to add music, sound effects, and a narration track to your movie. To work with sound, click the **Audio Viewer** tab to change to the Audio Viewer. You will see three possible sound tracks. The top one is for the sound track that came with your video clips. The middle one is for narration and sound effects you may want to add. The bottom one is for a music track you can record from an audio CD.

You can uncheck the check box at the end of any of these sound tracks to mute them. Otherwise, the sound effects work similarly to the transitions.

To add a music track from a CD, insert the CD you want to use in your iMac. Click the **Music** button on the effects palette. You will see a pop-up window showing the tracks on that CD. Use the controls to get to the portion of the music you want to use as a sound track. Play that music and click the **Record Music** button. Let the music record until it is the length you want it to be. When you are done recording, click **Stop**. To make the music track fade in or fade out, check the **Fade In** or **Fade Out** check boxes.

Now add a sound effect. Click the **Sounds** button to pop up the sound effects window. Drag a sound effect from the window to the middle sound track bar. The sound effect plays wherever your place it.

When you're done, you can see all the sound tracks in the Audio viewer window (see Figure 17.6).

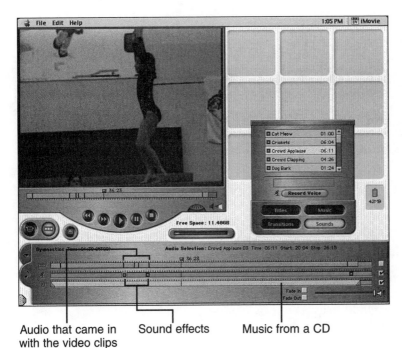

Figure 17.6
This video project now has a full sound track.

Audio that came in with the video clips

Sound effects

Music from a CD

Finish it Up

After you have finished your creation, make sure you save your project. You will probably want to export it to a more viewable format so you don't have to use iMovie to watch it. You have two choices. One is to save the movie to a DV camera. The other is to save it as a QuickTime movie that you can view with the QuickTime Player.

Open the **File** menu and choose **Export Movie.** In the Export Movie window, choose the option you want form the **Export to** pop-up menu. For example, to save it to a QuickTime movie, choose **QuickTime**. In the QuickTime dialog box, choose the format you want to use from the pop-up menu. The choices affect the size and quality of the movie. (The higher the quality, the larger the file size.) When you have your option selected, click **Export**. Give the QuickTime version of your movie a name, and save it. iMovie exports the movie into a QuickTime file.

iMovie can do much more for you; hopefully this section has been a jump-start for you into the world of digital video. You can get a lot more information about iMovie by running the iMovie Tutorial and using the iMovie Help Center. Both are available on the **Help** menu.

The Least You Need to Know

➤ You can listen to any audio CD on your iMac; use the Play CD Control Strip module for simple control or the AppleCD Audio Player to control your CDs like a disc jockey.

➤ You can watch DVD movies on your iMac using the Apple DVD Player; it features a full set of controls so you can make the most of your movie experience.

➤ You can use the FireWire ports on your DV iMac to connect a DV camera to it.

➤ iMovie is a full-featured digital video editor you can use to create and edit your own digital movies; you can even add music and sound effects!

Chapter 18

Games iMacs Play

In This Chapter

➤ Learn about the types of games you can play on your iMac

➤ Find out why multiplayer games are so cool

➤ Play multiplayer games using Ethernet

➤ Play games with people around the world on the Internet

Today's lifestyle is hard on everyone. With a lot of work to do, things to keep up with at home and school, and other responsibilities, there isn't much time for fun. And everyone deserves some time out for fun now and again. Many people (including yours truly) like to play computer games and today you can choose from thousands of games. And the games get even better when you play with others on a local network or the Internet.

With its preinstalled games, built-in stereo speakers, great graphics, powerful processor, and unmatched networking capabilities, your iMac is one great game machine.

Games You Can Play

There are so many different kinds of games you can play that the sky is not even the limit. Games that you can run on your iMac literally offer you the universe to choose from. Mac games fall into the following general categories; the type you prefer to play depends on your personality:

➤ **First person**—In first-person games, also know as first-person shooters, you literally become the game character. You see the game world through the eyes of your alter ego. Most first-person games involve some sort of carnage. The first successful first-person game was Id Software's Wolfenstein 3-D, in which you played a man trying to escape from a Nazi prison. Following on this success, Id released DOOM, which blew the first-person gaming experience into the next level (pun intended). DOOM was wildly successful and spawned DOOM 2. This was followed by Quake, Quake II, and Quake III. Other companies joined in the fray with games such as the Marathon series, Duke Nukem, Unreal, and so on. The carnage never ends.

First-person games found their real fulfillment in network play. On a network (including the biggest network of all, the Internet), you can face other people who become characters in your gaming world. There is nothing like competing against your friends as well as people whom you don't even know.

Take an iLook

First-Person Games and Real-World Violence?

First-person games tend to depict violence—and a lot of it. It has become fashionable to blame these games for everything from road rage to mass shootings. Whether these games bring out evil behavior in people or the evil behavior would come out anyway, I don't know. I play them myself, and see nothing wrong with them as long as they are kept in moderation. But be aware that some people see a strong link between violent games and violent behavior.

➤ **Third person**—Third-person games are similar to first-person games, except that you see the main character, usually from just above the character's shoulder. The most famous game in this motif is the Tomb Raider series, which features the adventures of Laura Croft as she explores the world and saves humanity.

➤ **Real-time strategy games**—These games involve more than just a single character. You can command armies, fleets of ships, or even entire governments. The world you live in (or die in, depending on how good you are) moves in real-time and the action can be intense. One of the best of these games is the Bungie's Myth series, in which you command armies of various creatures in battles with other armies commanded by the computer or (with network play) by other people.

Try Before You Buy

Many companies offer free demos of their games that you can download from the Net and play. This is a great way to see if a game is worth the money—before you buy it. You can download demos of great Bungie games from www.bungie.com. Find more fun demos from MacSoft's Web site at www.wizworks.com/macsoft/.

➤ **Turn-based strategy games**—These strategy games are modeled after board games in which each play takes a turn; a turn may involve many actions or only a few. These games focus almost exclusively on strategy and long-term thinking. If you are fond of action (as I am), you may not appreciate the pace of these games. However, many people really enjoy them (and you certainly aren't likely to develop a case of Carpal Tunnel Syndrome from them!).

➤ **Simulations**—If you can do it, there is probably a simulation game of it. With simulation games, you can play all sorts of sports, operate any sort of vehicle, manage towns and cities, and so on. The key difference between simulations and other sorts of games is that they try to model real life as much as possible. For example, many fighter simulations are almost as complicated to fly as the real-world aircraft they simulate.

Mix and Match

Some games involve combinations of the other types. For example, you may be exploring a 3D world like you do in a first-person game, but you also may have to solve puzzles as you do in arcade and video games.

➤ **Video games**—There are also all sorts of games that are similar to console and arcade games. These usually don't take advantage of the power of the computer as other games do, but they still can be a lot of fun.

➤ **Educational games**—Last, but not least, are so-called educational games. These are primarily aimed at young people, but having played a few myself, I know that they also can be a lot of fun. Educational games have the dual purpose of being fun and enabling learning to take place. There are many types of educational games, including those that teach reading, writing, arithmetic, history, geography, and so on.

It Only Takes Two to Network

A network can be as few as two computers connected together. So don't let the word "network" conjure up images of big corporations. You can set up your own two-computer network in seconds.

Playing by Yourself

Almost all games allow you to play by yourself. You usually battle computer generated foes of one sort or another. Playing a game by yourself involves little set up. Simply launch the game and get to it— you might want to read the instructions first (nah, you don't need them). You iMac comes with a couple of good games you can start playing right away, including the first-dinosaur adventure Nanosaur and the *Bug's Life*-like Bugdom. Open the Applications folder to get to Bugdom. You need to install Nanosaur from the Software Install CD that came with your iMac.

Playing with Others on a Local Network

Few things are more fun than including other people in your gaming sessions. Although the first-person combat games are the type that you are most likely to play with others, many other types of games enable you to play in multiplayer modes as well.

To play a game in the multiplayer mode, your iMac has to be able to communicate with other computers, which allows you to interact with the people with whom you are playing. Fortunately, your iMac makes this as easy as it can be. The following four steps are generally required to get a multiplayer game going:

1. Connect your iMac to a network.
2. Install the game.
3. Launch the game and configure it for a multiplayer session.
4. Get the other players to launch their games and sign on to the game you are hosting or sign on to a game someone else is hosting.

Multiplayer Games

Most games that allow multiple players include a license for at least two players with the game. This means you and a friend can enjoy multiplayer gaming with only one purchased copy of the game. Some games allow you to run one full copy of the game and provide a network–only version that you can install on the other person's computer.

If you want to play with more than one other person, you will need additional copies of the game.

Connecting with Ethernet Cable

The physical connection you use to connect to other computers is called Ethernet; Ethernet is a high-speed connection technology that enables your iMac to connect with other computers. There are a couple of ways to connect computers together so they can communicate via Ethernet.

What's in a Protocol?

A protocol is basically the language your computer is speaking at any particular time. You can run different protocols over a single physical connection (in this case, Ethernet). Different games communicate via different protocols. There are several that you may encounter. AppleTalk is the iMac's native communication protocol, and many games use it to talk to each other. Some games use TCP/IP (Transmission Control Protocol/Internet Protocol) to communicate with games running on other computers. Check the instructions that come with your game to see which you need to use.

No Crossover Cables Please

An Ethernet crossover cable works only when you are connecting two computers together. Don't try to use a crossover cable with an Ethernet hub.

If you want to connect to a single computer (to make a two-computer network), get an *Ethernet crossover cable* and plug one end into the Ethernet port on each computer. (The Ethernet port on your iMac is located on the right side of the machine and looks like a large telephone jack.) After the crossover cable is connected to each computer, they will be able to talk to one another and you can play a network game.

If you want to connect more than two computers together with Ethernet, you need to use an Ethernet hub. An Ethernet hub is a "block" that enables you to connect multiple Ethernet cables into it. You can connect as many computers together as there are ports on the hub. After all the computers are connected to the hub, they will be able to run the multiplayer game.

Cables...I Don't Need No Stinking Cables!

If you have an AirPort card installed in your iMac, you may not need any cables to play multiplayer games. If you want to play with other people who also have AirPort-equipped computers (such as G4 desktops or iBooks), you don't need any cables. Each computer that is equipped with an AirPort card can communicate with the network—and you have an instant, wireless, multiplayer game. One computer launches the game and sets up the session. The other AirPort-equipped computers simply join the game that is in progress (see Figure 18.1).

Figure 18.1

This is a network game of the excellent Myth: The Fallen Lords, in which you can join battle with up to 16 of your closest friends (or enemies).

If you want to connect your iMac to an Ethernet network (some people aren't fortunate enough to use an iMac), you can still take advantage of your AirPort capability. If you have an AirPort Base Station, you can connect that to the Ethernet network and then use the AirPort card to connect to the network. This is nice because you can move your iMac into a different room; as long as there is an electrical outlet, you have everything you need to connect to the gaming session.

With Apple's Access Point software, you can also use another AirPort-equipped computer to do the job of the Base Station. Connect that computer to the physical network, and then other AirPort-equipped computers can connect to the network through that machine.

Look Ma, No AirPort

If you have an older iMac, you don't have the capability to use an AirPort card. Check the manual that came with you iMac to see if it is AirPort-compatible (if it's a DV iMac, it is). Don't worry, though; all iMacs have an Ethernet port, so you won't be left out of the action.

Playing with the World

With many games, you don't need to connect to a local network to play multiplayer games because they enable you to play against other people over the Internet. This means you can literally play with people all over the world. The best of these games have dedicated Web sites to which you can connect to play the game against other people. You can also connect directly to other machines over the Internet, but this requires that you know the other machines' IP addresses. That can be a bit tricky, however, because the IP address changes for some people each time you connect.

Don't Ignore Windows PCs

Many games offer both Mac and Windows PC versions. If the game also has a multiplayer mode, you can play against Windows PC users as well as other Mac users.

To see what Internet play options your favorite game supports, check the manual that came with it. If you are fortunate, it will support Internet play as well as Bungie games, such as Myth: The Fallen Lords, does (see Figure 18.2).

Figure 18.2

The bungie.net *Web site enables you to play Myth games with people around the world.*

The Facts of Net Life

Most likely, you are connecting to the Internet with the iMac's 56K modem. Although this is great for cruising the Web and doing email, a modem is not very fast when you are trying to run a modern game. Although a modem on its own is only barely adequate to transfer the large amounts of data most games need to play, you also face network traffic. The bottom line is that you may find playing a game over a modem frustratingly slow. But try it for yourself to see how your favorite game fares on the Net.

The Least You Need to Know

➤ If you like fast-paced action and don't mind a little death and destruction, try a first- or third-person game (such as Quake, Unreal, or Tomb Raider).

➤ If you like action and strategy, one of Bungie's Myth games is a great choice.

➤ If you are into real life, try a simulation, such as F-18.

➤ Check the Web sites of game producers for games you think you might be interested in; download and play a demo to see if the game is a good match for you.

➤ Multiplayer games are really fun, especially on a local network that provides the speed you need.

➤ To play a multiplayer game, connect to a network using an Ethernet cable or AirPort, and then start the game and have the other players join it or join a game that someone else has started.

Part 4

Become an iMac Wizard

Now it's time for you to enter the next stage of your iMac development. In this part, you learn how to really make your iMac work like you want it to. You'll learn how to customize the Apple menu, use the Control Strip, manipulate the System Folder, and even make the Finder jump through your hoops. No iMac should have to stand on its own, and in this part you'll also learn how to share your files and to connect neat stuff to your computer to expand its capabilities. Finally, you'll learn what to do if your iMac gives you trouble.

By the time you reach the end of this part, you will truly ascend to iMac mastery. Get ready to be enlightened.

Chapter 19

NO?

There Are No Red Delicious on This Apple Menu

> ## In This Chapter
>
> ➤ Learn how to use the Apple menu (and why you should use it)
>
> ➤ Use the great stuff that is preinstalled on the Apple menu
>
> ➤ Make the Apple menu contain anything you want it to

If you have worked through many of the chapters in this book, you have already used the Apple menu. Mostly, you have used it to quickly access the Control Panels folder, to get to the Chooser to select a printer, to use Remote Access Status to connect to the Net, and open Sherlock to search the Web (see, you are an old hand with the Apple menu already). But the Apple menu enables you to do even more than this; with it, you can quickly and easily access any folder, volume, application, file, or any other item on your iMac. And when I said *any* I meant any. You can add your own items to the Apple menu so it becomes you own personalized menu.

Picking Apples from the Apple Menu

The Apple menu is easy to spot; it is always in the upper left corner of the screen no matter where you are working—in an application, on the desktop, in your System Folder, or wherever (see Figure 19.1).

Figure 19.1

Although what you get from the Apple menu doesn't keep the doctor away, you'll visit it every day anyway.

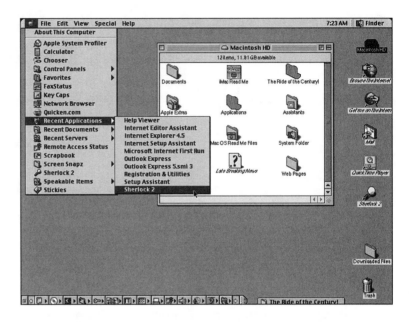

What—No Apple Menu?

Some programs, mostly games, hide their menu bars, including the Apple menu (because it is a part of every menu bar). Usually there is some way to activate the program's menu bar (often by pressing ⌘+**Spacebar**) and when you do, the Apple menu returns as well. Whew....

A standard Apple menu is available as soon as you start up your iMac and includes the choices you see in Figure 19.1. Also notice that some of the items on the Apple menu have a black arrow pointing to the right. As you learned earlier in the book, this means these are folders in the "hierarchical view" and when you choose one of these items, another menu pops out with additional choices.

The items you see on the Apple menu are determined by the Apple Menu Items folder within the System Folder (see Figure 19.2). Anything you place in this folder appears on the Apple menu, and conversely, if you remove something from this folder, it disappears from the menu. (Getting any ideas yet?)

Figure 19.2

Compare this figure with the previous one; you should notice the items in this folder correspond to the choices on the Apple menu.

You Don't Need a Ladder to Pick These Gems

Using the Apple menu is as easy as it gets. Just open the menu and choose an item to open that item. You have already done this several times, and I'm sure you have the hang of it. It's time to gather some low-hanging fruit.

You Guessed It

The expansion triangles you see next to some items enable you to see more (or less) information about that item. Click on them to open the additional information for any item.

Learning About This Computer

The first item on the menu is About This Computer. If you choose this, you will see a window that shows you how much RAM your iMac has and how it is being used. You'll learn more about this option later in the book.

Taking a Profile

The Apple System Profiler is a nice tool that helps you understand the hardware and software that make up your iMac. Open it by choosing it from the **Apple** menu. You will see a window with several tabs across the top. Click a tab to see information about that area of your iMac. For example, to see what disks and volumes you are working with, click the **Devices and Volumes** tab. You'll see a list of all the disks that are currently accessible (see Figure 19.3).

241

Figure 19.3

The Apple System Profiler tells you everything you need to know about your iMac.

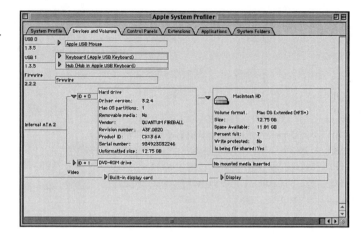

The best use for the Apple System Profiler is when you are asking for help. You can help someone trying to help you by using the Apple System Profiler to describe the version of the system you are running, how much RAM you have, and so on.

Calculating with the Calculator

The Calculator is one of those rare items that has been with the Mac since its inception in 1984. And from the way it looks, you can tell. I have often heard the

Cut or Copy

By the way, you can copy or cut a result from the Calculator's window. Whatever number you see in the window is placed on the Clipboard when you choose **Copy** (⌘+**C**) or **Cut** (⌘+**X**) from the **Edit** menu.

Calculator is a way to make your $1,500 Macintosh do *almost* as much as a $1.95 calculator. Although the Calculator is very, very basic, it is functional and I have used it myself many times over the years. When you need to do a simple calculation on-the-fly, the Calculator is often the best tool for the job.

To begin your own number crunching, open the **Apple** menu and choose **Calculator**. A calculator window appears. You can either click on numbers and operators using the pointer, or use either set of numeric keys on the keyboard. When you are done, press ⌘+**Q** to quit.

Choosing with the Chooser

The Chooser is an important utility you use to choose a printer or to mount a network volume on your desktop. You learned how to use it with a printer in Chapter 7, "The Paperless World—Bah!" You will learn how to use it with a network later in the book.

Making Life Easy with Favorites

The Favorites item enables you to quickly get to, well, your favorite items. Favorites can include files, applications, or even Web pages. When you make something a favorite, it appears under the Favorites hierarchical menu.

Adding and using your own favorites is child's play. Just for kicks, add AppleWorks to the Favorites menu so you can easily open it whenever you need to. Open your hard drive, open the Applications folder, and then open the AppleWorks folder. Click the **AppleWorks** icon to select it. From the **File** menu, choose **Add to Favorites**. Now open the **Apple** menu and choose **Favorites**. You will see AppleWorks as a menu choice (see Figure 19.4). To launch it, choose it from the hierarchical menu.

You Already Know About This

You learned about several choices on the Apple menu elsewhere in the book, so I won't bother you with them again here. These include the Control Panels, Remote Access Status, and Sherlock 2 choices.

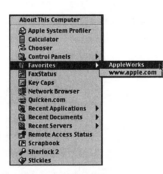

Figure 19.4
AppleWorks has been added to the Apple menu.

Following are some ideas on what you might want to include on your Favorites menu:

➤ **Documents**—If there are documents you regularly access, add them to the Favorites menu so you don't have to burrow into folders to get to them.

➤ **Folders**—Any folder you add to the Favorites menu becomes its own hierarchical menu (so you can access anything within that folder). This is especially neat for project folders because adding the project's folder to the Favorites menu means you can get to any of the files for that project from the Apple menu.

Using Contextual Menus Works Too

You can add any item to the **Favorites** menu by selecting it, pressing **Control**, clicking the mouse button, and then choosing **Add to Favorites** from the contextual menu.

243

➤ **Web sites**—By dragging a URL from the Address bar in Internet Explorer or from Sherlock to the desktop, you can create a link to that URL. To move to the site, double-click its icon. If you add the icon to the Favorites menu, you can move to the site by choosing it from the menu.

To remove something from the Favorites menu, open the **System Folder** and then open the **Favorites** folder. Drag the item you want to remove from this folder to the Trash (or elsewhere on your hard drive if you want to keep the item). It disappears from the Favorites menu.

Don't Clutter the Menu

Rather than have a bunch of Web sites cluttering up your Favorites menu, create a folder called something like My Favorite Web sites. Place the Web site icons in this folder and add the folder to the Favorites menu. Choose the folder, and you will see a neat pop-up menu of your favorite sites.

Figuring Out Fonts with Key Caps

Key Caps is a utility that enables you to locate special characters in the fonts that are installed on your system. For example, if you need to use the Return key symbol in a document you are writing, you can use Key Caps to help you find it.

Symbols and Fonts

The symbols you have available to you depend on the font you are using when you type. If you are using a different font in your working application, the symbol appears in that font rather than the one you were using in Key Caps. To see the symbol you want, you need to change the font in the working application to the same one you were using in Key Caps.

From the **Apple** menu, choose **Key Caps**. The Key Caps window opens. Choose the font you want to work with from the **Fonts** menu. You will see the font change on the Key Caps keyboard. Look for the symbol you need. If you can't find it, press a modifier key, for example, the **Option** key. The Key Caps keyboard changes to reflect the symbols that the modifier key provides. Continue trying keys until you find the symbol you are looking for. If you can't find the symbol, try a different font. After you find the symbol, you can either repeat the key combination in your document or simply copy and paste the symbol into your document.

Browsing Your Network

If you are connected to a network, you use the Network Browser to connect to the various servers you can see. Choose it from the **Apple** menu to begin browsing around (see Figure 19.5). (If you aren't on a network, you won't see anything, but you can open it anyway.)

Servers you can use on your local network   Add or view Favorites   Recent servers you have used

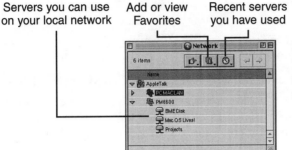

Figure 19.5

You can use the Network browser to see what is available on your network.

To log in to a server, click the expansion triangle next to its name. Enter the username and password for that server, and click **OK**. The server will be mounted on your desktop and you can work with it.

Visiting Your Recent Items

Your iMac tracks the most recent applications, documents, and servers you have opened and adds them to the Recent Items choices on the Apple menu. To go back to one of these recent items, choose it from the appropriate Recent Items menu (such as the Recent Documents menu).

Making Scraps with the Scrapbook

The Scrapbook is a good place to store graphics, text, sounds, movies, or other items you want to frequently re-use. The Scrapbook is always accessible via the Apple menu so you can quickly move to it, grab the item you want to reuse, and easily paste it into your document. Don't limit your use of the Scrapbook only to still images or text either. It works equally well for sounds, QuickTime movies, and so on.

Setting Recent Items

You can set the number of recent items your iMac remembers in the Apple Menu Options control panel. You can also turn off the hierarchical menu display using this control panel, but I have no idea why you might want to do that.

Drag and Drop

You can also add items to or use items from the Scrapbook by dragging them to or from the Scrapbook window.

To add something to the Scrapbook, select the item you want to use and press ⌘+**C** to copy it. Then open the Scrapbook and press ⌘+**V** to paste it into the Scrapbook.

To use something from the Scrapbook, open the Scrapbook and scroll until you see the item's window. Press ⌘+**C** to copy it from the Scrapbook. Move to your document and press ⌘+**V** to paste it into your document..

Getting Your Screen All Sticky

Stickies are the electronic equivalent of the sticky note pads that are so common in offices today. You can create a note and "paste" it on your screen. When you are done, you can close the note to remove it from the screen.

Defining How Your Stickies Work

You can use the **Preferences** command under the **Edit** menu to define certain aspects of how Stickies works; for example, whether it opens at startup or not.

From the **Apple** menu, choose **Stickies**. You will see some predefined notes appear onscreen. These notes provide some information about how Stickies work. When you are done reading these, close them by clicking their **Close** boxes. (If you don't save them, they are lost forever.)

To create a new note, from the **File** menu, choose **New Note.** A blank note window appears (it has the default font and color settings). Type your note. Use the **Text Style** command under the **Note** menu to set the font and style for the note. Use the **Color** menu to set the note window's color. The note remains on your screen until you close it.

Making the Apple Menu Your Own

You already know how to use the **Favorites** menu to add your own items to the **Apple** menu. You can also add items to it so you can choose them directly from the **Apple** menu.

Aliases and the Apple menu

An alias is simply a pointer to a file or folder. It is almost always better to add aliases to the Apple menu than the actual item itself, especially if the item is not a document. It is better not to clutter up the Apple Menu Items folder (which is in the System Folder, remember) with a bunch of big files and folders.

You can create an alias for any item by holding the **Option** and ⌘ keys down while you drag that item to a new location.

Find something you want to add to the Apple menu. For this exercise, use AppleWorks again (remember you made a favorite to it earlier in the chapter). Find the **AppleWorks** icon (it is inside the AppleWorks folder that is within the Applications folder) and select it. Hold down the **Option** and ⌘ keys and drag the **AppleWorks** icon onto the System Folder. Wait until the System Folder pops open, and then drag the icon onto the Apple Menu Items folder. Release the mouse button. Now AppleWorks appears on the Apple menu and you can select it without even needing to open the Favorites menu.

Organizing the Apple Menu

You can change the order in which items are listed in the Apple menu by changing their names. The Apple menu is sorted by alphabetical order.

To remove something from the Apple menu, drag it out of the Apple Menu Items folder.

The Least You Need to Know

➤ To use the **Apple** menu, simply open it and choose an option; it works just like every other pull-down menu you use except that it is always visible.

➤ There are lots of useful items preinstalled on the Apple menu including Favorites, the Chooser, the Network browser (assuming you are on a network of course), Recent Items, and even the lowly Calculator.

➤ You can add items to your Favorites on the Apple menu by selecting a folder or file and choosing **Add to Favorites** from the **File** menu; after you do so, the item will be listed under the Favorites menu on the Apple menu.

➤ You can also add an item to the Apple menu by placing an alias to it in the Apple Menu Items folder.

GoTCHA!!

Chapter 20

Get a Grip with the Control Strip

In This Chapter

➤ Understand the controls on the Control Strip

➤ Hide or show the Control Strip

➤ Move the strip around the screen

➤ Add or remove controls from the Control Strip

The Control Strip provides a fast and convenient way for you to control your iMac (thus, the name, I suppose). It appears at the bottom of the desktop as a series of buttons on which you click to activate whatever the button controls. As with most aspects of the iMac, you can customize the Control Strip as well as move and resize it. You can also add or remove control buttons from the Control Strip.

Touring the Strip

By default, the Control Strip appears across the bottom of your screen, and it contains quite a few controls (see Figure 20.1). Some of these will be useful to you and some may not be. After you use them for awhile, you can always remove the controls you don't use.

Figure 20.1

The Control Strip is a great way to access your favorite controls.

Collapse box   Scroll arrow   Scroll arrow   Collapse tab

For its controls to always be available to you, the Control Strip floats on top of all other windows so you can access it at all times.

To access any of the controls on the Control Strip, click a button. From the pop-up menu, choose a command or a setting, or open a control panel. You learned how to use the Audio CD Player control back in Chapter 16, "Watch Some QuickTime Movies and Then Make Your Own"; the other controls work similarly. The following is a quick overview of what each button does:

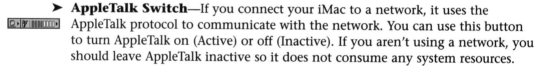

➤ **AppleTalk Switch**—If you connect your iMac to a network, it uses the AppleTalk protocol to communicate with the network. You can use this button to turn AppleTalk on (Active) or off (Inactive). If you aren't using a network, you should leave AppleTalk inactive so it does not consume any system resources.

➤ **Audio CD Player**—This control enables you to play audio CDs. (You learned about this one in Chapter 16.)

➤ **Energy Settings**—You use this button to manage your iMac's current energy use and to open the Energy Saver control panel (see Chapter 2, "You Never Need to Dust This Desktop," for the details).

➤ **File Sharing**—If you connect your iMac to other iMacs or to another network, you can share your files with others. You'll learn more about file sharing in Chapter 22, "Don't Be Stingy—Share Your iMac and Its Files."

➤ **Keychain Strip**—This one helps you manage your Keychain. The Keychain is a feature of Mac OS 9, so if you are running Mac OS 8.6, you won't see this button on your Control Strip. See Chapter 21, "Not-So-Stupid Finder Tricks" to learn about the Keychain.

➤ **Apple Location Manager**—The Location Manager enables you to quickly adapt your iMac to various locations in which you might use it. You will learn more about it in Chapter 21.

➤ **Monitor Color Depth**—If you need to change the number of colors that are displayed on your iMac's screen, use this button. (It does the same thing as the color depth section in the Monitors control panel.)

➤ **Monitor Resolution**—Using this control, you can change the screen resolution. (This does the same thing as the resolution control in the Monitors control panel.)

➤ **Printer Selector**—Unless you use a printer that supports one of the Apple
print drivers (such as a laser printer that uses the Apple LaserWriter driver), this
control is useless. If you do use a printer that supports desktop printing, you
can set a default printer with this button.

➤ **Remote Access**—This is a useful button because you can use it to connect to
the Net, change the account you use, and access connect controls. You can
choose to show your connection time in the button as well, which can be helpful if you tend to lose track of the amount of time you are spending online. You
learned about this control in several chapters of Part II, "The 'i' in iMac Is for
Internet" of this book.

➤ **Volume**—Click this button and drag the slider to change your volume level.

➤ **Sound Source**—This button enables you to change the source of the sound on
your iMac (for example, from the CD player to the microphone). Your iMac
automatically chooses a sound source for you, and most of the time it picks the
right one. Use this button if it doesn't, or when you want to be sure which
sound source you will use (when you are recording sounds for example).

➤ **Web Sharing**—Your iMac can serve Web pages to a network to which it is connected. Use this button to manage your Web sharing by turning Web sharing
on or off and opening the Web Sharing control panel.

Controlling the Strip

You can make your Control Strip be what you want it to be. You can change its
appearance, move it around the screen, and even determine which buttons it
contains.

Collapsing and Expanding the Control Strip

The Control Strip is open by default, but you can collapse it if it is getting in your
way. Then if you want to use a control on it, you can expand it again. To collapse the
Control Strip so you just see its "stub," click the collapse control on either end of the
Control Strip (see Figure 20.2). To expand it again so you can use its controls, click
the tab and it pops open.

Figure 20.2

Clicking the collapse controls at the end of the Control Strip collapses it down to a "stub."

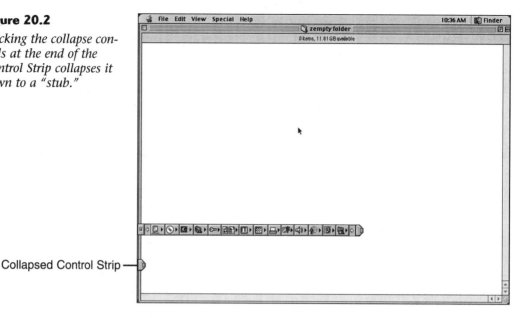

Collapsed Control Strip ——

Resizing the Strip

If the Control Strip is not the length you want it to be, you can shorten or lengthen it. Click the tab at the end of the Control Strip toward the middle of the screen. Drag the end until the Control Strip is the length that you desire. Note that you can't make the Control Strip any longer than the last module that is installed. If you make it shorter than the last module installed, use the left and right arrows to scroll through the modules.

More Control of the Strip

You can use the Control Strip control panel to show or hide the strip, set a key combination to show or hide it (such as ⌘+Control+S), and change the font settings it uses. To access this control panel, open the **Apple** menu, choose **Control Panels**, and then choose **Control Strip**. Use the radio buttons and pop-up menus to change the Control Strip's settings. Close the control panel when you are done.

Moving the Strip

To move the Control Strip, hold the Option key down, click the tab at the end of the Control Strip, drag it to a new location, and release the mouse button. You are somewhat limited in where you can move it; it has to be anchored on one side of the desktop or the other. If you move it all the way across the desktop, it flip flops so that the tab is always projecting towards the center of the desktop.

Moving Modules

You can move modules around on the Control Strip (changing the order in which they appear) by holding the **Option** key down while you drag a module to its new location. (The cursor changes to a closed hand while you hold down the **Option** key.) The rest of the modules move to accommodate the new order.

Stripping the Strip

You can easily remove any Control Strip modules that you don't use. Open the Control Strip Modules folder that is within the System Folder. Drag the useless modules out of the folder and put them in a different folder. (You might want to create a folder to store them rather than throwing them out.) Restart your iMac. The buttons you removed no longer appear on the Control Strip.

Fast Access to the System Folder

A quick way to access the System Folder is to open the About This Computer window (the command is on the **Apple** menu), and then double-click the small **Mac OS** icon. When you do so, the System Folder opens.

Building Up the Strip

You can re-install modules you already have or you can add new functions to your Control Strip by adding modules to it. Control Strip modules are available in many places, including the Internet. After you find a module you want to add to the Control Strip, drag it onto your closed System Folder and your iMac puts the module into the Control Strip Modules folder (or you can place it there yourself). Restart your iMac and the new controls are available on the strip.

If you find yourself wishing that some feature you use regularly had a Control Strip module for it, it probably does. Do a search on the Internet (remember Sherlock!) in your favorite Mac shareware sites to see what modules are available. It is likely that a module exits that does what you need. Just install it, and you can quickly access that function from the Control Strip.

The Least You Need to Know

➤ To use the Control Strip, click its buttons to reveal pop-up menus containing commands and controls.

➤ To hide the Control Strip, click either end of it; click again to open it up.

➤ Hold down the **Option** key and drag the tab to move the strip around on the screen.

➤ Hold down the **Option** key and drag a module to move it around on the strip.

➤ You can add or remove modules from the Control Strip by adding or removing them from the Control Strip Modules folder.

➤ Look around on the Net for additional modules that you can download and add to your Control Strip.

Chapter 21

Not-So-Stupid Finder Tricks

In This Chapter

➤ Make your iMac tell time accurately—all the time

➤ Set your function keys to open files, applications, servers, and Web pages

➤ Create and use Keychains to store all your network and Internet passwords so you have to remember only one

➤ Configure locations to make moving around easier

The Finder is the underlying application that controls how your iMac works. When you are working on the desktop, moving files, creating folders, and so on, you are working with the Finder. In addition to all-too-obvious tricks, the Finder has a lot of other useful tricks up its electronic sleeves. Although these tricks probably won't get your iMac on the *David Letterman Show*, they are certainly worthy of being in your studio.

Take an iLook

It's About More Than Just Telling Time

Aside from making it easy for you to see what time and date it is, having the correct time and date information is important for your iMac. In addition to setting the time and date on all the files you create and modify, your email is also time- and date-stamped when you send it.

Telling Time (and Date)

I am sure you have noticed your iMac has a nice little clock in the upper-right corner of the desktop; this is handy for keeping track of time as you work. When you used the Mac OS Setup Assistant, you told your iMac what time it was, and after your iMac's clock was set, it began keeping track of the time for you. You also set the date in the Assistant; you can click on the time to see the current date.

The Finder has a couple of time tricks that may not be so obvious to the casual iMac observer.

Setting the Time and Date on Your Own

The Date & Time control panel controls the iMac's internal clock. To get to it, open the **Apple** menu, then the **Control Panels** folder, and then the Date & Time control panel (see Figure 21.1). At the top of the window are controls you can use to set the time and date as well as the formats in which they appear. To make a change, click the number you want to change and use the up and down arrows to change it. To change the formats, click the appropriate button and set it to look as you want it to.

Figure 21.1

You can use the Date & Time control panel to make sure iMac is always on time.

In the Time Zone area, you should tell your iMac about the daylight savings status in your area. If you pick a city in your time zone and tell your iMac to set Daylight-Savings time automatically, you won't ever have to remember when to spring forward and when to fall back.

Setting the Time with a Server

You may have set your iMac's time with your watch or other clock that may or may not be accurate. Being an iMac owner, I am sure you want your iMac to be as accurate as possible, right? I am glad you feel this way because your iMac can use a time server to set its time accurately and keep it that way. All you need is your Internet account.

Open the **Date & Time** control panel. Check the **Use a Network Time Server** check box. Click the **Server Options** button. You will see the Server Options dialog box. Choose **network time server** from the pop-up menu at the top of the dialog box. You can use one of Apple's time servers or add one of your own.

Making Your Clock Pretty

Click the **Clock Options** button at the bottom of the Date & Time control panel, and you can set all sorts of options for the way the clock works, including how it looks, what it displays, chimes, and so on.

Test

If you don't see any difference in time when you tell your iMac to Set Time Now, it may be that your clock is already synchronized with your Network Time Server. To test your configuration, change your Mac's time so it's wrong. Then try synchronizing your iMac to the Network Time Server. If you have used a valid Network Time Server, the time on your iMac will be updated.

Use the radio buttons to determine at what times the time is set. You can have your iMac automatically update its time setting, check it at a specified interval, or only when you tell it to. Use the **Set Time Now** button to have your clock synchronized. Your iMac connects to the Net and sets its clock. Click **OK** to close the dialog box and then close the control panel.

Talking Trash

One of the most recognizable features of the Mac OS is the Trash. Ever since the first Mac was introduced, the Trash has been a part of the Mac experience. As you know, the Trash is actually a special folder on your Mac that has certain unique features, those being that you can delete files by placing them in the Trash and then emptying it, and unmounting a network volumes and ejecting disks by dragging them there.

Take an iLook

The iMac Is Fairly Intuitive, But...

After you learn you can eject a disk by dragging it to the Trash, you don't have trouble with the idea. But it is far from intuitive to do this. Why would anyone think dragging a disk to the Trash would do anything other than delete the files on it? I'm not sure how this idea became part of the Mac, but it sure is contrary to how intuitive the rest of the iMac is. I guess no one, or no computer, is perfect.

The Trash is pretty easy to work with. The following are some things to keep in mind when working with the Trash:

➤ If the warning when you empty the Trash annoys you (like it does me), you can turn it off. Select the **Trash**, press ⌘+**I**, and uncheck the **Warn before emptying** check box. The next time you empty the Trash, it will be emptied without warning you first.

➤ There are many ways to move things into the Trash. You can drag something there. You can select a file or folder and press ⌘+**Delete**. You can select a file or folder, press **Control**, click the mouse button, and choose **Move to Trash** from the contextual menu.

➤ If you try to Empty the Trash when it contains something that is locked, you will see a dialog box telling you the locked item can't be deleted. Hold down the **Option** key while you choose **Empty Trash** to delete locked items.

➤ There are also a couple of ways to empty the Trash. One is to select **Empty Trash** from the **Special** menu. You can also select **Trash** and use its contextual menu to choose **Empty Trash.**

Doing a Lot with a Single Key Press

You probably don't use the function keys on the keyboard very much. However, you can set these keys to do what you want. For example, because you will be checking your email frequently, you may want to be able to open Outlook Express by pressing a function key. To do this, you use the Keyboard control panel.

Open the **Apple** menu, then the **Control Panels** folder, and then the **Keyboard** control panel. At the top of this dialog box, there are controls you can use to configure the keyboard layout for particular countries. In the middle of the window are sliders you can use to set key repeat rates and delays. These controls can be useful, but the good stuff is under the **Function Keys** button. Click this button and you will see a function key map (see Figure 21.2). Using this map, you can open any file, application, or even AppleScript with the push of a button.

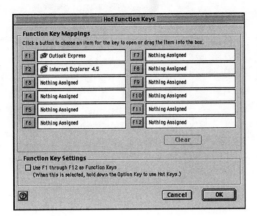

Figure 21.2

You can use this function keyboard map to assign your own actions to the function keys. (You can see that I have set F1 to open Outlook Express and F2 to open Internet Explorer.)

AppleScript?

AppleScript is the Mac's built-in scripting language that enables you to automate many actions. You can build complex macros that will perform complex tasks for you. When you run a script, the task is accomplished with no further action on your part. Your iMac comes with a number of AppleScripts ready for you to run. These are located in the Automated Tasks and More Automated Tasks folders in the AppleScript folder within the Apple Extras folder. To run an AppleScript, double-click it or assign it to a function key.

To map an action to a function key, click the function key you want to press for that action. In the **Assign Key** dialog box, move to the item you want to open, such as a file, application, server, or AppleScript. Select the item and click **Assign**. When you return to the function key map, you will see that your item has been assigned to that key. Set the additional function keys in the same way. When you are done, click **OK**. Then close the Keyboard control panel.

To open an item you have assigned to a function key, press the assigned function key. Cool, isn't it!

Quick Way to the Web

If you create an Internet Location file to a Web site (by dragging its URL from Internet Explorer to the desktop), you can assign it to a function key. To access that site, press the function key. Internet Explorer opens and moves to the site. It doesn't get any easier than that.

Driver Update

If you connect a USB device for which you do not have the appropriate driver installed, the Software Update finds and downloads the appropriate driver for you.

Keeping Your iMac Up-to-Date

Apple is continually updating and upgrading the software that makes your iMac hum. You don't have to worry about keeping your iMac up-to-date because it can do that for itself.

Open the **Software Update** control panel. To manually update your software, click the **Update Now** button. Your iMac logs on to the Net and searches for any updates. If it finds some, they are downloaded to your iMac.

For added convenience, you can have your iMac automatically check for software updates. Click the **Update software automatically** button and then the **Set Schedule** button. Set your schedule—you can have it checked daily if you want to, but that is a bit much. Once a week is reasonable. When you have the schedule set, click **OK**. If you want the process to be handled automatically, uncheck the **Ask me before downloading new software** check box. Otherwise, you will have to be on your iMac to give it permission to download what you need. Close the control panel. Your iMac will now look after itself software-wise.

Remembering Passwords— Who Needs It!

In today's world, everyone is connected to Web sites, network servers, and so on. For security and other reasons (such as making online shopping more convenient), you usually need usernames and passwords to access these resources. After using a few, you will have a pile of usernames and passwords that you have to remember. Unless you are a world-class rememberer (Is that a word?—I can't remember!), you will struggle to remember which username and password set goes with which resource. Fortunately, your iMac lets you store all of your usernames and passwords in a Keychain. You can then apply your Keychain to whatever resource you want to use and the appropriate information is provided to access what you need. All you need to remember is the password that unlocks your Keychain.

Creating a Keychain

Open the Keychain Access control panel. If you have not already created a Keychain, you are prompted to do so. (If you want to create a new Keychain, open the **File** menu and choose **New Keychain**.) In the **Create Keychain** dialog box, name your Keychain and enter a password you will use to unlock the Keychain. (Pick something longer than six letters and has both numbers and letters in it—try to make it something you can remember but that other people won't be able to guess.) Click **Create**. You will see the Keychain Access window with the name of your Keychain in the title bar (see Figure 21.3).

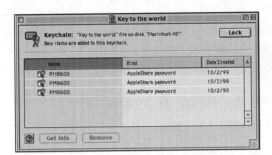

Figure 21.3

This Keychain has the passwords in it that I need to access the PM8600 computer on my network.

Locking and Unlocking Your Keychain

When your Keychain is locked, it can't be changed or even used. If other people have access to your iMac, you should always keep your Keychain locked. When you need to use it, or when you want to make changes to it (such as adding a new resource), you need to unlock it.

There are several ways to lock a Keychain. The fastest is to use the **Keychain Access** button on the Control Strip. Click the button and choose **Lock All Keychains** from the menu. (You can also lock a Keychain individually by selecting it from the menu.) You can also click the **Lock** button in the Keychain's window to lock it.

As you might guess, there are a couple of ways to unlock a Keychain as well. Click the **Keychain Access** button on the Control Strip and choose **Unlock Keychain**. Enter the Keychain's password and click **Unlock**. You will see the Keychain's window. You can also open the Keychain Access control panel, choose the Keychain in the **Unlock Keychain** pop-up menu, enter your password, and click **Unlock**.

After a Keychain is unlocked, passwords can be added to it or removed from it and you can use it to access secured resources.

Where Are My Keys?

The Keychain files are stored in the Keychains folder in the Preferences folder in the System Folder. You can unlock and access a Keychain by double-clicking its file. You can also add these files to the Favorites or Apple menu for easy access. You can quickly access the Keychain folder by choosing **Show Available Keychains** from the **Keychain Access** button on the Control Strip.

Adding Passwords to Your Keychain

There are a couple of ways to add passwords to your Keychain. But before you learn how to do that, you need to know that not all applications support Keychain Access. If these steps don't work, check the documentation that came with the application you are trying to work with to see if it does support a Keychain.

Keychains Are Cool, But...

The power of a Keychain is that you have to remember only one password to access many secured resources. The bad thing about a Keychain is that you have to remember only one password to access many secured resources. Remember that when your Keychain is unlocked, anyone who can access your iMac can also access what the Keychain can. This can be dangerous, so make sure if your iMac can be used by others, you always keep the Keychain locked.

Some applications provide a dialog box that enables you to add a resource to your Keychain from a dialog box. A good example of this is the dialog box you see when you log on to an AppleShare server. If you are on a network, open the **Chooser** and click on the **AppleShare** icon. Your iMac searches for available servers and displays them in the right side of the Chooser window. Choose a server and click **OK**. You see the AppleShare connection dialog box. Enter your name and password, check the

Add to Keychain check box, and click **Connect**. In the next dialog box, choose the items to which you want to connect, click the **Save My Name and Password in the Keychain** check box, and click **OK**. The volumes are mounted on your desktop. Close the Chooser. Move back to your Keychain and you will see that the resource has been added to it.

The other (and easier) way to add passwords to your Keychain is by dragging and dropping the resource onto the Keychain's window. When you do, you are prompted to enter your username and password for that resource. Enter them, and then click **Add**. That resource is added to your Keychain. This works for both AppleShare resources and Internet sites.

Move to an Internet site for which you need a password (such as a shopping site). Enter your password and username and log into the site. After you are logged in, drag the URL from the Address bar in Internet Explorer to your desktop to create an Internet Location file for that site. Drag that file from your desktop onto your Keychain. Enter the username and password you need for that site. The Internet site is added to your Keychain.

Unlocking the World with Your Keys

The whole point of having a Keychain is to use it, right? As with most things Macintosh, there is more than one way to use your Keychain.

Open your **Keychain**, unlock it, and double-click on a resource. You will see an information window for that resource (see Figure 21.4). Click the **Go There** button. A dialog box appears asking for confirmation that your iMac should allow the Keychain to be used—choose the settings you feel most comfortable with. Allowing access without warning requires the least action from you, but is the most unsecure. When you have decided on your access settings, click **Allow**; your Keychain is applied to that resource and the resource is opened for you. If it's a volume on your network, it is mounted on your desktop. If it's a Web site, your iMac connects to it and you can view the site.

Figure 21.4

*Clicking the **Go There** button takes you to a resource on your Keychain.*

You can also drag a resource on your Keychain to your desktop to create a locator file to it. To access the resource, double-click the file, enter your Keychain password (if it is locked), and the resource opens in the appropriate window (for example, Internet Explorer if the resource is a Web page).

After you have acquired a password or twenty, the Keychain capability of your iMac will make your life a lot easier. You are likely to end up with dozens of usernames and passwords from the Internet alone. Being able to access all of these with a single password is a lifesaver for the memory-challenged (like me).

Viewing Passwords

Should you forget the password to a site and need it again someday, you can click the **Verify Password** button. After you enter the password for your Keychain, you will see the password to the resource.

Using Your iMac in Many Locations

The iMac is a luggable computer—its all-in-one design and carrying handle make it relatively easy to move around. Although you wouldn't want to try to carry it around an airport, you can easily take it with you and use it in new locations. (For example, you might want to lug it to a friend's house for a quick gaming session.) However, the iMac settings are dependent on where you happen to be at the moment. For example, the number you use to connect to the Internet may be different at different locations; it may be a different number or you may need to add an area code or special dialing codes.

With the Location Manager, you can set up different configurations and easily switch between them. This prevents you from having to manually reconfigure your iMac each time you move around with it.

Setting Up a Location

Before you configure a location, you need to configure your iMac as you want it to be when it uses that location. When it is set up, open the **Control Panels** folder and then open the **Location Manager** control panel (or use the Location Manager button on the Control Strip). Choose **New Location** from the **File** menu. Name your location and click **Save**. You return to the Location Manager window and see the various settings you can configure as part of a location.

Click the check box next to an area of settings that you want to be part of the location. You will see information relating to those settings in the Values pane. Click **Edit** if you want to change the settings for that area. If you have to use a control panel for that area, you will be able to open it from within Location Manager. (Some settings cannot be edited from within Location Manager.) When you are finished editing the settings, click **Apply** to apply them to the location. (They will overwrite the current settings.)

To learn more about an area, select it and click **Get Info**. Click **OK** when you are done reading about it. Repeat these steps for each area you want to be set by the location. When you are done defining a location, press ⌘**+S** to save it. Quit Location Manager.

Changing Locations

After you have your configurations established, it is simple to switch among those locations to reconfigure your iMac. Click the **Location Manager** control on the **Control Strip**. Choose the location you want to use from the pop-up menu. You will see a window showing you the progress of all the settings being changed to the location's values.

Take an iLook

Another Way

If you don't use the Control Strip, you can open **Location Manager** and choose a location from the **Current Location** pop-up menu at the top of the control panel window.

If the location change involves extensions, control panels, or other components loaded into the system, you have to restart your iMac by clicking **Restart**. If not, click the **OK** button to close the window. Your iMac is now configured for your new location. If you regularly work from different locations, setting up locations using Location Manager can be a great labor saving tool.

The Least You Need to Know

➤ Use the Date & Time control panel to set the correct time and date.

➤ If you really want to be accurate, use a time server to keep your iMac's clock on time all the time.

➤ Getting rid of the annoying warning when you empty the trash is easy; choose **Trash**, press ⌘**+I**, and then uncheck the check box.

➤ Use the Keyboard control panel to assign files, servers, and scripts to the function keys on your iMac; then you can open these items with a single button push.

➤ Use Keychains so you have to remember only one password; this may be the greatest feature of them all.

➤ Use the Location Manager so you can quickly change between configurations for different areas from which you use your iMac.

FILES!! FILES
FOR EVERYONE!!

Chapter 22

Don't Be Stingy— Share Your iMac and Its Files

In This Chapter

➤ Set up multiple user accounts on your iMac. (You may find yourself having to share your iMac more than you want to!)

➤ Access resources on a network using the Chooser and the Network Browser

➤ Use File Sharing to enable others to access resources on your iMac

Your iMac is meant for sharing. From being able to create custom accounts for everyone who uses your machine to its excellent networking capabilities that you can use to share files, your iMac definitely gets high marks for citizenship.

Letting Others Use Your iMac—the Worry-Free Way

Your iMac is one of the most attractive computers ever made. With its appealing looks and great features, people will have a hard time keeping their hands off your machine. And with Mac OS 9, you can let other people use your machine without being concerned that they will change something you don't want them to. You can create custom accounts for everyone who uses your machine; you determine which accounts can access which applications, files, CD-ROMs, and so on.

No Multiple Users Allowed

If you are running Mac OS 8.6 on your iMac, you won't be able to create multiple accounts. This feature was added in Mac OS 9; if you want this feature, you will have to upgrade your operating system software. (To check which version you are running, open the **Apple** menu and then choose **About This Computer**.)

Setting Up User Accounts

The first thing to do when designating individual accounts on your iMac is set up user accounts. To do this, open the **Apple** menu, then the **Control Panels** folder, and then the **Multiple Users** control panel. In the dialog box that appears, you will see that a user account has been created with your name—as you entered it when you used the Mac OS Setup Assistant (see Figure 22.1). The password for the account is also the same as you entered in the Mac OS Setup Assistant. This account can access *everything* on your iMac, so be careful to whom you give this password!

Figure 22.1

When you first open the Multiple Users control panel, you will see an owner account with your name.

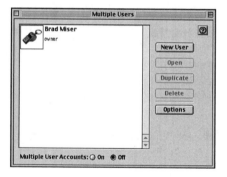

To enable multiple user accounts, click the **On** radio button. Then click the **New User** button. You will see the **Edit New User** dialog box. Enter the user name for the new account, press **Tab**, and enter a password. Click **Show Setup Details**, and you will see the Setup Details window (see Figure 22.2).

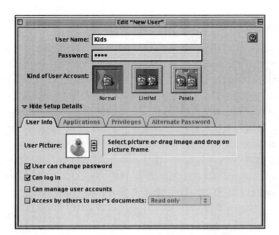

Figure 22.2

You use the Setup Details window to control the options of each user account.

Next, choose the kind of user account this user will have by clicking the appropriate button. The following three types of user accounts are available:

➤ **A Normal account**—Enables the user to access the hard disk and all applications on the startup disk, but not the documents in other users' document folders. Normal accounts provide the most access to your iMac, so use Normal accounts only for those people who know how to use a Mac fairly well. Normal accounts are the easiest to set up.

➤ **A Limited account**—Enables the user to access only limited Finder functions and features and a defined set of applications (not to mention only being able to access his own documents). The interface a Limited user sees will look just like the one a Normal user uses.

What's in a Password?

You probably don't need to get too complicated with your password. Remember to keep the user in mind when you create it—if you want young children to be able to log on, you need to keep the password simple.

➤ **A Panels account**—Provides the user with panels in the Button view (single clicking a button opens the item). There is an Items panel that contains the applications the user can access. There is also a panel for the user's document. If the user can access network disks, there will be a panel for each network resource. If there are too many panels to fit on the screen, some panels will appear as pop-up windows at the bottom of the desktop.

Setting the Details

Click the **User Info** tab. (If you choose a Normal account, this is the only tab you can select.) Choose a picture for the account (this will appear next to the account name in the logon window) by clicking the up and down arrows (or you can drag a picture you want to use onto the User Picture window). Check or uncheck the other check boxes as appropriate to the user. If you want the user to be able to select her own password, check the **User can change password** check box. You should always leave the **Can log in** box checked. Leave the **Can manage user accounts** check box unchecked unless you want another user to be able to set up and change user accounts. If you want other users to be able to access documents created by this user, check the **Access by others to user's documents** check box and choose an access option from the pop-up menu (such as Read only or Write only).

Not Everyone Needs Their Own Account

Remember that an account is a set of access privileges and is not necessarily tied to an individual. For example, if you have kids and you want them to be able to use your iMac, you can create a single account for all of them to use. You can create another account for your spouse (that would presumably have greater access than the kids' account).

Limiting Access

If you choose a Limited or Panels account type, click the **Applications** tab. You use this tab's window to determine which applications the user will be able to access. Scroll down the list and check the box next to the applications you want the user to be able to use.

If you want the user to be able to access most of the applications in the window, click the **Select All** button and uncheck the boxes next to the applications you don't want the user to access. If the file or template you want to allow access to is not shown in the list, click the **Add Other** button and move to the application to select it. Use the **Show** pop-up menu to determine which applications are shown in the window.

Click the **Privileges** tab. Check the check boxes next to the items you want this user to be able to access. For example, if you don't want the user to be able to use control panels to change the operating system, make sure the **Control Panels** check box is unchecked. If you want the user to be able to access network resources, check the **Chooser and Network Browser** check boxes. If you want to limit access to CD-ROMs to specific material, check the **List for restricted users** radio button.

Speaking Your Way onto the iMac

You can allow users to speak a phrase to log on to their account rather than typing their information. This is cool, and it can also be helpful for very young users. To allow this, click the **Options** button back in the Multiple Users dialog box and check the **Allow Alternate Password** check box. (Make sure that Voice Verification appears in the pop-up menu.) Click **Save** and move back to the Edit New User dialog box.

Now click the **Alternate Password** tab. Click **Create Voiceprint**. Click **Change Phrase**. Type the phrase you want the user to speak (each user can have their own phrase); you should use a phrase that contains at least five words. Click **OK** and then click **Continue**.

Now record the phrase the user will speak—you have to have the user who will be using this account speak the phrase while it is being recorded. Click **Record First**. You will see the Recording window. Click **Record** and have the user speak the phrase shown at the top of the window. When she finishes speaking it, click **Stop**. Click **Play** to hear the phrase. If it sounds right, click **Done**. Continue this until you have made four recordings.

Now click **Try It**. You are prompted to speak the phrase. Speak it or have the user speak it if you are creating an account for someone else. If the iMac recognizes the phrase, you will see a dialog box saying the voiceprint is good. If not, you will have to re-record the phrase.

When you have all the options set for this user, close the window. You will see the user account that you created listed in the Multiple Users window.

Setting Global Options

You can set global options that affect all user accounts. To set these global options, click the **Options** button in the Multiple Users window, and you will see the Global Multiple User Options window (see Figure 22.3). Click the **Login** tab to set the login options. Enter a welcome message and use the check boxes to select the other options you want to set. For example, if you want the user to be logged out after a specific period of inactivity, check the **If the user is idle for** check box, enter the time period, and click the **Log out** user radio button.

Figure 22.3

You can use the global options settings to enter options that will apply to all accounts (such as my clever welcome message).

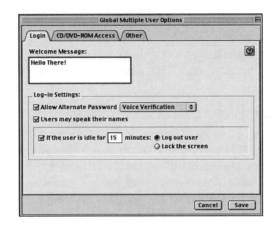

To limit access to CD-ROM material for restricted users, click the **CD/DVD-ROM Access** tab, insert the CD into the iMac, and click the **Add to List** button. Use the Restrict Content To window to limited access of particular files on the CD. The items you choose in this window will affect all the users for whom you clicked the List for Restricted Users radio button when you set up the account.

Don't Forget Your Password!

As the administrator of your iMac, you need to make sure you can remember your password. If not, you won't be able to change the options set for other accounts, including your own. You won't even be able to log on to your own account! You may have a lot of trouble recovering from this, so remember your password!

Click the **Other** tab and use the radio and check boxes to set the options you want. You probably won't need to change any of these options. For example, you probably will want users to be able to click on their account in a list rather than having to type their names to log on. Click **Save** when you are done.

You change the settings for any account by selecting it in the Multiple Users window and then clicking **Open**. You will see the same window you saw when you created the account, and you can change any of the account's settings.

Close the control panel. You need to log out or restart the iMac to make the accounts active. From the **Special** menu, choose **Logout**. Click **Yes** in the dialog box and you are logged off your iMac.

Logging On with a User Account

When you are logged off, you will see the login window (see Figure 22.4). Notice that your login message appears at the top of the window and that the pictures you chose appear next to the account names. To log on under an account, click on the account and then click the **Log in** button. Enter the password for that account and click **OK**. If you allow the user to speak a phrase to logon, he is prompted to speak the phrase. If you enter the correct password or if the voiceprint is recognized, the iMac initializes the options you chose for that account.

Figure 22.4

The login screen greets you each time your start up your iMac or when you log off of it.

The desktop reappears, and you will notice two folders on the desktop that relate to the account under which you logged on. One folder, called *Items for username*, contains aliases to all the applications that the user can access. The other folder, called *username*, is where the user can store documents. If you enabled the user to share documents, the documents the user can share will be within a folder called Shared Documents that is within this folder.

If the account is a Panels account, the desktop will look quite different. You will see the various panels containing the items you can access. To use an item, click its button.

When you are done with this account, open the **Special** menu and choose **Logout**. You will move back to the Login window. Choose a different account or click the **Shutdown** button to turn the iMac off.

273

Sharing and Sharing Alike

With its built-in Ethernet port and its amazing AirPort technology, your iMac is ideally suited for networking so you can share files. With file sharing, you can access files and other resources on other computers just as if those resources were installed on your iMac. And you can make the resources on your iMac available to other computers on the network.

Adding Your iMac to a Network

There are several ways to gain access to a network. One is to use an Ethernet crossover cable to connect the Ethernet port on your iMac to an Ethernet port on another computer. Another is to use a "regular" Ethernet cable to connect the Ethernet port on your iMac to an Ethernet hub on a network. Yet another way is to connect an AirPort Base Station to a network using an Ethernet cable; then you can

use your iMac's AirPort card to wirelessly connect to that network through the Base Station. Lastly, you can use your AirPort card to wirelessly connect to other AirPort equipped devices (such as other iMacs or G4 desktop Macs that have an AirPort card installed) that are connected to a network.

After the physical connection (or wireless one if you are using AirPort) is made, all you have to do is tell your iMac where to look for the network. You do this in the AppleTalk control panel. Open the **Apple** menu, choose **Control Panels**, and then choose **AppleTalk**. Use the pop-up menu to choose the location through which your iMac should connect to the network. For example, to use the physical Ethernet port, choose **Ethernet** from the pop-up menu. When you are done, close the control panel and save your changes.

Do You Do Windows?

You can connect to networks based on other computers, such as Windows NT, but those networks will have to be configured to allow your iMac to access them. You will need to talk to the network's administrator to see if you can connect your iMac to that network.

Your iMac will now be able to access other computers and resources that are on the network.

Borrowing from Others

You can access files that others on your network make available to you. The following steps get you there:

1. Get the username and password you have been assigned for the resource you want to use. (These must be provided by the owner of that resource.)

2. Use the Chooser or the Network Browser to select a drive containing the files you want to use.

3. Enter your username and password to log on to that shared volume. That resource appears on your iMac's desktop.

4. Use the files you want to share. (What you can do will depend on the permissions you have been assigned.)

Take an iLook

Transferring Instead of Sharing

If you want to transfer a folder or file to your iMac instead of sharing it, simply drag it to your desktop or hard drive just as you would from a CD-ROM or other removable media. The folder or file is copied to the volume to which you drag it. Any changes you make to it will not affect the original, and you don't need to be connected to the network to use your copy of it.

Managing Your Connections with the Chooser

The following two basic steps enable you to use the files and folders on a networked computer:

1. Use the Chooser to log on to a file server. (A file server is simply another computer on the network that is sharing its resources with other computers on the network.)

2. Choose the volumes on the server that you want to work with. Those volumes will be available for your use.

Be an iMac Wizard

Volume?

A volume is sort of like a disk except that a volume is an electronic construct rather than a physical device. A physical disk can be electronically divided into partitions, and each partition looks and acts just like a physical disk. These partitions are called volumes.

To log on to a file server, choose **Chooser** from the **Apple** menu. In the left pane of the Chooser window, click **AppleShare**. In the right pane of the window, you will see a list of currently available file server names that you can use. Click a server name in the right pane and click **OK** (or double-click the file server name). You will see the **Connect to** dialog box. Enter your username and password and click **Connect**.

Now you will see a list of volumes that are on that file server and that you can access. To use a volume, double-click it. It appears on your desktop, and you can work with it just like you do the hard drive that is part of your iMac.

Mounting

By the way, logging onto a file server is often called *mounting* it on your desktop. When you mount a file server or removable disk (such as a CD-ROM), it becomes visible on your desktop and you can work with it.

Use a Keychain

You can set up a Keychain to be able to quickly access shared resources. See Chapter 21, "Not-So-Stupid Finder Tricks," for details about the Keychain.

Putting Away Shared Volumes

You can also "unmount" a shared volume by selecting it and pressing ⌘+Y (the Put Away command).

If you will regularly use this resource and want it to be mounted each time you start up your iMac, check the check box next to the volume's name when you select the items you want to use. Use the radio buttons to determine that your username or username and password are remembered so you don't have to type them each time a volume is mounted.

When you are done, close the Chooser.

When you return to the desktop, you will see the volume mounted on your desktop. You can treat a mounted volume just like you treat a mounted floppy disk, Zip disk, or whatever. Double-click on the volume's icon to open its window. Use any files that you can access. (You may be limited to certain folders or you may only be able to read files rather than change them.) When you want to terminate your connection to the remote machine, just drag the server's icon into the Trash.

Managing Your Connections with Network Browser

The Network Browser enables you to connect to various machines on your network as well as on the Internet. You can also use it to create favorites for quick access to servers, and it presents a consistent interface for network devices.

From the **Apple** menu, choose **Network Browser**. Its window opens, and you will see all the neighborhoods (such as the AppleTalk neighborhood for the local network) that are available for sharing. (If one or more of the neighborhoods are on the Internet, your iMac dials out to connect to your Internet account.)

To log on to a file server on a local network, click the expansion triangle next to the AppleTalk icon. You will see the servers available to you. To use a server, double-click its icon. You will see the **Connect to** dialog box. Enter the name and password you were assigned by the owner of the shared item and click **OK**. You will see a window representing the file server that shows all the volumes of the server that are available to you (see Figure 22.5). Double-click a volume to work with the files on it.

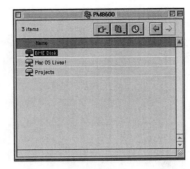

Figure 22.5

The PM8600 file server has three volumes I can access.

The Network Browser has some nice features, including the following:

➤ **Expansion triangles**—If you click the expansion triangles next to a file server or volume in the Network window, the item will be expanded. (If you aren't logged on, you will have to do so before the item will expand.) This works just like a Finder window in List view.

➤ **Shortcuts button**—This button enables you to access the Network window and the Connect to Server command. The Connect to Server command enables you to connect to an AppleShare server with an Internet Protocol address or a Uniform Resource Locator address.

➤ **Favorites button**—The Favorites button enables you to add file servers to your Favorites folder (on the Apple menu) for quick access. You can also access your favorite file servers by selecting them from this menu.

➤ **Recent button**—This button enables you to move back to recently used file servers.

➤ **Back and Forward buttons**—These buttons move you back or forward to previously viewed items.

Sharing Your Good Stuff

To share the resources on your iMac with others, follow these steps:

1. Set up File Sharing on your iMac.
2. Share folders and files that live on your iMac.

Setting Up File Sharing

Before you can use File Sharing, you have to turn it on. Open the **File Sharing** control panel (see Figure 22.6). You should see the Owner name, password, and computer name you entered in the Mac OS Setup Assistant. Under the File Sharing section, click **Start**. You will see a status message telling you that File Sharing is starting. The start-up process may take a little while, depending on your iMac and the network to which you are connected. Close the control panel. After File Sharing has finished starting up, your iMac is ready to share.

Figure 22.6

The File Sharing control panel enables you to share your treasures with the world.

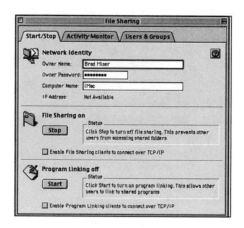

Sharing Files and Folders

After File Sharing is active, you can share individual items on your iMac with the people on your network. For each item, you will assign one of the following four privileges levels:

Control Strip

You can also turn File Sharing off or on with the **File Sharing** button on the Control Strip.

➤ **Read & Write**—When you assign someone to have Read & Write privileges to an item, they can do anything to the item.

➤ **Read only**—This level means they can read the item, but can't make any changes to it.

➤ **Write only (Drop Box)**—When you choose this level, users can place things in the folder, but cannot see anything that is contained in it.

➤ **None**—When you choose None, users will not be able to see the item.

You can assign these items to the following three categories of user:

➤ **Owner**—This is the person who controls the item. For most of the items that exist on your iMac to be shared, this should be you.

➤ **User/Group**—These are specific users or a group to whom you assign privileges for an item.

➤ **Everyone**—Everyone on the network shares these privileges.

In the Finder, select the item you want to share. From the Finder's **File** menu, choose **Get Info** and then **Sharing**. You will see the Sharing pane of the Get Info window for that item (see Figure 22.7).

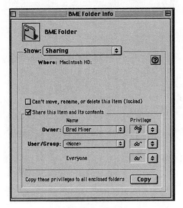

Figure 22.7

The Sharing pane of the Get Info window enables you to set the sharing options for a particular item.

Check the **Can't move, rename, or delete this item (locked)** check box if you don't want users to be able to do any of these things. Check the **Share this item and its contents** check box. Ensure that your name appears in **the Owner** pop-up menu, and choose the level of access you want the owner to have; normally, this will be Read & Write access (the glasses and pencil icon). Set the level of sharing privilege for Everyone on the network (for example, Read Only so other people can't change the item). If you want to copy all of the sharing settings for this item to each item within it, click **Copy**. The window displays the sharing privileges you have set for this item. Close the Info window.

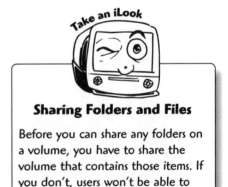

Sharing Folders and Files

Before you can share any folders on a volume, you have to share the volume that contains those items. If you don't, users won't be able to share any contents of that volume.

279

Users and Groups

Rather than equally sharing an item with everyone on a network, you can define users and groups and set permissions for that group for an item. For example, you can define a read-only group and assign users to it. When you share a folder with this group, people can read things in the folder but can't change them.

Because you aren't likely to need to do this with a small network, I don't cover the details of setting up user accounts in this chapter. However, here's a thumbnail sketch of how to do it: To set up user accounts, open the **File Sharing** control panel and click the **Users & Groups** tab. This window enables you to define user accounts and to place users in groups. You can set access to items for these users and groups with the **User/Group** pop-up menu in the Sharing pane of the Info window for an item.

The icon of the item changes to reflect the sharing privileges you have applied to it, and now the item can be accessed by others on the network as you have indicated.

The Least You Need to Know

➤ Setting up multiple user accounts is useful when several people will be using your iMac and you don't want everyone to be able to access everything on the machine.

➤ To set up multiple accounts, use the Multiple Users control panel.

➤ To use network resources, connect your iMac to a network, get the username and password you have been assigned, use the Chooser or Network Browser to log on to available files servers, and mount the volumes containing the resources you want to use.

➤ To share your files with others, connect to a network, turn File Sharing on, select the item you want to share, and use the Sharing pane in the Get Info window to share the item.

Chapter 23

Beating the System

In This Chapter

➤ Master the mysterious System Folder

➤ Learn how to manage the all-important RAM

➤ Install cool USB devices

Your journey toward iMac wizardry is almost complete. Now it's time to explore the inner depths of your iMac and learn from where all its secrets and mysteries come— the System Folder.

Beat the System by Understanding the System Folder

The System Folder is a special folder; it contains all the software that makes your iMac work (see Figure 23.1). The files in the System Folder determine most everything about how your iMac runs as well as what it can do—as goes the System Folder, so goes your iMac. If something serious gets messed up in the System Folder, your iMac may not even start up. (No worries; you'll learn how to handle this situation in the Appendix.)

Figure 23.1

The System Folder is the heart of your iMac; get comfortable with it and you will be way ahead of the iMac game.

To be an iMac wizard, you need to understand and be comfortable with the System Folder. During the preceding chapters, you manipulated quite a few parts of the System Folder, especially control panels. You also learned about some of its folders, such as the Apple Menu Items folder.

Be Afraid?

You should maintain a good level of caution about messing around in the System Folder. If you change something without knowing what you are doing, you run the risk of making your iMac unusable. There are only a couple of files in the System Folder that can lead to this situation, and after you know what those are, you should feel fairly comfortable inside the System Folder.

It's time to take a more comprehensive view of the System Folder so you know what it contains. In the following sections, you'll learn about some of the folders you are more likely to need to understand.

In your System Folder, you are likely to see other folders or files than those I describe in this chapter. Some of these are part of the Mac OS, but I didn't think there was much chance you would need to fuss with them. You may also see other items that are installed by third-party software packages.

Appearance

In Chapter 14, "Giving Your iMac an iMakeover," you learned to use the Appearance control panel to change the way your iMac's desktop looks. The Appearance folder contains several folders that are used to store the files related to this control panel. These include the desktop pictures, sound sets, and theme files. You aren't likely to need to access the Appearance folder very often. The most likely case is one in which you are installing additional themes (which go in the Theme Files folder) or additional desktop pictures (which can be stored in the Desktop Pictures folder, but don't have to be).

Apple Menu Items

You also already know about the Apple Menu Items folder. In Chapter 19, "There Are No Red Delicious on This Apple Menu," you learned about the Apple menu. The Apple Menu Items folder contains all the files and folders (or their aliases) that appear on the Apple menu. Put files or folders in this folder to have them appear on the Apple menu; take files and folders out of this folder to remove them from the menu.

Contextual Menus Items

Contextual menus are cool because they enable you to quickly access menus that are specifically related to what you are doing at the moment. The iMac's Contextual menus are provided courtesy of the Contextual Menus Items folder. If you open the Contextual Menus Items folder, you will see that it contains several contextual menu files. You can add additional commands to the iMac's built-in contextual menus by adding contextual menu files to the Contextual Menus Items folder. Removing these files removes the contextual menus).

Control Panels

Control panels are pieces of software that are added to the operating system when it starts up. These control panels provide additional functionality that you can adjust by using a control panel to change settings. You have used all sorts of control panels throughout the book to control many aspects of your iMac. Mostly, you accessed the control panels through the convenient alias to the Control Panels folder on the Apple menu.

Take an iLook

Installing System Folder Stuff

The System Folder is smart enough to recognize most of the files you are likely to install in it, and the iMac automatically places them in the correct folder. For example, to install a control panel, simply drag the control panel icon onto the closed System Folder. Your iMac asks you if it is okay to put the file in the Control Panels folder. When you say **Yes**, your iMac places it there for you. This works with many of the other files you may install, such as extensions, Sherlock search sites, and so on.

The control panels themselves are stored in the Control Panels folder. This works just like other folders in the System Folder. To remove a control panel from the system (so its software does not load), remove it from the Control Panels folder. To install a control panel so it provides additional functionality, place it in the Control Panels folder.

Take an iLook

Disabled Folders?

You may also see twins to some of the folders in the System Folder except that they contain "(Disabled)" in their names, such as Control Panels (Disabled). These folders are holding areas for items you do not want to load during system startup but that you don't want to permanently delete. Extensions Manager (which you will learn about later in this chapter) creates the (Disabled) folders.

Open your Control Panels folder so you can see all the control panels that are installed. As you add third-party software to your iMac, the list of control panels will get even longer.

Control Strip Modules

The Control Strip provides quick access to lots of handy controls. Each button on the Control Strip has a file in the Control Strip Modules folder. To add a button to the Control Strip, add its file to this folder. (I'm sure that by now you can figure out how to remove one.)

Open the Control Strip Modules folder. You may see several buttons that do not appear on your Control Strip. That is because some of the modules are not applicable to the iMac. For example, the Media Bay module controls the media bays on PowerBook computers. Because you don't have a media bay, this control does not appear on your Control Strip.

Extensions

Like control panels, extensions are additional pieces of software that are added to the OS when your iMac starts up. Extensions also provide additional functionality to your iMac. The difference between an extension and a control panel is that you cannot adjust an extension. The software is either on (it's installed in the Extensions folder when you start your iMac) or it isn't (the extension is not in the Extensions folder when your start your iMac).

Open the Extensions folder to see the many extensions that are installed. You are also likely to add more extensions when you add additional third-party software to your iMac.

Take an iLook

March of the Icons

When you start your iMac, you will see a bunch of icons marching across the bottom of the screen. These icons show you the control panels and extensions that are installed on your iMac.

iWarning You

Troublemakers

Be aware that control panels and extensions are the most likely causes of problems you will experience. Actually, I should be more specific and say that *conflicting* control panels and extensions are the most likely cause of problems you experience. Sometimes certain control panels and extensions will not play well together. When this happens, all sorts of bad things can occur. You can usually fix the problem by disabling the offending control panel or extension. You will learn how to do this later in this chapter.

Favorites

The Favorites folder contains the files that will appear under the Favorites menu. Place items in this folder to add them to your Favorites or remove them from this folder to take them from your Favorites.

Finder

Ah, the Finder. The Finder is the application that manages most everything about your iMac. Never do anything with this file; if you mess it up, your iMac won't work.

I Was a Bit Hasty

When I said *never* do anything with the Finder file, I should have said never do anything with it unless you know what you are doing. There are utilities that enable you to make changes in the Finder (such as adding keyboard shortcuts to commands). Use one of these only if you are *really* comfortable with the innards of your iMac.

Fonts

One of the neat things about using an iMac is that you can use all sorts of fonts in your document. To make a font available, install it in the Fonts folder. To remove a font, remove it from the Fonts folder.

Internet Search Sites

As you learned in Chapter 13, "Sleuthing Around the World with Sherlock," Sherlock is the coolest way to search the Internet. The search sites you can use with Sherlock are stored in the Internet Search Sites folder.

Preferences

Most software you use has settings you can change to make the software better fit your personal preferences. These preferences are stored in preferences files in, you guessed it, the Preferences folder. Knowing about the Preferences folder can occasionally be useful. For example, if you have made so many changes to an application's preferences settings that it is no longer useful to you, you can sometimes remove its preferences file and all the settings will return to the default position.

Shutdown Items

Placing items in this folder causes them to be opened when your iMac shuts down. You may want to place a system sound file in this folder so you have a audible clue when the iMac is being turned off.

Startup Items

This works just like the Shutdown folder, but the files and folders you place in this one open after your iMac starts up. Putting sound files in this folder gives you an audible clue that your iMac is ready to work. If you use the same application every time you start your iMac, place an alias to that application in the Startup Items folder. The application will be opened automatically for you each time you start up your iMac. (Your email or Web browser applications might be good choices.)

Placing an Alias—the iMac Wizard Way

To quickly place an alias to a file in one of these folders, select the item for which you want to create an alias. Hold down the **Option** and ⌘ keys and drag the file onto the System Folder. Wait for the System Folder to spring open, then drag the icon onto the folder you want to place it in. When that folder springs open, release the mouse button. An alias is created in that folder. Close the folder.

System

The System file is a special type of file called a *suitcase*. A suitcase file is simply a container for other files. The System's suitcase contains system sounds and keyboard layouts. You can add system sounds to your iMac (that you can use as Alert sounds) by placing them inside the System file.

Extensions Manager Can Help You Deal with All of This

You can manually add or remove items from the folders in the System Folder to turn off or turn on capabilities. But this can be a bit of a pain, especially if you want to make these sorts of changes regularly. Extensions Manager is a utility that can help you manage your system software by making it easier to turn individual system items on or off. You can also create sets of configurations so you can switch between them easily.

Open the Control panels folder (use the **Apple** menu) and choose **Extensions Manager**. You will see the Extensions Manager window (see Figure 23.2). In the window, you can click the check box next to an item to turn it off. (If the check box has an "x" in it, the item is turned on.) When you are done changing settings, click the **Restart** button. After your iMac restarts, the system components you turned off will be off and you will not be able to use them. You can use Extensions Manager to turn them on again.

Figure 23.2

Extensions Manager enables you to turn control panels, extensions, and other system software off or on.

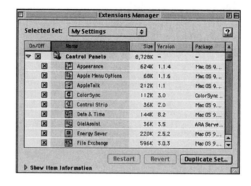

No Saving Necessary

There is no need to save a set after you create it. It is saved automatically.

Extensions Manager has a lot of nice features, including the following:

➤ **Sets**—You can create Extensions Manager sets, which are groups of system extensions, control panels, and other system files that are turned on. This can be useful when you want to switch several of them off at one time and then be able to turn them on again quickly. To create a new set, open the **File** menu and choose **New Set**. Name the set and save it. Configure the set by turning system components off (or on). When you are done, click the **Restart** button to restart using the new set. When you want to switch to another set, choose the set from the **Selected Set** pop-up menu.

➤ **List view**—The Extensions Manager window appears in a list view that works just like folder windows in List view (sorting, changing column widths, and so on).

➤ **Views**—You can change the window's view using the **Views** menu. You can view the items as **Folders** (according to the folders in the System Folder), as **Packages** (all the files related to a technology, such as QuickTime), or as **Items** (by filename).

➤ **More information**—The purpose of many control panels and extensions is not clear from the item's name. If you don't know what an item does, select it in the Extensions Manager window. Click the **Show Item Information** expansion triangle and you will see a description of the item as well as additional information about it (see Figure 23.3).

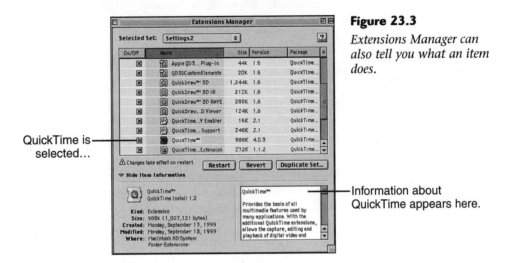

QuickTime is selected...

Figure 23.3

Extensions Manager can also tell you what an item does.

Information about QuickTime appears here.

You may be wondering why you would want to use Extensions Manager. There are primarily two instances when it comes in very handy. The first is when you are managing your iMac's memory, which you will learn about in the next section. The second is when you are troubleshooting problems, which you will learn about in the Appendix.

Beat the System by Managing Your RAM

Random Access Memory (RAM) is one of the most critical parts of your iMac because it is the area into which your iMac stores all the information with which you are working. Managing your RAM effectively can make all the difference between iMac bliss and iMac purgatory.

What Is RAM? (Hint: It Has Nothing to Do with Sheep.)

RAM is a special type of memory your iMac uses to temporarily store information with which it is working. (Other types of memory include long-term storage such as your hard drive.) For example, when you open an application, its code is copied into the iMac's RAM and it runs from there. Your basic system also loads into RAM during the startup process.

RAM Is Volatile

RAM requires power to be able to store information. When you shut down your iMac (and when you quit an application), the data in RAM is purged. That is why applications prompt you to save your changes before you quit. After something is removed from RAM and it has not been saved to your hard drive, it is gone forever.

RAM is provided to your iMac through RAM memory chips. Your iMac writes data to these chips as it works. The amount of space (memory) on a chip determines how much information it can hold. When it comes to RAM, one rule is always true: more is better. Because your iMac is constantly writing to and reading from RAM, the more RAM it has to work with, the better it works.

A Great Source of RAM

The Chip Merchant is a great place to buy a RAM chip for your iMac. Check it out at www.thechipmerchant.com. You can also get a price quote from www.macseek.com.

Some iMacs, such as the top of the line DV iMac, come with plenty of RAM (128MB). Other models come with less, all the way down to the basic non-DV iMac that only has 32MB of RAM. This amount is sufficient to run the system and an application. If you want to make your iMac run even better (faster), the best thing you can do is add a RAM chip to its open RAM slot. You can add a single RAM chip to your iMac, such as a 64MB chip (which would give a basic non-DV iMac a total of 96MB of RAM). See the user manual that came with your iMac for details on how to do this and what type of RAM chip you need.

Your iMac can also write to its hard drive as if the hard drive is RAM—this is known as virtual memory. Sounds good, right? The problem is that your hard drive is many times slower than RAM, and using virtual memory means your iMac will work a lot more slowly than if it is using "real" RAM. You can control virtual memory through the Memory control panel.

Ideally, you will have enough RAM to be able to use *most* of the applications you like to run at the same time. You can use virtual memory for those times when you are running more than you usually do.

iMac RAM Is Like a Pie

When your iMac starts up, it has a total amount of RAM with which to work. The system occupies a certain amount of this memory pie. Each time you open an application, the system carves out a slice of RAM from the amount of free RAM remaining and creates a RAM space for that application to work in. When you close an application, its RAM returns to the unused portion and is available for other applications.

To see how this works, open the **Apple** menu and choose **About This Computer**. In the About This Computer window, you will see information on the version of the OS you are running as well as the physical RAM you have installed (also called built-in memory). You will also see the amount of virtual memory available and the largest unused block (consisting of RAM and virtual memory) available.

In the lower part of the window, you will see how the total RAM pie has been allocated. If you aren't running any applications, you will

An Ideal World

In an ideal world, you will install enough physical RAM to be able to run all the applications that you want. If you do so, turn off virtual memory (use the Memory control panel). Your iMac runs at its top speed if it uses only physical RAM.

see that the Mac OS is using a fairly big chunk (probably around 30MB if you haven't added or removed any system software, which is why you will probably want to add more RAM). Now open several applications. It doesn't matter which; just open two or three of them. Then go back to the About This Computer window and you will see a listing of the open applications, how much RAM each has been allocated (how big its piece of the RAM pie is), and how much of that RAM allocation the application is actually using (see Figure 23.4). Quit one of the applications and go back to the About This Computer window. You will see that the RAM that was allocated to that application has returned to the unused block. (Compare the block size before and after you close the application.)

Physical RAM installed
Virtual memory space
Available RAM

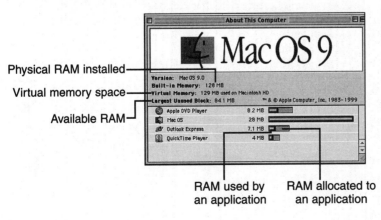

RAM used by an application   RAM allocated to an application

Figure 23.4

As applications are opened, you can see how much RAM they are allocated in the About This Computer window.

Mac OS 9 Only

These About This Computer tricks only work with Mac OS 9; if you are using 8.6, you can skip these tips.

The About This Computer window does more than just tell you about memory; it's a veritable gold mine of shortcuts and tricks, including the following:

➤ Turn on Balloon help (choose **Show Balloons** from the **Help** menu) and point to an application's RAM allocation bar. You will see the exact amount of RAM being used by that application and how much is allocated to it. Turn off the balloons by choosing **Hide Balloons** from the **Help** menu.

➤ Double-click an application's icon to move into that application.

➤ Hold down the **Option** key and double-click an application's icon to move to that application and close the About This Computer window.

➤ Press **Control** and click an application's icon to show a contextual menu that enables you to move to the application, open its Info window, and so on.

➤ Hold down the ⌘ key and click the **Mac OS 9** logo to move to the Mac OS 9 home page.

➤ Double-click the **Mac OS** icon to jump into the System Folder.

Control How Your iMac's RAM Is Used

One of the most important factors that affects how an application works is the amount of RAM it has to work in. When you install an application, it is preconfigured to use a certain amount of memory. If the application is not running very well (it seems slow or it keeps crashing), you can increase the amount of memory that application is allocated when it opens. This gives the application more RAM working room, and it may run better.

To change an application's RAM allocation, select its icon. From the **File** menu, choose **Get Info** and then **Memory** from the hierarchical menu. You will see the Memory window (see Figure 23.5).

There are two settings you can change. The **Minimum Size** is the smallest block of RAM that needs to be available for the application to be able to open. This should never be set lower than the **Suggested Size** amount or you will likely have problems. The **Preferred Size** is the largest block of RAM that will be allocated to the application (assuming that much is available). To change these values, enter new numbers and close the window. The next time you launch that application, the new settings will be used. (An application must be closed before you can change this information.)

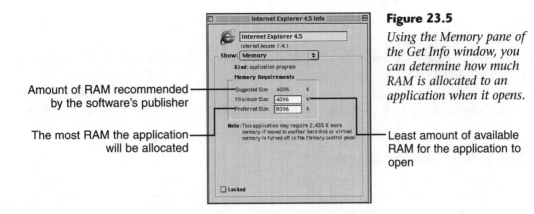

Figure 23.5

Using the Memory pane of the Get Info window, you can determine how much RAM is allocated to an application when it opens.

Amount of RAM recommended by the software's publisher

The most RAM the application will be allocated

Least amount of available RAM for the application to open

Use Extensions Manager to Trim Your System's RAM Requirements

Every control panel and extension that is loaded during startup consumes some amount of RAM—even if you don't use the functionality that software provides. A good way to make more RAM available to applications is to reduce the amount used by the system. You can do this by using Extensions Manager to turn off parts of the system you don't use. Open Extensions Manager and create a new set (call it something like RAM Optimized). From the **View** menu, choose **as Packages**. Look through the packages and see if there are some you don't use and turn those packages off. (For example, if you aren't using personal Web sharing, turn that package off.)

Take an iLook

Using RAM to Solve Problems

If an application is not working well, try increasing the amount of memory it is allocated. This will often solve the problem.

Open the **View** menu and choose **as Items**. The list will be a lot longer, but the process is the same. Look through the list and turn off any items you don't use. (Remember that you can use the Item Information window to see what an item does.) When you have turned everything off that you want to, click the **Restart** button. Your iMac restarts in its fighting-trim state and it has more RAM for applications. (If you have lost some functionality that you find you need, go back into Extensions Manager and turn it on again.)

Beat the System by Adding Cool Stuff to Your iMac

Your iMac is a self-contained system. You don't need to use anything else to be able to do a lot. But there are all sorts of great USB peripherals you can add to increase your iMac's capabilities. The following are some examples of devices you may want to add:

➤ **Input devices**—You can add a different mouse, trackball, different keyboard, and so on.

➤ **Storage devices**—You can add tape drives, additional hard drives, Zip drives, and so on.

➤ **Output devices**—These include printers, but you can also add CD-RW (which stands for Compact Disc, Rewritable) drives so you can create your own CDs.

How It Usually Works

You add peripheral devices to your iMac using its USB ports (the flat rectangular ports located on the right side of the iMac and on each end of the keyboard). There are two general steps needed to install such devices:

1. Connect the device to a USB port.

2. Install the software (a driver and any applications) that came with the device.

Hot-Swaps

USB devices are hot-swappable, which means you can plug and unplug them while the iMac is running.

Your iMac comes with four USB ports (two on the computer and two on the keyboard). Of course, your keyboard and mouse consume two USB ports, so you have only two free USB ports. However, you can attach a USB hub to one so you can attach more than four USB devices at the same time.

In Chapter 7, "The Paperless World—Bah!," you learned how to install a printer. Installing other devices is similar.

An Example: Adding a CD-RW Drive

Wouldn't it be cool to be able to create your own CDs? In addition to customized music CDs, you can use CDs to back up your important files, to archive files, to share files with others, and so on. Adding such a drive is simple. In this example, I am using the excellent LaCie CD-RW drive.

Remove the drive from its box and install it where you want it to be. Plug in the power cable and connect one end of the USB cable to the port on the drive and the other end to one of your iMac's USB port. Turn the power switch on. Your iMac should recognize the new drive and tell you it cannot find the necessary software to use it. Click **OK**.

Insert the CD that came with the drive into the iMac. Run the Toast Installer. Open the LaCie Utilities folder and drag the Silverlining control panel and the two extensions (in the System Extensions folder) onto the System Folder (answer yes to the prompt). Restart your iMac. When it starts up, launch Toast and begin creating your own CDs (see Figure 23.6)!

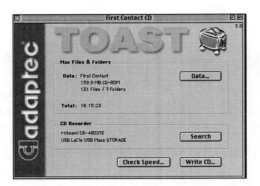

Figure 23.6

Using a USB CD-RW drive and CD mastering software, such as Adaptec's excellent Toast, you can create your own data and audio CDs!

The Least You Need to Know

➤ The way your iMac works is determined by the system—in this case, system doesn't mean some corrupt bureaucracy, but the set of software your iMac uses to operate.

➤ The System Folder is where the vital system software is stored; it contains numerous folders and files, many of which are easy to understand.

➤ Everything with which your iMac works is stored in RAM while it is being "processed," such as applications you launch and the system itself.

➤ You can adjust your iMac's RAM usage by adjusting how much RAM applications are allocated and how much the system uses; you can add an additional RAM chip to your iMac to make more RAM available.

➤ To add a USB device to your iMac, set up the device, install the software, and restart your iMac.

➤ Add a USB hub if you want to connect your iMac to more than four USB devices at a time.

When a Good iMac Goes Bad

Your iMac is a great machine. But as good as it is, you're going to have trouble with it at some point. It will crash, an application won't run, or things just won't work the way they are supposed to. As frustrating as it is, you are better off accepting this fact. Then when a problem does occur, you won't get frustrated as easily. A frustrated person is not good at problem solving.

What Could Happen—It's an iMac After All?

The Mac OS is one of the most stable and reliable operating systems around. Apple hardware usually is high quality. Likewise, Mac software is usually well-crafted. Nonetheless, iMacs are sophisticated systems with technology that is always changing, thus creating fertile ground for problems.

Any problems you experience will be one—or a combination—of five general types of problems.

You Are Your Own Worst Enemy

Many problems are the direct result of a user (this means you) doing something improperly—or not doing something properly. The biggest single cause of these problems is the failure to read and follow instructions. As tough as it can be, try to follow instructions when you add something new to your iMac.

Buggy Software

Sometimes the cause of a problem is a "bug" inherent in the design of the products involved. The bug can be a design flaw, a manufacturing problem, or a conflict with some other part of your system. Although companies often do the best they can to prevent bugs, there usually is no way to prevent all the possible bugs in a product. Bug-induced problems usually are solved by a maintenance/bug fix release of software.

Battling Software

Another common cause of problems is conflicting software; some programs just don't play well with others. Conflicts often are associated with control panels and extensions because they modify the low-level operations of the system. If you call for technical support, this is likely to be the cause that the support person tries to identify first. Software conflict problems usually can be solved by shutting down or removing the software that is responsible for the conflict.

Nasty Viruses

Although fairly rare—especially if you use a good anti-virus program—your computer can sometimes get infected by a virus. Viruses can cause all sorts of problems, from simple and silly messages appearing to strange dialog boxes to major system crashes and even hard disk deletions or failures.

The best cure is to prevent infections, but if you do get a virus, you will have to rely on an antivirus program to get rid of it.

Hardware Failures

The most unlikely cause of problems is a hardware failure. Although hardware does fail now and again, it doesn't happen very often. Hardware failures are most likely to occur immediately after you start using a new piece of hardware or near the end of its useful life. Sometimes, you can induce a hardware failure when you upgrade a machine or perform some other kind of maintenance on it—for example, if you install new RAM in a machine, but fail to seat a RAM chip properly. Unfortunately, the solution to most hardware failures is to have the hardware repaired by a professional or to replace it.

Living Virus Free

The best way to protect yourself from viruses is to get (and use!) a good antivirus program. One of the better ones is Norton AntiVirus.

Disk Failures Are Bad

If you do have a major hardware failure, such as a disk drive failure, and you don't have a good backup, you are in big trouble. You usually can kiss all your data goodbye, although there are services that can try to recover your data—at a high price.

How Do I Fix This @#$(@#$ Computer?

Now that you understand the general sources of problems, it's time to learn how to go about solving them.

Solving Problems You Create

When you run into a problem, one of the first things you should think about is what you were doing or maybe what you *weren't* doing that you should have been. If you take a close look, you may discover that you are indeed sometimes your own worst enemy.

RTFM

If you don't check the manual and ask a question somewhere, you may get a terse response "RTFM." This stands for "Read The Fudgy Manual" (Okay, so it isn't really "fudgy," but, hey, this is a family book!). Anyway, the point is that sometimes the information you need is right in front of you; people often don't make a decent effort to find information on their own before asking a question. Don't be one of those people.

Fixing Quits and Type Whatever Errors

Sometimes, the application you are using suddenly quits. You may or may not get an error message saying something like, "The application has unexpectedly quit because of an error." When this happens, you lose all the changes you made to any open documents since the last time you saved them. This is not a good thing.

When an application quits unexpectedly, there isn't much you can do about it—except try to prevent future quits. The program is simply gone. Sometimes, you can recover your data; sometimes, you can't. The most likely way to prevent future quits is to give the problem application more RAM (see Chapter 23, "Beating the System") or figure out whether there is a software conflict (you will learn how to do that in a moment). Also, check the manufacturer's Web site to see whether a patch is available.

Fixing Hangs and Freezes

Sometimes software errors cause your application—or iMac—to *freeze*, also known as a *hang*. When this happens, your machine seems to lock up, and you can't make the pointer move on the screen. This is also very bad if you haven't saved your work lately.

When an application hangs, you can attempt to shut it down by pressing ⌘+**Option+Esc**. This is called a force quit and sometimes enables you to shut down the hung application. When you attempt this, you see a dialog box asking whether you want to force the application to quit. If you click **Force Quit**, the iMac attempts to shut down the problem application. If it works, you are returned to the desktop. You need to immediately save all the work in other open applications and restart your iMac. A force quit is only a last-resort measure and will cause problems for the system. Make sure your restart after you use it—after saving any open documents.

If the Force Quit doesn't work, you must reboot your Mac. You can do a *soft* restart by pressing **Control+⌘+Power key** (the round key in the upper-right corner of the keyboard that has a partial circle with a line in it).

If the soft restart doesn't work either, you have to do a hard reset. If you have a DV iMac, press the **Reset** button (it is a small button located near the FireWire and modem ports, with a black triangle on it). If you have a non-DV iMac, straighten a paperclip and gently press one end into the small hole located near the Ethernet port (the hole is marked with a small triangle) and gently press the paperclip in to click the **Reset** button (which is inside the hole). After you press the Reset button, your iMac will restart.

One of the most frequent causes of problems like this is an application not having enough RAM to run. Likely symptoms of a RAM problem are either unexpected quits (with some blather about a type xx error) or certain functions of the application not working. Often, increasing the RAM allocation for a particular application solves its problems.

Bringing Peace to Battling Software

The more extensions, control panels, and applications you use, the more likely it is that some of this software will conflict. What happens when software battles it out? You lose. You can experience startup errors when conflicting software tries to load into the system, or you may experience quits, hangs, and performance problems. The most likely sources of conflicts are extensions and control panels.

Military Intelligence

Known conflicts are often listed in ReadMe files and on Web sites for software you install. Check these sources for known conflicts before purchasing or installing new software.

To find out if battling extensions and control panels are the cause of your woes, you can restart your iMac with all its extensions and control panels turned off. To do this, hold down the **Shift** key while your restart your iMac. As your iMac starts up, you will see Extensions Off on the start up screen. All extensions and control panels will be disabled when your desktop appears. If the problem goes away, you know some extension or control panel (or combination thereof) is causing your troubles. Of course, if the problem occurs while you are using an extension or control panel, you won't be able to recreate the problem because they will be turned off.

You can use Extensions Manager to find out which software is conflicting. Open Extensions Manager and create a new set. Scroll through the lists of control panels, extensions, and other items, clicking the **On/Off** check boxes for those that might be related to your problems. Continue this process until you have turned off about half of the items you see in Extensions Manager. Restart the iMac by clicking **Restart**.

Try to focus on items that are related to the application or function you were using at the time of the problem. For example, if you were having problems with a communications program, choose the items that are related to modems. Use the Package view to see items grouped together so you can easily see related items and can turn off several of them with a single click.

After the machine is running, try to duplicate the problem. If the problem doesn't happen again, you know that the problem item is in the group you turned off. If it does happen again, you know the problem item is still on.

If the problem is gone, go back to Extensions Manager and turn on about half of those items that you turned off the first time. If the problem still happens, turn off about half of those items that are still on.

By the way, you can move into the Extensions Manager during the startup process by holding down the spacebar while your iMac starts up.

Consider the Preceding

The most likely cause of conflicting software is the software you installed most recently. If you install new software and begin having problems shortly thereafter, try un-installing that software first. If the problem goes away, you have the offender.

Restart the computer to see if the problem occurs again. If it doesn't, you know the problem isn't caused by one of the items you turned back on, and the culprit is still off. If it does happen, you know the culprit is still on.

Repeat these steps until the problem happens again. Continue turning items off and on until you finally isolate the piece of software that is causing trouble.

The Better Way

Casady & Greene's excellent Conflict Catcher can automate this process for you. You will be way ahead if you get a copy of Conflict Catcher. You can download a demo version of Conflict Catcher from the Casady & Greene Web site at http://www.casadyg.com.

Eventually, you will identify the software that is causing the problem. To correct the problem, you can do one of the following:

➤ **Live without it**—If you can do without the problem software, you can solve the problem by leaving the item off.

➤ **Get an upgrade**—You can try to get a patch or an upgrade for an item to see if the conflict has been resolved.

➤ **Change the loading order**—You can rename items to change the order in which they load into the system. (Try adding a "z" or spaces to the item's name.) Sometimes, changing the loading order can eliminate conflicts.

Fixing Buggy, Poorly Designed, and Conflicting Applications

Some applications are just plain buggy. Symptoms of buggy software problems can include quits, hangs, and odd performance. In the case of a buggy application, the only real solution is to get a bug fix release of the application, assuming that the publisher issues one, of course. You may just have to live with the problem or live without the application. If it conflicts with another application you also need, one of them may have to go.

Solving "General Weirdness" Problems

Sometimes, your iMac will do weird things that don't seem to be related to any specific applications. These kinds of problems usually are either easy to solve or darn near impossible. In either case, they won't take much of your time because if you are able to solve them, it won't take long. If you can't solve them, you won't need to waste much time trying.

There are several problems that can be lumped under the "general weirdness" category. These include the following:

➤ **Generic icons**—One of the great things about the iMac is that it keeps track of which applications can be used to edit specific documents so you don't have to worry about it yourself. You open a document by simply double-clicking it. Each icon has a distinctive look based on the type of file it is (for example, Word documents have the Word document icon). Sometimes, the iMac will seem to lose its mind and all the icons will suddenly become generic (just a plain looking rectangle).

➤ **Lost time or date**—Your iMac always—almost always anyway—keeps track of the time and date. This is important for many reasons, the most significant of which is date-and-time stamping the files and email that you create and modify. Once in a while, your iMac may seem to lose its watch and won't know what time it is.

➤ **Lost preferences**—You make your iMac your own by setting various preferences that tell it how you want it to work and look. Occasionally, you will find all of your preferences gone.

These problems almost always are solved by one of two simple actions: rebuilding the desktop or zapping the PRAM.

Rebuilding the Desktop

The iMac associates documents with applications through its desktop database, which links particular files with the applications that create those files. This linkage is indicated by the custom icons on files. When these icons go generic—they lose the custom icons and become plain rectangles—you need to rebuild the desktop database. This helps the iMac "remember" which files go with which applications. This also restores the custom icons.

An easy way to rebuild the desktop database on your disks is by holding down the **Option** and ⌘ keys and then restarting your iMac. When the iMac restarts, you are asked if the desktop should be rebuilt. Answer **Yes**, and your icons should look "right" again.

Zapping the PRAM

Parameter RAM (PRAM) is the area of your iMac where the information is stored that needs to be retained when the power to the computer is turned off. These settings include time and date, system preferences, and so on. Rarely, your iMac will start acting oddly and will seem to lose its mind every time you restart it. If you have problems with your date and system preferences, try zapping (clearing) the PRAM.

Think Before Zapping the PRAM

Note that if you zap the PRAM, you will lose a lot of your system settings and will have to reconfigure things that you changed from the defaults. Make sure you need to do it before you do.

To zap the PRAM, hold down ⌘+**Option+P+R** while you restart your iMac. When it starts back up, the PRAM is cleared. You will then have to reset some of your custom settings.

If zapping the PRAM doesn't work (you lose your settings the next time you restart), it may be that the internal battery in your iMac has expired. Your iMac uses this battery to maintain its PRAM. If this battery dies, your PRAM is cleared each time you shut down the machine. The solution is to replace the battery. (You will have to have a service person do this for you.)

Solving the Startup Problem

One of the worst problems you can have is when your iMac won't start. This can be caused by many things, including software conflicts, buggy software, failed hardware, or a combination of all of these. This problem is the failure of your iMac to boot to the desktop. When instead of loading the system it just sits there and flashes a disk icon with a question mark in the center, it means that your iMac can't find a suitable System Folder to use to start up the machine. Or you might get errors during the startup process that prevent your iMac from getting to the desktop.

There are several things that can cause your iMac to be unable to find a usable System Folder. One is that there is a problem with the system software that is installed. Another may be a faulty disk with a corrupted disk structure. Or the hardware itself may have failed. In any case, you must provide the iMac with a different startup disk for it to start up. In this case, you need to startup using the System Restore CD and then repair the System Folder.

Booting from the System Restore CD

If your iMac won't start up and instead you get error messages or perhaps a flashing disk icon, the most likely cause is a problem with the System Folder. Insert the System Restore CD into your DVD or CD-ROM drive (this CD is part of the software package you received with your iMac).

Upgraders Take Note!

If you have upgraded the version of the system software you use, from 8.6 to 9 for example, you need to use the installation CD-ROM that came with the upgrade rather than the System Restore CD. The System Restore CD restores the System Folder to the version that shipped with your iMac. This is not good if you have upgraded your system.

You can use the system software installer on your upgrade CD to repair or replace your System Folder.

Restart your iMac. If you have made it to the desktop, use the **Restart** command. If your iMac is locked up, press **Control+⌘+Power key** to restart it. If this doesn't work, use the hard reset button.

As your iMac restarts, hold the C key down. The iMac uses the System Folder on the CD and you should eventually see the desktop (although you will see a different desktop because you are now running on the CD's System Folder). The System Restore CD appears in the upper-right corner of the desktop and opens to reveal the Apple Software Restore application.

Restoring the System

Launch the Apple Software Restore application. In the application's window, you will see the following three options:

➤ **Restore, saving original items**—This option installs new software, but it saves everything that is on your hard drive in a folder called Original Items.

➤ **Restore in Place**—With this option, items with the same name as in the restore application are replaced by "fresh" versions.

➤ **Erase "Your Hard Disk's Name" before restoring**—This option *completely* erases your hard disk before the new System Folder is installed.

Losing Your Mind

When you use the first or third option, you will *lose* all of the files in your System Folder. This means you will have to re-install any third-party software you have installed as well as any configurations you have done. Be sure you really need to restore your System Folder before you do this because it will take quite a bit of work to get back to where you were before the problem happened. Try the second option first. If that doesn't work, try the first option. If that fails, you will have to use the third option—this requires you to lose *everything* on your hard disk, so make sure you have saved important files elsewhere first. (You should keep your important files backed up to a USB storage device, such as a Zip drive, or to a network.)

Choose an option by clicking its radio button, and click **Restore**. The software performs the required installations and you should be able to start your iMac normally. You will likely have to re-configure it—remember to use the Assistants to make this process less painful.

Where Can I Get Some Help?

You are not alone. Somewhere in the world, there probably is someone who has either experienced the same problem you have or who knows how to solve it. One of the most important things you need to know is how to get help when you need it. The following are some sources of information that you should consider:

➤ **The manual and online help**—Most applications come with a paper manual, online help, or both. You should peruse this information to help you understand what you are doing and help you prevent and solve problems. (Remember the Mac Help Center!)

➤ **People**—There are many people you can ask for help. You can ask people you know or the tech support group for the "problem" application. It often pays to make friends with a geek who lives and breathes Macs.

➤ **The Internet**—You can also use the Internet to look for help via email, Frequently Asked Questions (FAQs), newsgroups, and of course, Web sites. There are also lots of good mailing lists you can join.

A Couple of Web Pointers that Might Help

The first place you should go, especially when experiencing trouble after adding a new piece of software (which is the most likely time) is the Web site for the manufacturer of that software. There are also Web sites that are dedicated to solving Mac problems. One of the best is **www.macfixit.com**.

➤ **Books and magazines**—There are a lot of books and magazines that contain information that will help you with problems.

Glossary

AirPort   The technology that enables your iMac to wirelessly connect to a network or the Internet. To use AirPort, you need to install an AirPort card in your iMac. Then you can wirelessly communicate with the AirPort Base Station or with another AirPort-equipped computer (other iMacs, iBooks, or G4 Macs).

alias   A "pointer" file that you can create to help you organize your computer. An alias acts just like the "real" file; for example, when you double-click an alias, the original file opens. Alias files are very small, so having a lot of them is not likely to consume much space.

allocated memory   Allocated memory is that portion of your computer's RAM that is set aside for a particular application (including the system software). When the application is launched, the allocated memory block is opened and can be used only by that application.

Apple Computer   The maker of Macintosh computers (including the iMac) and the Mac OS. Apple's Web site is at **www.apple.com**.

AppleScript   The iMac's built-in scripting language that can be used to automate many processes and tasks. AppleScript is very powerful, but its language does take a bit of effort to learn (even though it is perhaps the most English-like scripting/ programming language around). Most iMac users are better off running the AppleScripts that are provided as part of the Mac OS, and using a macro utility, such as the excellent QuicKeys macro utility, to create their own macros.

application   Software that enables you to perform some task (for example, word processing, Web browsing, and so on). An application is the same as a program.

CD-ROM   Compact Disc-Read Only Memory; CD-ROM discs store digital data for audio, video, and other data. CD-ROM discs are widely used to distribute software, especially multimedia applications.

Clipboard   Where iMac stores any information that you cut or copy. You can view the contents of the clipboard from the Finder.

color depth   The number of colors a device can display or output. The number of colors is determined by raising 2 to the power of the number of data bits that can be displayed on each pixel. For example, 8-bit color results in 256 colors (2 raised to the power of 8).

compression   A scheme that makes files smaller, usually by finding a pattern and substituting shorthand for the pattern. Most files that you download from the Internet or receive via email are compressed to make them transfer more quickly. You need a decompression utility to use the files. The dominant compression scheme on the Mac is the StuffIt format, which is identified by the extension .sit. Aladdin Systems' StuffIt Expander is freeware that enables you to decompress .sit files.

control panel   A piece of software that provides your iMac with specific capabilities that can be adjusted via the control panel. A number of control panels are part of the Mac OS. There also are many third-party control panels that can be added to your machine to increase its capabilities.

Control Strip   The Control Strip is a bar across your desktop that enables you to quickly access certain controls. You can add or remove modules from the Control Strip to customize the controls it offers.

crash   When an application suddenly and unexpectedly stops working. A crashing application can also cause the OS to crash or sometimes the OS can crash on its own.

Creator   The application that creates a specific type of document. Every Macintosh file contains information on its "creator"; when the file is double-clicked, the Mac looks for the creator application to use to open the file. If it can't be found, the Mac's built-in file translator tries to help you locate an application that can be used to open that file.

desktop   The main interface of the Mac OS where you see all the drives, the Trash, and so forth. The desktop is controlled by the Finder.

DV   Using Digital Video (DV), video and audio data is stored digitally instead of in analog format (such as a VCR uses). Digital video has much higher quality than analog and it can be manipulated more easily. DV iMacs are ideally suited to edit digital video, which can be input from a DV camcorder via the DV iMac's FireWire port. DV iMacs come with iMovie, which is a digital video editor.

DVD   Stands for Digital Video Disc, Digital Versatile Disc, or just DVD. A DVD can hold almost 10 times as much data as a CD-ROM disc. DVD discs can contain DVD movies that you can watch on DV iMacs or programs and files that work just like a CD-ROM disc (holding a lot more data, of course). DVD drives can read all the discs that a CD-ROM drive can (but CD-ROM drives cannot read DVD discs).

encoding   When you send a file over the Internet, it is converted into a plain ASCII text file (which consists of a seemingly incomprehensible string of characters) so it can be transmitted across the Net. This process is called encoding. There are different encoding schemes; the Mac uses binhex while Windows uses uucode. Email applications and Web browsers do the necessary encoding and decoding for you, but you should know which encoding scheme to use.

Ethernet   The networking technology that is widely used for local networks. The iMac has a high-speed Ethernet port and the AirPort can also access high-speed Ethernet networks.

extension   A piece of software that adds additional functionality to your iMac. You cannot adjust the operation of an extension as you can with a control panel. An extension is either on or off.

Extensions Manager   This control panel enables you to turn various parts of the operating system off or on in order to troubleshoot or tailor the iMac's performance.

Favorites   Favorites are folders, files, volumes, and other items that you use regularly. You can add items to your Favorites folder with the Add to Favorites command. You can access your favorites in several places, including the Apple menu and the Navigation Services window that you will see when you save or open files. Internet Explorer also uses Favorites to enable you to quickly move to a Web site without typing a URL.

file extension   All PC files have a three-letter file extension appended to their names. Windows uses the file extension to determine which application opens when a file is opened. Your iMac also uses extensions when you open a PC file.

file format   The way in which data is stored in a file. There are many, many file formats. Fortunately, you will usually only deal with a few main types. The iMac makes dealing with file formats simpler than it is on other computers.

File Type   One of the two codes associated with all iMac files (the other is the Creator code). The File Type code indicates what kind of file it is—for example, a text document or a jpeg image.

Finder   The main application that controls your iMac; it provides the desktop and manages all activity on your computer.

FireWire   A high-speed input and output technology, primarily intended for high bandwidth data needs, such as digital video. DV iMacs have two FireWire ports to which you can connect DV cameras, high-speed hard drives, and so on.

floating window   A window that "floats" on top of all other windows.

font   A definition of how characters will appear onscreen and in print. There are many font families you can use. The Mac OS comes with many font families, and there are hundreds more available.

G3   The processor used in your iMac. The G3 is one of the most powerful processors available for a personal computer.

G4   The next generation of processor for Macintosh computers. The G4 is the first supercomputer processor to be used in personal computers.

Get Info   The command that provides information on folders and files that you select, including the sharing information for a file or folder.

hang   When an application or the operating system "freezes" and won't respond to anything you do (move the pointer, use the keyboard, curse, and so on). You can sometimes recover from a hang by force quitting (⌘+Option+Esc).

HTML   Hypertext Markup Language; the set of commands used to mark up documents with standard elements so they can be displayed and read on the World Wide Web by different browsers on different computers.

hub   A hardware device that enables you to connect multiple devices together. You can use a USB hub to connect more than four USB devices to your iMac at one time. You may also use an Ethernet hub to set up a local network.

inkjet printer   A printer that uses small particles of ink to produce output. Inkjet printers are low cost, and they produce output that is sufficient for most uses.

Internet   The world wide conglomeration of various networks that provides various services such as email, the World Wide Web, and so on.

Intranet   A local area network (LAN) that is used to provide services similar to the Internet; access to those services usually is limited to members of the organization that creates the intranet.

Key Caps   The application that shows you particular symbols associated with a font family.

LAN   Local area network; a network usually associated with a single office, building, or organization.

laser printer   A printer that uses a laser to produce text and graphics. Laser printers are more expensive than inkjet printers, but they also produce higher quality output.

Mac OS   The collection of software that enables Macintosh computers (including the iMac) to operate. The current version is Mac OS 9.

Mac OS X   The next evolution in the Mac OS. Mac OS X is based on Rhapsody/NeXT technology and will be a modern OS that offers excellent features such as preemptive multitasking, protected memory, and more PowerPC code.

MacinTalk   The technology that enables your Mac to speak.

memory   An area in which data is stored. Your iMac uses all sorts of memory in different areas, for example, RAM, the hard drive, ROM, and so on. Each memory type is used for a specific purpose.

Microsoft   The company that produces software that dominates several markets including spreadsheets and word processing. Microsoft also produces the most widely used operating system, Windows. Many of the features that the Mac pioneered have appeared in Windows as well. A few features have also made their way from Windows to the Mac.

minimum size   The smallest amount of RAM that has to be available for an application to open.

mount   Making a disc or other resource available to be used. For example, when you insert a CD-ROM disc, it becomes mounted on the desktop and you can see its icon. A disk must be mounted to be used.

multitasking   The capability to do two or more things at once. The iMac currently has some multitasking (cooperative multitasking) capabilities, but the actions of open applications affect the other open applications. In a true multitasking environment, each application is provided with resources by the OS so that both performance and stability are better. Mac OS X will feature true multitasking.

Parameter RAM (PRAM)   The memory in which data that needs to be maintained across system shut down is stored (PRAM uses battery power even when the iMac is turned off). For example, the time and date and mouse settings are stored in PRAM.

patch   A piece of software that fixes a bug in a specific application. Usually, a patch application is provided by the software manufacturer. You run the patch and the bug is squished (hopefully).

pixel   Picture Element; the smallest block of data displayed on a monitor or captured by an imaging device, such as a digital camera. All digital images are made up of dots. On a monitor, digital camera, or scanner, these dots are called pixels. The more pixels that a device can work with, the higher its resolution and the more detail it can provide.

PlainTalk   The technology that uses MacinTalk to enable your iMac to speak to you (and enable your iMac to understand verbal commands when you use the microphone).

plug-in   Plug-ins are software components that extend an application's capabilities—giving you, for example, the ability to play audio samples or view video movies from within a Web browser. Generally, plug-in installation requires you to save the plug-in to your hard drive and then double-click the saved file to start the installation. You tell your application which type of plug-in you have installed, and it knows from then on what to do when it comes across this type of file.

preferred size   The maximum amount of RAM that will be allocated to an application when it is opened.

QuickTime   The technology that enables your iMac to display time-synchronized data such as digitized video and animations. Unlike many other technologies developed by Apple, QuickTime has been widely adopted on the PC as well.

RAM   Random Access Memory; RAM is the place where your iMac stores any information with which it is currently working. The RAM available to software on your iMac is one of the major determinants of how well your iMac works. If the RAM you are using is not sufficient, you will experience many more problems and the capabilities of your iMac will be limited. Fortunately, RAM prices have been drastically reduced so you can add more RAM to your machine for a relatively small amount of money.

RAM allocation   The amount of RAM that is set aside for a particular application.

RAM disk   A scheme whereby RAM is used to store information that usually would be written to a hard drive. This speeds up the operation of the computer.

removable media   Storage media that can be removed (for example, floppy disks, Zip disks, and so on) from the respective drive.

Reset   Using the Reset button resets the iMac's hardware and software. An iMac should be reset if nothing else recovers a hung machine.

resolution   The number of pixels that can be displayed by a device in specific color depths (for example, 800 pixels×600 pixels with millions of colors). Resolution is a key measurement of the output of monitors, printers, digital cameras, and other devices.

Restart   The process of shutting down the computer and starting it again. This is best done with the Restart command on the Finder's Special menu.

ROM   Read Only Memory; The information on your iMac that is permanent is stored in the ROM. For example, the information stored in ROM tells your iMac how to look for an operating system to use.

Scrapbook   A utility that stores clippings that can easily be re-used.

sleep   Putting the computer to sleep powers down the hard drive and blacks out the monitor to conserve power.

suggested size   The minimum amount of RAM required for an application according to the application's manufacturer.

System Folder   The folder that contains all the software your iMac uses to run. You should understand what is in the System Folder so you can tune your iMac to your personality and so you have a better idea of how to solve problems you may experience.

themes   Themes are collections of interface customizations such as the desktop pattern or picture, menu appearance, fonts used in menus, and even sounds. You can define themes to include many of these customizations and then easily switch among "looks" by choosing a different theme.

updater   An program that "updates" an application to a newer version. It is similar to a patch except that updaters usually solve multiple problems or add new functions.

upgrade   The process of replacing an older version of an application with a newer one for many reasons, including to get more features and better stability. Most software companies make a large portion of their income from upgrades. You can also upgrade hardware by adding RAM, larger hard drives, and other items.

URL   Uniform Resource Locator; a standard address for a file or location on the Internet. URLs always begin with an Internet protocol (FTP, Gopher, HTTP), followed by an Internet host name, folders, and the destination file or object.

USB   Universal Serial Bus; USB is a modern interface that enables you to connect all sorts of peripherals (mice, keyboards, scanners, hard disks, tape drives, and so on) to the same port. The iMac determines what kind of device is connected to the USB port and configures itself appropriately. In addition to making life simpler for the user, USB ports also offer better performance than many of the ports they replace. You can also chain multiple USB devices through a single hub.

Uucode   An encoding strategy used to prepare Windows files to be transmitted over the Internet. You can also use uucode to encode Mac files, but it is more appropriate for Windows files.

315

virtual memory   Technology that enables your iMac to use a hard drive as it would RAM. Although this enables you to do things for which you may not have enough physical RAM, virtual memory is much slower than physical RAM.

volume   A disk space that can be mounted on your iMac. A volume may be a partition on a drive connected to your machine or it may be a drive that is connected to your iMac via a network.

Warm start   The process of restarting your iMac without turning off all power to it.

Windows NT   A higher-end version of Windows 95/98. Currently, it is mostly used on servers, but eventually Windows 95/98 will be replaced by versions of Windows NT. Windows NT is a stable operating system and is perhaps the most modern OS that can be used on a personal computer (until Mac OS X).

zip drive   Iomega's removable drive that stores 100MB of data on a 3.5-inch disk.

Index

323

331

335